DIMITRI JELEZKY

PRINT DESIGN FOR TEXTILES

Step-by-Step Methods for Fashion & Home Decor

Dimitri Jelezky, Hamburg 2025

Bibliografische Information der Deutschen Nationalbibliothek: Die Deutsche Nationalbibliothek verzeichnet diese Publikation in der Deutschen Nationalbibliografie; detaillierte bibliografische Daten sind im Internet über dnb.dnb.de abrufbar.

Die automatisierte Analyse des Werkes, um daraus Informationen insbesondere über Muster, Trends und Korrelationen gemäß §44b UrhG („Text und Data Mining") zu gewinnen, ist untersagt.

©2025 english Edition Dimitri Eletski

Publisher: BoD · Books on Demand GmbH, Überseering 33, 22297 Hamburg, bod@bod.de

Print: Libri Plureos GmbH, Friedensallee 273, 22763 Hamburg

ISBN: 978-3-8192-4907-5

Table of contents

1.0 INTRODUCTION

With more than 25 years of professional experience, 15 years as a dedicated educator, and a mastery of multiple design disciplines, the author of this book stands as a towering figure in the field. His career is a testament to the power of creativity, perseverance, and a commitment to excellence. Through his work, teaching, and writing, he has not only shaped the design industry but also inspired countless individuals to pursue their own creative journeys. This book "Print Development for the Design Sector" teaches basic and advanced techniques for working with Adobe Illustrator and Adobe Photoshop in print development. It is designed specifically for the field of textile design. An indispensable reference work for designers, illustrators and students at design schools. Important tools, program functions and techniques in Adobe Illustrator and Adobe Photoshop are explained step by step. Most of the steps are shown graphically so that a quick and precise realization of the respective project is easy and everyone can understand the structure of a print, whether it is an all-over print or a placement print.

In this book, the author does not go into all aspects of print development, this topic is too extensive for that. This book should rather serve as a practical and inspirational book and provide the reader with knowledge for everyday use.

The textile industry offers a range of printing methods for printing artwork on textiles. Every one of these printing techniques has its advantages and disadvantages. **Block printing**, **digital printing**, **heat transfer printing**, **screen printing**, and **rotary printing** are the most widely used techniques for printing on fabrics.
There are countless finishing methods and over 20 different printing techniques. The majority of fashion companies employ these techniques, and designers must take these printing techniques characteristics into consideration when creating an artwork.

Direct printing, discharge printing, and resist printing are the three different **types** of printing. In **direct printing**, colored pastes are imprinted directly onto the fabric. For **discharge printing**, the fabric is first dyed with a background color that is later removed using reagents. In order to prevent the printed areas from taking on color, a chemical called a resist is initially printed on the fabric in the **resist method**. The fabric is colored or pigment-padded only in the areas that were not printed using the resist.

The outcome of an artwork is greatly influenced by the appropriate technical approach used in its creation. Always select the appropriate technique at the beginning of the design process. Although there are many analog and digital techniques to prepare an artwork for printing, an artwork that is intelligently organized from the beginning is always advantageous. Planning the proper approach and the most important steps beforehand is always the best course of action. As a result, you can quickly correct some work processes while also saving a lot of time.

The printing processes of textiles has advanced greatly in the past decades, requiring the talents of designers and artists.
When creating artwork, there are numerous factors to take into consideration. Along with linework, aesthetically pleasing forms, harmonious object proportions, textures, and of course, the right colors. Therefore, it is important, among other things, to have a good grasp of the rules of proportion and color theory and to always follow them. In addition, a designer should always be experimenting with new trends in order to produce contemporary and high-quality artwork. It's also crucial to continuously explore new directions in analog and digital drawing because practice makes perfect.

Prints are a crucial component of almost every collection. Prints and graphically designed surfaces (such as embroidery) lend a garment the allure of a finished work of art, whether they are placement prints or allover prints, small and discrete or large and covering the entire garment. The garment may be simply cut, but a beautifully designed print gives it that extra touch.

Now more than ever, prints are essential and important in the fashion industry because they can highlight any collection what gives a significant competitive advantage in the current market.
Fashion designers and artists need to be continuously innovative in order to create beautiful artworks.

To have excellent sketching skills is also very advantageous for a designer as it covers a vast area in the creation process of a collection.

Many benefits are provided by textile printing to the designer, enabling him to present his works to clients or customers in an exquisite manner.
This makes it easier for the designer to draw customers' attention to his/her well-designed clothing.

1.1 PRINT METHODS

BLOCK PRINTING:

Block printing is a traditional printmaking technique where an image or design is carved into a block of material, such as wood, linoleum, or rubber. The raised (uncarved) areas of the block are then inked, and the design is transferred onto paper, fabric, or another surface by pressing the block onto it. This process can be repeated to create multiple copies of the same image.

DIGITAL PRINTING:

Digital printing is a method of printing from a digital-based image directly printed on to the surface of fabric. Since the ink is applied directly to the fabric when printing digitally using large-format or high-volume laser or inkjet printers, it is not a heat transfer. Because the design does not need to be reduced to a specific number of colors and there is no need to create a screen for each color, digital printing is simpler than screen printing. Unlike screen printing, digital printing doesn't use screens (stencil) and therefore can produce prints with much more details and reduces the cost factor in the preparation process of the design itself. In the final stage, it is still usually more expensive than rotary printing. This depends on the number of items ordered.
The choice of printing technology is heavily influenced by the complexity of an artwork. If the artwork has too many details, colors, effects, the artwork must be often simplified by the designer, which is one of the trickiest steps in the design process, otherwise it can only be printed digitally. However, as a result, digital printing is not as

high-quality; for instance, because the ink is applied thinner, the colors may lose their vibrancy after several washings.

HEAT TRANSFER PRINTING:

Heat transfer printing is a printing technique that enables you to imprint a design onto a piece of clothing. It is also referred to as thermal printing. Using transfer printing techniques, a design is moved from one medium to another. The most popular type is heat transfer printing, where the design is first printed using standard printing equipment on a special paper. The paper is then heated in close proximity to the fabric, causing the dyes to vaporize and transfer to the fabric.

SCREEN PRINTING:

Screen printing is a printing method where ink is transferred onto a substrate using a mesh, with the exception of areas where a blocking stencil has rendered the substrate impermeable to the ink.
Screen printing involves making a screen that is used as a stencil to apply multiple layers of ink to the printing surface. Each color used in the design requires a different screen, which must be used sequentially and in combination to produce the desired result. When printing on a dark surface or a specific product and the design needs a high level of vibrancy, screen printing is the best option. Larger orders are typically printed on screens. Screen printing uses a thicker application of the dye color than digital printing, which produces a brighter color even on darker shades.

ROTARY PRINTING:

The rotary screen is a cylindrical-shaped screen. While the rotating screen is in use, the color/printing paste is applied from the inside. The paste can transfer to the fabric thanks to the pressure of the screen and the central cylinder. Rotary screen printing is the most appealing method for printing designers and fashion apparel fabric due to the high quality it can achieve.

1.2 OTHER IMPORTANT TERMS

FLOWER PRINTS

In most womenwear collections, flowers are one of the main themes. Even if this theme graphically differs from very subtle to very expressive from one season to the next.

Expressionistic or accurate lines and shapes created analog or digital, vintage or 3D genereted flowers, oversized or millefleur, expressive placements or with abstract almost unrecognizable floral elements. Variety is provided by both the motifs and how they are used, which can be used to create eye-catching looks with colored overlays, depth generated effects, minimal color printing, silhouettes, or unexpected contrasts.

MILLEFLEUR FLOWER PRINTS

Millefleurs flowers: A typical print theme that is used for dresses and blouses almost every season.

Compared to the typical large-scale flower prints millfleur flower prints are less striking and despite the abundance of tiny flowers, it is also less colorful and restless.

BIG FLOWER PRINTS OR LARGE SCALE FLOWER PRINTS

Large scale flowers are not a big trend every season but compared to the millefleur flowers, designers have more artistic freedom (art techniques) in creating large-scale flowers. The diversity of this pattern group is all the more varied.
Large floral patterns are unlike other designs such as millefleur pattern types. They tend to feature often but not necessarily a lot more details. Compared to millefleur flower pattern types, large-scale flower patterns are one thing above all: a statement, because this eye-catching flower pattern immediately catches your attention.

ALLOVER PRINT OR AOP

Allover print or AOP is a repeat pattern, where a design continuously repeats across the length and width of fabric. An all over print is most often printed directly onto the fabric, before it is cut and made into a product. Allover print consists of motifs (e.g. lines, shapes, abstract or figurative motifs) that are created and placed within a rectangle or square (called repeat rectangle or rapport), ensuring they join seamlessly at each edge of the rectangle or square. This gives the viewer the impression of a never-ending motif.

An alloverprint can be also engendered for a placement on a specific garment area like a placement print. That ensure that a motif (for example big flower, bird etc.) will be placed only on a convenient area on a garment to avoid any inappropriate areas for a motif (for example figurative motif in the crotch area of a garment). This method can be also be appled for different sizing (pattern grading). But this has a disadvantage because the unnecessary empty areas in the fabric as a result of this method increase the production costs, that's why big fashion brands try to avoid individual sizes and placements for all over prints on the clothing.

When designing an all over print you will need to consider a lot of specifications for example beautiful, aesthetic transition between elements and not only a clean seamless alignment on all sides of the repeat rectangle (rapport).

PLACEMENT PRINT

Different to a repeat print (AOP), which features continuous tiling of artwork a placement print rellies on artwork done to the scale of a product and then being cut in a particular position to control the placement of a print.

A placement or engineered print is a type of print that is specifically placed onto the fabric and garment on an exact controlled position without repeating itself. In contrast to an allover print (repeat print), which involves continuously tiling artwork, a placement print relies on artwork that is scaled to a product before being cut in a specific location to control the placement of the artwork. Placement prints are one of the main topics in streetwear fashion and fast fashion industry. A t-shirt print with a front or back print is the most common example of a placement print also called "graphic tees" as generic term.

Different sizes for placement prints:
Keep also in mind different sizing of the garment. Often a placement print should be resized for different sizes of the garment to keep the same aesthetic proportions of the product and to avoid any technical errors in the produc-

tion process (for example if the motive is too near to a cutting edge it can happen that it will be cropped on the seamline do to the size differences of the pattern).

RAPPORT/ REPEATING RECTANGLE

The motif for an alloverprint is alway placed in a rectangle or square at the end, even if it was created inside another geometric shape templates like a hexagon. This ensure a seamlessly repetition at each edge of an allover print.

COLORWAY

A color combination used to create different color options for existing artwork or a print. Each season, multiple color options of the same print are created for almost every artwork. This ensure a trend-oriented selection and at the same time the client receive an overview with an extended color selection of the same artwork.

1.3 DIFFERENT COLOR SEPARATION TECHNIQUES FOR SCREEN PRINTING

Screen printers employ a few different separation procedures. It can be easier for you to consistently carry out successful separations if you are aware of the various separation types and the difficulties they present. The following color separations are typical for screen printing:

SPOT COLOR.

Spot color separation is the most typical type of color separation used in screen printing. For vector images, spot color separation technique is a standard procedure. Spot color separations, though usually solid, may contain some halftone dots to add shading. Typically, CorelDRAW, Adobe Illustrator or other vector programms are used to create spot color separations.

FOUR-COLOR PROCESS.

Cyan, magenta, yellow, and black (CMYK) halftone dots are used in the four-color process to produce finely detailed, photorealistic images. These separations are typically made in Photoshop, and it can be challenging to correctly print four-color separations and create process color separations.

SIMULATED-PROCESS COLOR.

Halftone dots are used in simulated-process color separations, just like in conventional four-color process separations, to produce extremely detailed or photorealistic images. Simulated process color separations differ in that they employ a variety of ink colors. Unlike four-color process separations, they can be printed on darker materials and have a tendency to be more vivid than four-color process prints. Simulated-process color separations are done usually in Photoshop, just like four-color process separations.

INDEX COLOR.

Index color separations produce color shading instead of halftone dots by using square pixels of the same size. Process separations may be more difficult to perform than index color separations for printing. However, producing a photorealistic print frequently requires using more colors. Photoshop is usually used to perform the separations, but CorelDRAW, Adobe Illustrator or other pixel or vector programms can also be used to transfer images with ease.

1.4 DIFFERENT TYPES OF REPEATING RECTANGLES (RAPPORT)

STRAIGHT REPEAT/FULLDROP/BLOCK PATTERN REPEAT

One of the most common and simplest pattern repeat styles is the straight repeat or full drop repeat. The repeat unit has a layout where the repeat appears on the same horizontal and vertical plane to the original pattern unit (grid format). It can be created with a square or rectangular unit. It´s also called a block or a drop repeat.

All other pattern repeat styles you can find here can be subsumed under the straight repeat pattern style because every repeat block at the end will be set up as rectangle shape for the supplier in digital form.

HALF DROP PATTERN REPEAT

The half drop repeat is another widely used surface pattern repeat. A pattern layout in which the initial pattern unit repeats on the same vertical column but then offset by half in the next vertical row. Half drops make it much easier to conceal the repeat pattern, giving it a more organic and less formal appearance.

The Brick pattern repeat is very similar to the Half Drop pattern repeat, with the exception that the original pattern unit repeats horizontally on the same plane and then when it repeats vertically, it appears halfway over, resembling a brick wall. As a result, just like with the half drop pattern repeats, brick repeats allow a design to look more organic and less formal

DIAMOND PATTERN REPEAT

A diamond pattern repeat consists of repeating diamond shape. Diagonal rows or lines are used to arrange design elements in a diamond repeat pattern.

OGEE PATTERN REPEAT

Similar to the diamond repeat, an ogee pattern repeat has points at the top and bottom but rounded edges on the sides.

TOSSED/RANDOM PATTERN REPEAT

In a random pattern repeat the elements of the design are placed randomly.
An unstructured, tossed pattern creates a very organic, non-linear design. In general, designers prefer that look particularly for floral prints.

STRAIGHT REPEAT HAS AN IMPORTANT SUBDIVISION:

A hexagon shape is frequently used to construct millefleur patterns, which are then set as a straight repeat.
In order to keep the repeat transition invisible to the viewer, the elements are organized into groups by the hexagon shape. Because the visible **repeat adjacent transitions** are one of the biggest mistakes that can be made in a allover print.

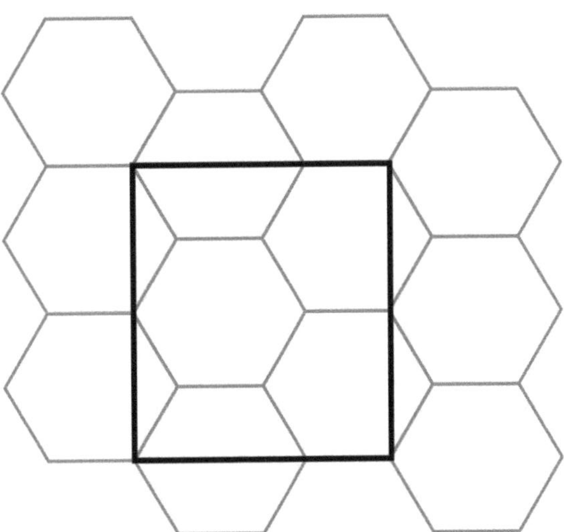

A hexagon pattern repeat consists of repeating hexagon shapes. Diagonal rows are used to arrange design elements in a hexagon repeat pattern.

The final artwork must always be digitized cleanly, regardless of whether a pattern was created exclusively digitally or analog by hand using brushes, for instance.
Therefore, different repeat settings for allover prints serve as the foundation for seamless repeat.

The examples given here do not attempt to explain the technical repeat design process in relation to different printing techniques.
This overview of different repeat settings explains which settings should be used for the final **digital** repeat rectangle for the supplier.

These are the typical construction methods used by designers.

1.5 OTHER IMPORTANT LITERATURE

FASHIONDESIGN - Digital drawing with Adobe Illustrator: Techniques & Tips

Pages: ca. 140 pages
ISBN: 978-3945549223
Language: English
Price: 29,90 EUR

MODEDESIGN - Digital Zeichnen mit Adobe Illustrator: Techniken & Tipps

Pages: ca. 140 pages
ISBN: 978-3945549124
Language: German
Price: 24,90 EUR

FASHION DESIGNER'S SKETCHBOOK - women figures

Part 1 Women Figures
Pages: ca. 108 pages
ISBN: 978-3945549414
Language: English
Price: 24,90 EUR

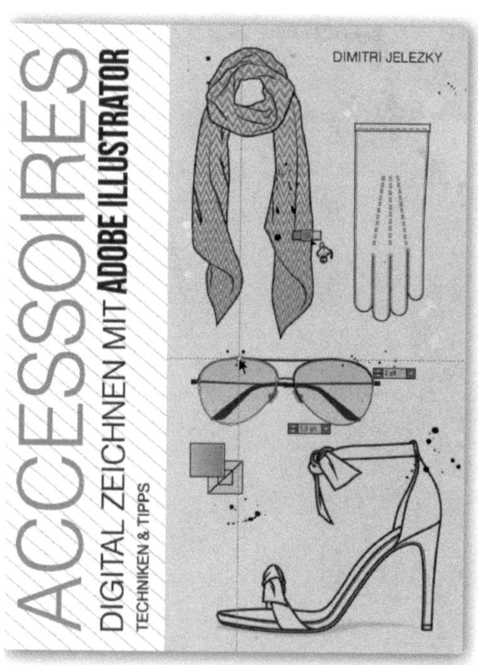

ACCESSOIRES - Digital Zeichnen mit Adobe Illustrator: Techniken & Tipps

Pages: ca. 156 pages
ISBN: 978-3945549391
Language: German
Price: 29,90 EUR

2.0 DIFFERENT PATTERN NAMES

ABORIGINAL PATTERN

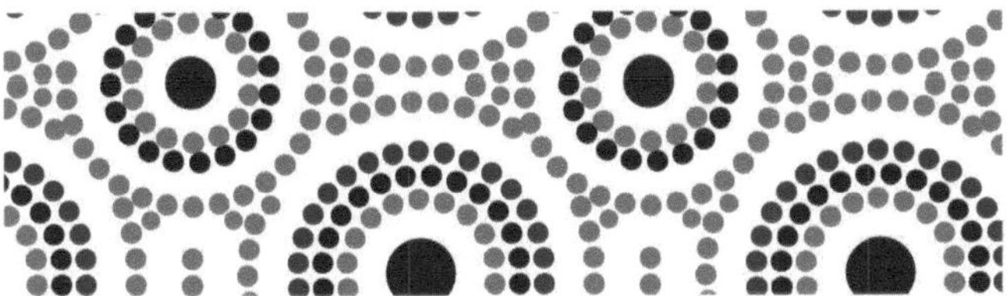

Aboriginal patterns reflect the rich cultural heritage, dreamtime stories, and connection to the land of Indigenous Australians . These patterns often feature intricate and vibrant designs that depict dreamtime stories, totems, animals, plants, and landscape elements.

ABSTRACT PATTERN

An abstract pattern is a non-representational, often geometric or stylized, visual design. Instead of depicting recognizable objects or scenes, it relies on elements like lines, shapes, colors, and textures to create a composition.

ADAPTATION PATTERN

In textile design, adaptation patterns involve modifying and integrating existing motifs, designs, or techniques to create something new . This process allows designers to blend historical and cultural elements with modern innovations, resulting in unique and evolving textile patterns.

AFRICAN PATTERN

Also known as Tribal pattern or Ankara. African pattern designs use vibrant, vivid colors that are associated with African culture.

ALLOVER PRINTS

An allover pattern in textile design features motifs (such as Flora&Fauna) and colors distributed across the entire surface of the fabric without a specific direction . These patterns create a seamless and balanced look. There are numerous allover pattern types.

ANIMAL PATTERN

Animal patterns are those that resemble the skin or fur of an animal. They can be further classified according to the animal the pattern tries to imitate.

ANTHEMION PATTERN

The anthemion pattern is a decorative motif commonly found in architecture, furniture, and textiles. It resembles a stylized honeysuckle or palm leaf Ancient Egyptian and Greek art frequently uses anthemion patterns.

ARABESQUE PATTERN

An arabesque pattern is a form of intricate, decorative artwork characterized by flowing lines, interlacing geometric shapes, and elaborate, often symmetrical motifs. It is deeply rooted in Islamic art and architecture.

ARGYLE PATTERN

An argyle pattern is a design made of interlocking diamonds of different colors, often including a superimposed grid of diagonal or criss-cross lines. The pattern typically uses a limited palette of colors.

ART DECO PATTERN

An Art Deco pattern is characterized by sleek, geometric, and stylized designs that reflect the modernity and luxury of the 1920s and 1930s . These patterns often incorporate bold, symmetrical compositions with stylized motifs and luxurious materials.

ART NOUVEAU PATTERN

An Art Nouveau pattern is characterized by its use of long, sinuous, organic lines and flowing natural forms . Flourishing between 1890 and 1910, this style often incorporates intricate details and motifs inspired by nature, mythology, and symbolism.

ASYMMETRICAL PATTERN

An asymmetrical pattern is a design where the elements are intentionally arranged unevenly, creating a lack of symmetry and a sense of dynamic visual interest . Unlike symmetrical designs, where elements are mirrored or evenly distributed around a central axis, asymmetrical patterns achieve balance through the strategic placement of dissimilar elements.

AWNING PATTERN

On a light background, the awning pattern consists of broad, vertical stripes of a solid color.

AZTEC PATTERN

An Aztec pattern is a design style inspired by the art, architecture, and textiles of the Aztec civilization. These patterns are characterized by geometric shapes, bold colors, and intricate motifs.

BASKET WEAVE PATTERN

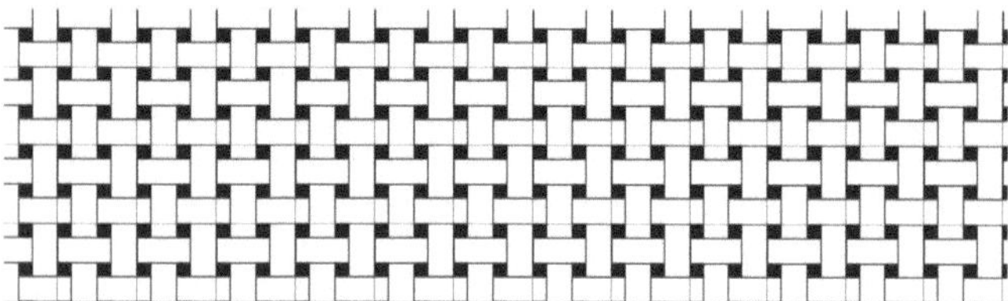

A pattern called a basket weave has a design that resembles a woven basket.

BATIK PATTERN

A batik pattern is a design created on fabric using a wax-resist dyeing technique. Molten wax is applied to cloth, and the waxed portions resist dyes, creating patterns. This process can be repeated multiple times with different colors to achieve complex and layered designs.

BAYADERE PATTERN

Vibrant horizontal stripes of different widths are used in the Bayadere pattern.

BEAD AND REEL PATTERN

Oval and round shapes alternate with elongated oval or cylindrical shapes in a bead and reel pattern.

BIRD´S EYE PATTERN

Bird's eye patterns consist of four or more carefully positioned tiny diamond shapes with a dot or blank space in the center.

BOHEMIAN PATTERN

A bohemian pattern, often called a "boho" pattern, is characterized by its eclectic mix of colors, patterns, and textures, reflecting a free-spirited and unconventional style. These patterns often draw inspiration from nature, global cultures, and vintage designs.

BOTANICAL PATTERN

A botanical pattern features designs inspired by plants, flowers, leaves, and other botanical elements . These patterns can range from realistic, detailed illustrations to stylized, abstract interpretations of plant life.

BOTEH PATTERN

The eardrop-shaped boteh pattern has a curved upper end. This shape is used in paisley patterns along with additional ornamentation and decorative elements.

BUFFALO CHECK PATTERN

A plaid pattern known as a "buffalo check" is made up of sizable blocks created by the intersection of two different colored yarns, usually red and black.

BULL´S EYE PATTERN

A bull's-eye pattern is a design featuring concentric circles radiating from a central point, resembling the target on a dartboard.

CALICO PATTERN

A calico pattern is characterized by small, densely packed, all-over floral designs, often printed on a light or white background. The term "calico" originally referred to cotton cloth from Calicut, India, but now describes the specific print style.

CAMOUFLAGE PATTERN

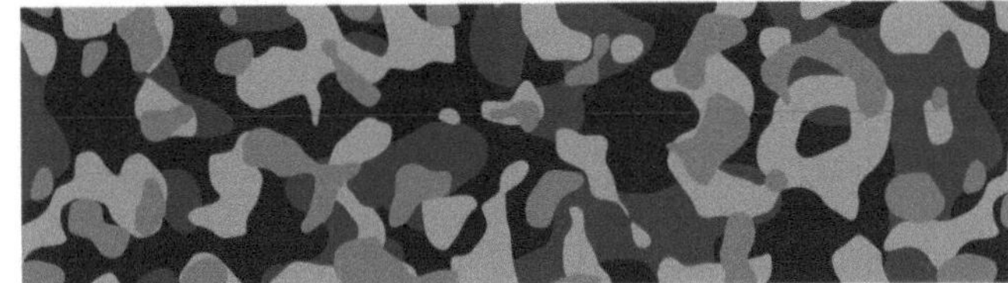

A camouflage pattern is a design that uses a combination of colors, shapes, and sometimes materials to conceal or disguise something, making it blend into its surroundings.

CANING PATTERN

A Caning pattern is a traditional weaving technique used in furniture making to create intricate designs on the surface of chairs, cabinets, and other wooden items.

CARTOUCHE PATTERN

An oblong design known as a cartouche pattern resembles a frame, table, or scroll that is inscribed.

CELTIC KNOT PATTERN

The Celtic knot pattern, also known as the Everlasting Knot pattern, makes use of numerous interlocking lines or ribbons that flow into one another and seem to never end.

CHEQUERED CHECKS PATTERN

Squares of contrasting color, texture, or material are used to create the chequered check pattern.

CHEVRON PATTERN

A chevron pattern is a design that consists of two or more stripes or lines that meet at an angle, typically forming a zigzag or V-shape.

CHINOSERIE PATTERN

Chinoiserie is a decorative style in European art and design that imitates, interprets, or evokes motifs and techniques from Chinese and East Asian art.

CHRISTMAS PATTERN

A Christmas pattern is any of several patterns with a Christmas theme, such as stars, reindeer, holly, etc., typically using the colors green and red.

COLLAGE PATTERN

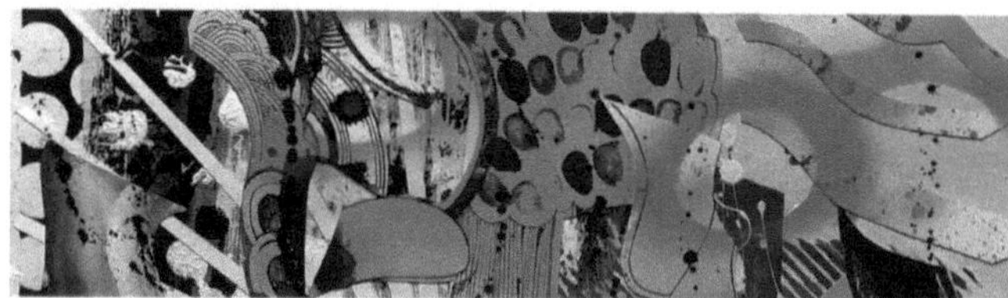

Glued scraps, pictures, drawings, or other objects give the appearance of a collage pattern on fabric.

COMPOSITE OVERLAY PATTERN

A composite overlay pattern layers two or more different patterns.

CONFETTI PATTERN

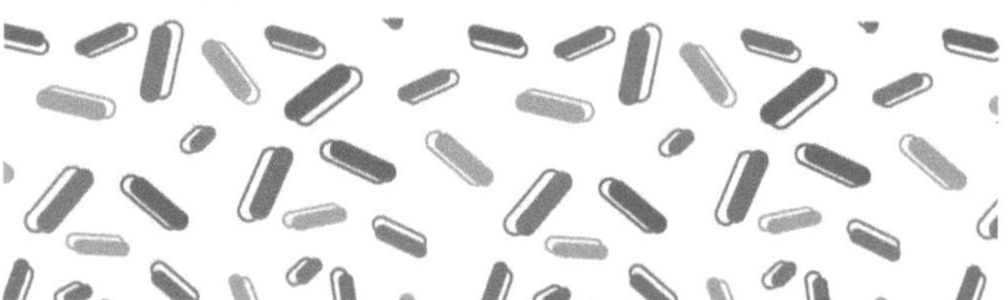

A confetti pattern is a design motif characterized by a scattered arrangement of colorful, small, and irregularly shaped shapes resembling confetti.

CONTOUR PATTERN

A contour pattern outlines the key features of a figure's shape.

CONVERSATIONAL PATTERN

A conversational pattern in textile design, also known as a novelty print or object print, features recognizable, non-traditional motifs like objects, scenes, or characters that serve as conversation starters. Instead of typical motifs like flowers or geometric shapes, these prints incorporate unusual elements that catch the eye and spark discussion.

COUNTERCHANGE PATTERN

A counterchange pattern involves a symmetrical arrangement where a motif and its background reverse in color. It's a two-color pattern where the positive and negative spaces trade hues, creating a visually balanced and often striking effect.

DAMASK PATTERN

A Damask pattern is a versatile design characterized by intricate patterns of flowers, fruit, and other shapes and typically featuring a reversible design.

DESIGNER PATTERN

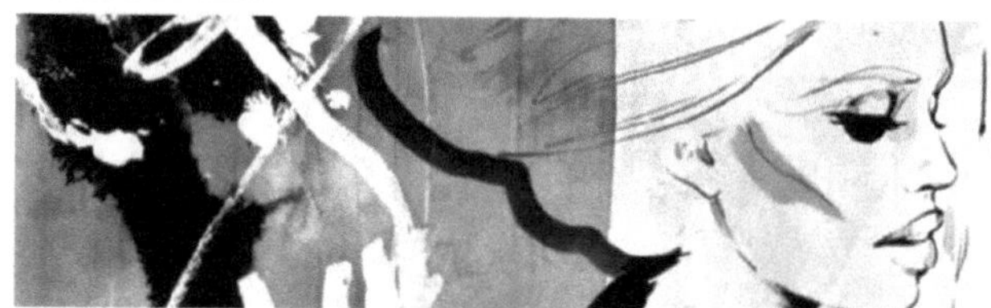

A unique pattern that is typically protected by designer's copyright is called a designer pattern.

DIAGONAL PATTERN

The motif of a diagonal fabric pattern includes diagonal lines.

DIAMOND PATTERN

A diamond pattern is characterized by the repetition of diamond shapes, often arranged in diagonal rows.

DIAPER PATTERN

The diaper pattern is made up of tiny, closely arranged forms that interlock with one another, usually in a diamond pattern.

DIGITAL PATTERN

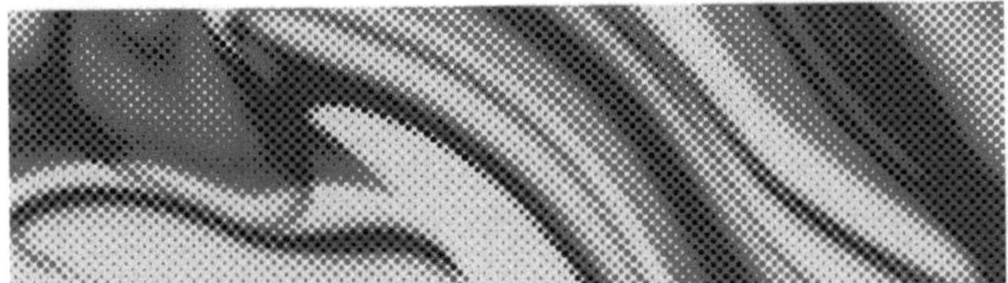

A digital pattern is one that contains components that were created by a computer. They frequently have fractal shapes or are artistically pixelated.

DIRECTIONAL PATTERN

Any pattern in which the motifs are oriented in one or more specific directions is known as a directional pattern.

DITSY PATTERN

Also known as ditzy, ditsie, or Ditsies. A ditsy pattern design featuring tiny, scattered motifs, often floral, distributed randomly across the fabric.

DOTTED SWISS PATTERN

Small, elevated dots are used to create the dotted Swiss pattern. Typically, the pattern is applied to a thin fabric that contrasts with the thicker dots.

DUPPLINS CHECK PATTERN

The Dupplins check pattern is an example of a District check (checks within checks) that alternates dark and light checks, frequently using framed lighter check motifs.

EVERLASTING KNOT PATTERN

The term "everlasting knot pattern" most likely refers to the endless knot, also known as the eternity knot or mystic knot.

FAIR ISLE

A Fair Isle pattern is a traditional knitting technique originating from Fair Isle, a small island in the Shetland Islands of Scotland . It's characterized by geometric patterns with multiple colors, typically knit in the round.

FIGURATIVE PATTERN

Either human or animal elements form the figurative pattern.

FLEUR DE LIS PATTERN

A fleur de lis pattern is a stylized design of a lily flower with three or four petals.

FLORAL PATTERN

A floral pattern in textile design features flowers as the primary design element, ranging from realistic botanical illustrations to abstract, stylized representations.

FOCUS PATTERN

A focus pattern it's something that we focus on over and over. Mostly the print has only one focus area.

FOULARD PATTERN

A foulard pattern is characterized by small, repeated, evenly spaced geometric or floral motifs.

FOUR-WAY LAYOUT PATTERN

The motifs that face left, right, up, and down are known as four-way patterns.

FRET PATTERN

A fret pattern features interconnected and symmetrical geometric motifs, often based on right-angle lines that form a repeating, maze-like design . It is also known as a Greek Key pattern.

FRIEZE PATTERN

An elongated vine or stranded rope are examples of frieze patterns, which repeat in a single direction.

GEOMETRIC PATTERN

A repeating pattern of geometric shapes, such as diamonds, squares, or cubes, is called a geometric pattern.

GINGHAM CHECK PATTERN

An all-over weaved block or check pattern known as the Ginham pattern is produced by overlapping stripes of the same width.

GLEN CHECKS PATTERN

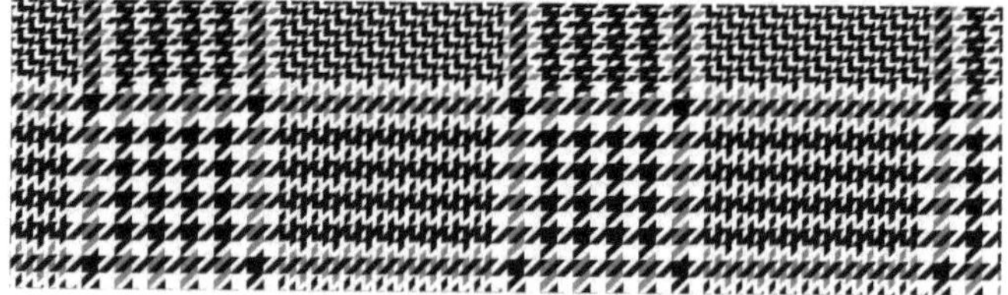

A type of District check known as Glen checks or also as Glen plaid or Prince of Wales check, is a classic woven fabric design characterized by a pattern of small and large checks typically features broken check areas at the intersection of darker and lighter stripes.

GRADATION PATTERN

A gradation pattern involves a gradual change or transition in color, tone, size, or motif density across the fabric.

GRAPH CHECK PATTERN

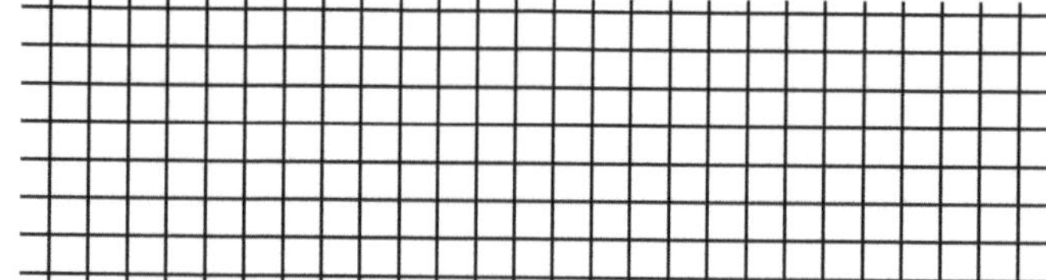

A graphic check pattern is a design featuring a grid-like arrangement of crossing lines, typically in two or more colors which has a solid background.

GRAPHIC PATTERN

Graphic patterns often draw inspiration from graphic art and design, featuring a combination of shapes, lines, and colors to create a visually striking effect.

GUILLOCHE PATTERN

A guilloché pattern involves intricate, repetitive geometric patterns mechanically engraved or digitally created to mimic engine-turned designs.

HAIRLINE PATTERN

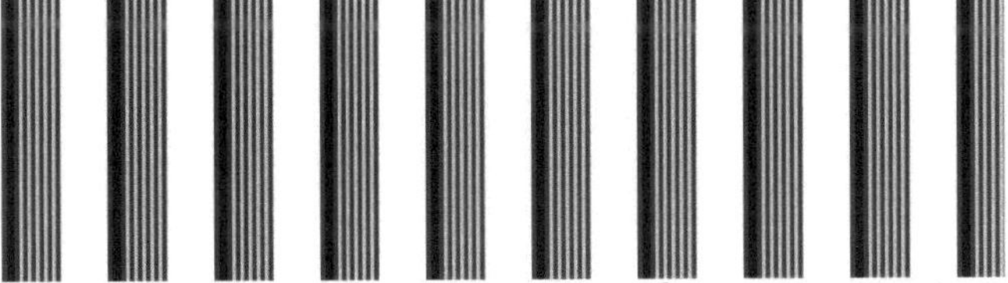

The hairline pattern features a series of very narrow stripes.

HARLEQUIN PATTERN

The harlequin pattern is a repeating design of long squares or constricted diamonds arranged in a lattice-like arrangement.

HERRINGBONE PATTERN

A herringbone pattern, also known as a broken twill weave, is a distinctive V-shaped weaving pattern commonly found in twill fabric.

HEXAGONAL PATTERN

The hexagonal pattern uses hexagonal shapes in an allover arrangement.

HOUNDS TOOTH PATTERN

Houndstooth is a distinctive duotone textile pattern characterized by broken checks or abstract four-pointed shapes. The pattern is made of alternating light and dark checks.

IKAT PATTERN

An ikat pattern is a textile design created using a resist dyeing technique on the yarns before the fabric is woven. This means the pattern is dyed onto the threads themselves, rather than printed on the finished fabric.

ILLUSION PATTERN

An illusion pattern utilizes visual tricks to create the perception of depth, movement, or altered shapes on a flat fabric surface.

INTERLOCKING PATTERN

The motifs are closely connected by an interlocking pattern. It is impossible to move one motif in this pattern without affecting another.

IRREGULAR REPEAT PATTERN

The irregular repeat pattern resembles brick layout and half drop patterns, with the exception that repeated units are spaced a certain distance apart.

JACOBEAN PATTERN

A Jacobean pattern characterized by elaborate and flowing designs, often featuring floral and plant motifs, along with birds and other animals, inspired by the "Tree of Life".

LANDSCAPE PATTERN

The landscape pattern features landscape scenes.

LANE´S NET PATTERN

Each diamond in the Lane's net pattern is rotated 45 and 90 degrees, and the pattern is usually filled with thin lines that radiate from opposite ends.

LATTICE PATTERN

Lattice patterns are crisscrossed, interconnected designs with holes that resemble squares or diamonds.

LIBERTY STYLE PATTERN

The liberty style pattern is a highly stylized allover design with tiny floral motifs.

LOGO PATTERN

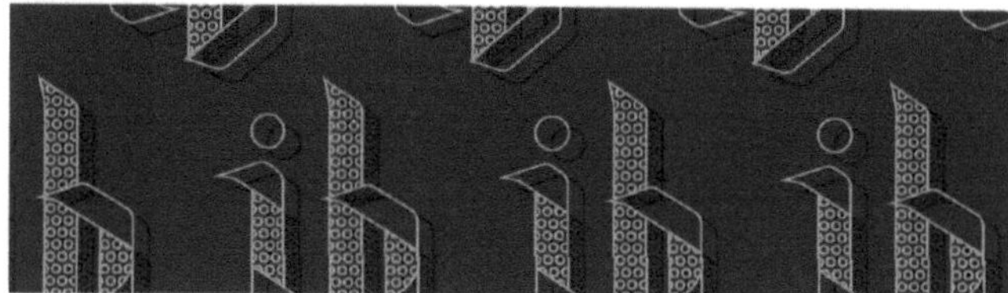

Any pattern made from a logo is called a logo pattern.

MANDRAS CHECK

A Madras check pattern is a colorful, typically plaid design, characterized by uneven checks formed by bands of colors crossing each other.

MAZE PATTERN

A Maze pattern is a seamless abstract pattern with curved lines, lines that look like a labyrinth from above.

MATELASSÉ PATTERN

Matelassé is a textile pattern and weaving technique that creates a quilted or padded appearance without actual stitching. The fabric is woven with multiple layers of threads that interlock and crinkle during the finishing process, producing a raised, textured surface.

MINI CHECK PATTERN

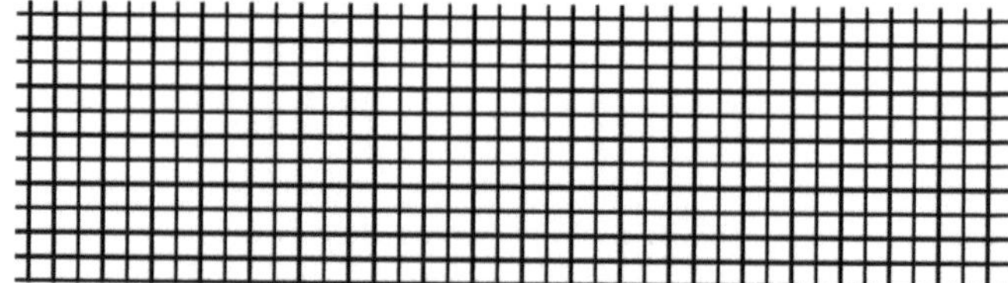

Small checks are used to create the mini check pattern. The checks' size is in the middle of a pincheck and a gingham check.

MOIRE PATTERN

A moire pattern is a visual effect that occurs when two similar patterns are overlaid at a slight angle or when they have slightly different spacings . This creates a new pattern of interference fringes, often appearing as wavy lines or shimmering effects.

MONOPRINT PATTERN

A monoprint is a single impression of an image made from a reprintable block. Printmaking techniques which can be used to make mono-prints include lithography, woodcut, and etching.

MOSAIC PATTERN

A mosaic pattern involves arranging small pieces of different materials, colors, or textures to create a larger, cohesive design. This technique mimics the art of mosaic, where small pieces of glass, stone, or other materials are assembled to form an image or pattern.

NATURAL PATTERN

A natural pattern draws inspiration directly from the natural world, incorporating motifs and elements found in nature, such as plants, animals, landscapes, and organic forms.

NAVAJO PATTERN

A Navajo pattern in textile design refers to a distinctive style of weaving and design that originates from the Navajo people. Navajo textiles, particularly their rugs and blankets, are renowned for their intricate patterns, vibrant colors, and cultural significance.

NEATS PATTERN

A "neats" pattern is an allover, small-scaled, spaced pattern featuring floral or geometric motifs, typically printed in one or two colors on a white or colored background.

NON DIRECTIONAL PATTERN

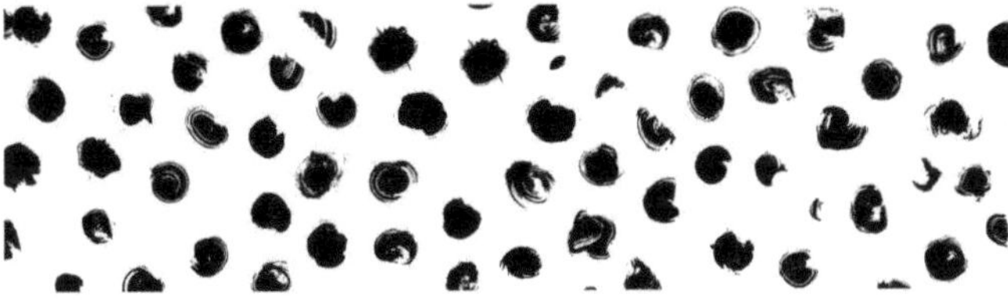

A non directional pattern is a pattern that looks the same from any direction.

NURSERY PATTERN

A nursery pattern in textile design is specifically created for items intended for babies and young children.

OGEE PATTERN

An ogee pattern is a decorative motif characterized by a curved shape resembling an elongated "S," formed by two opposing arcs—one concave and one convex.

OMBRE PATTERN

An ombre pattern is a shade effect in which the coverage gradually shifts from open to closed and from dark to light.

OP ART PATTERN

An Op Art pattern, short for Optical Art, uses geometric patterns, high contrast, and precise arrangements to create visual illusions of movement, vibration, or depth on a flat surface . The goal is to engage the viewer's eye and create a dynamic, sometimes disorienting, visual experience.

ORIENTAL NET PATTERN

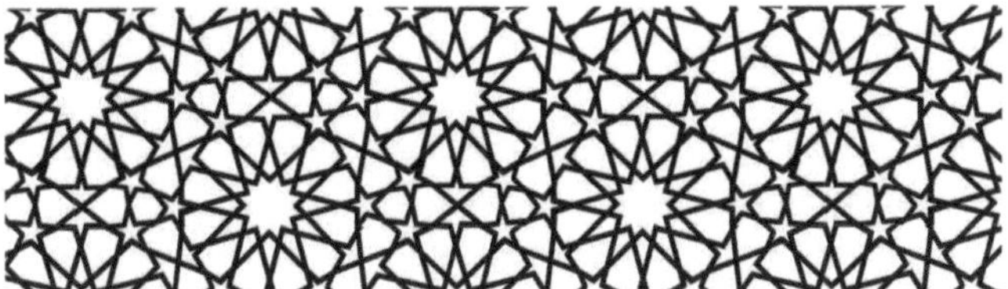

An elaborate design from Indian culture, usually a medallion, is called an oriental net pattern.

PAISLEY PATTERN

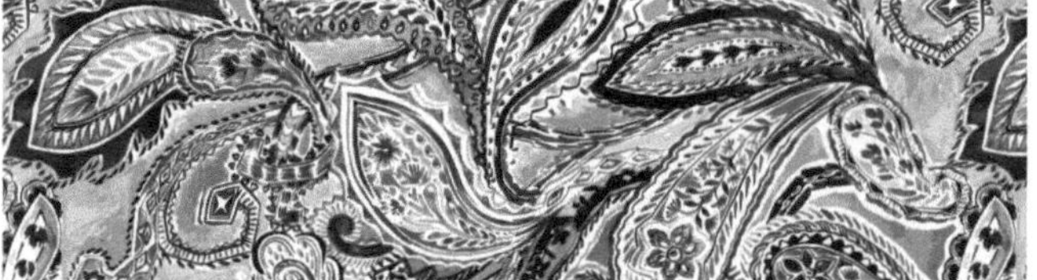

A paisley pattern is a distinctive ornamental textile design characterized by a teardrop-shaped motif with a curved upper end, known as a "boteh" or "buta". Paisley pattern can be simple or very complicated.

PALMETTE PATTERN

The stylized form of fan-shaped palm tree leaves is known as the palmette pattern.

PATRIOTIC PATTERN

Patriotic patterns include a theme that symbolizes a particular nation.

PEACOCK PATTERN

The peacock pattern is a mesmerizing design motif inspired by the distinctive plumage of the peacock bird.

PENCIL STRIPES PATTERN

Lines that are roughly the width of those drawn with a pencil make up pencil stripe patterns.

PHEASANT´S EYE PATTERN

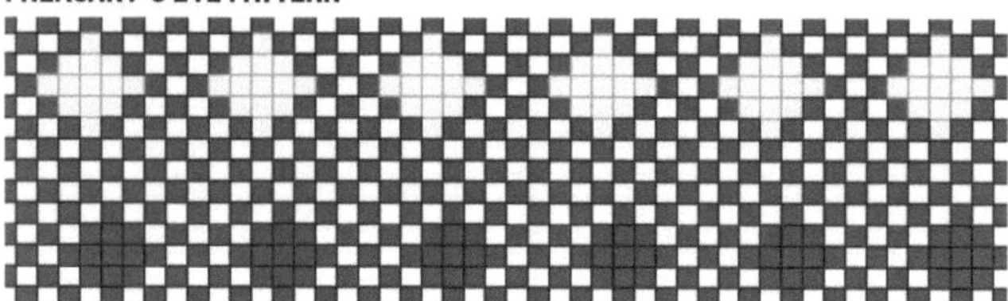

The weave pattern known as "Pheasant's Eye" forms a diamond shape that is slightly larger than the bird's eye pattern.

PIN CHECKS PATTERN (NAIL HEAD CHECK)

Pin-sized stripes that are just one or two yarns thick are used in the pin check pattern to form intersecting pins.

PIN DOT PATTERN

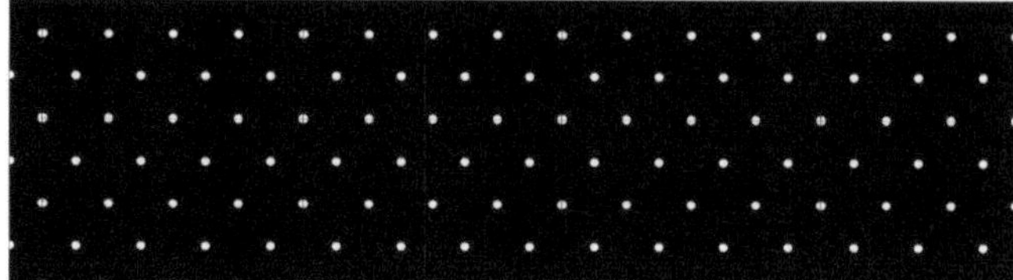

A polka-dot pattern of very small dots is called a pin-dot pattern.

PINSTRIPE PATTERN

Pinstripe is a type of stripe pattern with thin, one- or two-yarn-thick lines that do not intersect but can occasionally break.

PLAID PATTERN

A plaid pattern is a design featuring a pattern of horizontal and vertical stripes that cross each other to form different sized checks.

POLKA DOT PATTERN

A polka dot pattern is a classic design consisting of an array of large, filled circles, typically of the same size, arranged in a regular or evenly distributed manner . Traditionally, polka dots feature a single, bright color on a white or off-white background, or vice versa.

POP ART PATTERN

A Pop Art pattern is characterized by its use of bold colors, recognizable imagery from popular culture, and a playful, often ironic, approach to design. Inspired by the Pop Art movement, these patterns often incorporate elements from advertising, comic books, and everyday objects.

POSITIVE-NEGATIVE PATTERN

In a positive-negative pattern, both the positive motif and the negative motif have identical shapes.

QUATREFOIL PATTERN

Quatrefoil pattern means „four leaves", it looks like four similar sized overlapping circles.

RANDOM PATTERN

A random pattern in textile design, also known as a tossed or irregular pattern, features design elements scattered seemingly without any predictable order or symmetry . This unstructured arrangement results in an organic and non-linear design.

REGENCY STRIPES OR BENGAL STRIPES PATTERN

The regency stripes pattern or bengal stripes pattern has alternating light and dark stripes of the same width. The stripes are thinner than awing stripes but wider than candy stripes.

REGIMENTAL STRIPES PATTERN

A regimental stripe pattern features stripes using colors from respectivea regiment. The stripes consist of a combination of thick and thin lines.

RETRO PATTERN

A retro pattern draws inspiration from past decades, typically the mid-20th century, particularly the 1950s, 1960s, and 1970s . These patterns evoke a sense of nostalgia and often incorporate characteristic colors, shapes, and motifs from those eras.

ROMAN STRIPES PATTERN

Bright, multicolored, and highly contrasted vertical stripes make up the Roman stripes pattern.

SCALE PATTERN

The scale pattern, also known as the clamshell pattern, is made up of overlapping arcs that resemble the scales of fish or snakes.

SCROLL PATTERN

A scroll pattern includes spirals and vine-like curves.

SERPENTINE STRIPES PATTERN

The serpentine stripes pattern consists of aligned and wavy stripes.

SHEPHERD CHECKS PATTERN

A shepherd's check pattern, also known as shepherd's plaid, is a simple, uniform check pattern traditionally woven in white and a single dyed color, most often black . The pattern typically features small, equally sized checks formed by the intersection of light and dark threads.

SPRIG PATTERN

The sprig pattern resembles small shoots of young tree branches and repeating sprigs.

STIPPLE PATTERN

A stipple pattern is created using numerous small dots or specks to form an image or design . The density of the dots determines the tonal value, with more dots creating darker areas and fewer dots creating lighter areas.

STRIAE PATTERN

A striae pattern features subtle, irregular stripes or streaks. These stripes are usually soft and diffused, creating a textured, striated effect on the fabric.

SUZANI PATTERN (MANDALA PATTERN)

A suzani pattern is inspired by the traditional, hand-embroidered textiles of Central Asia. These patterns are characterized by bold, colorful, and often floral or geometric motifs, showcasing a rich cultural heritage.

SWIRL PATTERN

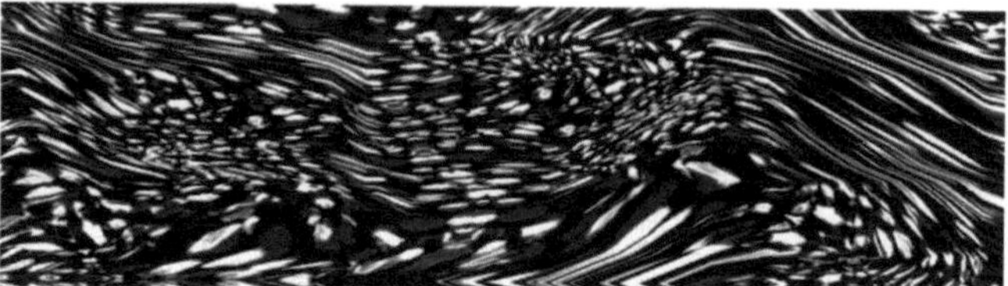

A swirl pattern features a repeating motif of circular or spiral shapes that create a dynamic, flowing, and often mesmerizing visual effect. These patterns evoke a sense of movement and energy and can range from simple, abstract swirls to more elaborate, organic designs.

TARTAN PATTERN

The terms checked patterns, plaid, and tartan are frequently used interchangeably. These days, tartan is a kind of plaid design. In contrast to other plaids, traditional tartans differ primarily in the repeat of the pattern. For tartans, the vertical stripe's pattern usually corresponds to the horizontal stripe's pattern.

TATTERSAIL PATTERN

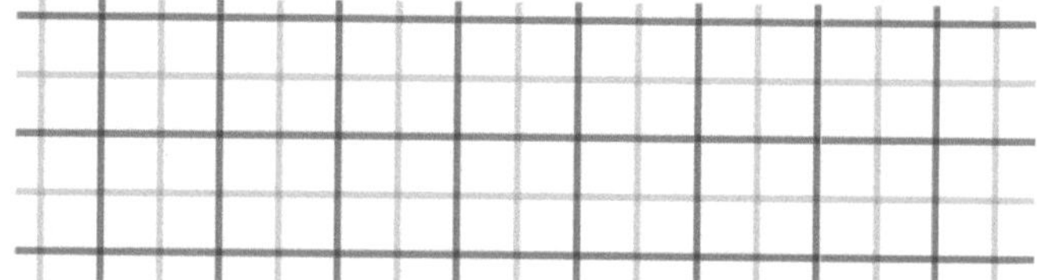

Tiny check patterns of thin, uniformly colored lines spaced regularly make up the tattersail pattern.

TESSELLATIONS PATTERN

A tessellations pattern is an infinitely extendable repeating pattern of interlocking shapes.

TEXTURE PATTERN

A texture pattern is a pattern that looks like surface of an object such as old paper, wood, or other materials with unique surface.

TOILE DE JUOY PATTERN

Toile de Jouy is a fabric design characterized by a repeated, monochromatic, typically intricate scene printed on a light-colored background. The motif of the Toile de Juoy pattern is usually of a French countryside.

TREFOIL PATTERN

A Trefoil pattern is characterized by a flower or leaf with three petals.

TRELLIS PATTERN

A trellis pattern features a network of interconnected elements that resemble a garden trellis, typically used to support climbing plants, often forming diamond or square shapes, which may include stylized vines or floral motifs.

TRIBAL PATTERN

A tribal pattern is inspired by the art, culture, and traditions of indigenous or tribal communities from various parts of the world. These patterns often feature bold, geometric shapes, intricate lines, and symbolic elements that hold cultural significance.

VERMICULAR PATTERN

An irregular pattern of twisted lines is called a vermicular pattern.

WATERCOLOR PATTERN

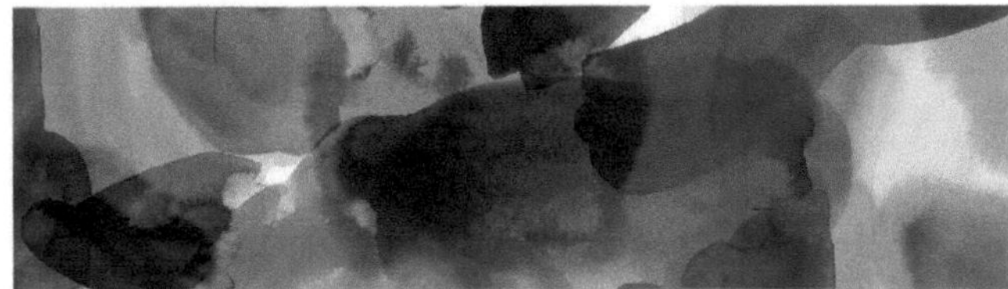

A watercolor pattern mimics the soft, fluid, and translucent effects of watercolor painting . These patterns often feature blended colors, gentle washes, and delicate details, creating a dreamy and artistic aesthetic.

WINDOWPANE CHECK PATTERN

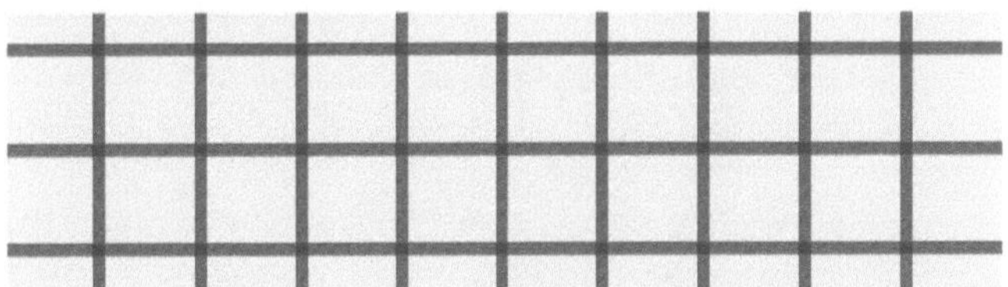

A windowpane check pattern features large, widely spaced lines that intersect to form large squares, resembling the panes of a window.

WREATH PATTERN

The circular patterns of entwined flowers or leaves are known as wreath patterns.

ZIGZAG PATTERN

The zigzag pattern consists of jagged, interconnected straight lines that are angled.

3.BASICS

This introduction will only cover Adobe Illustrator, as most of the final steps (such as repeat rectangle and style sheets) are completed in Illustrator. The relevant Adobe Photoshop-related steps are explained directly in the respective tutorial.

3.1 CREATING A NEW DOCUMENT (ADOBE ILLUSTRATOR)

10. Click "More Settings" to open another window.

11.Color Mode: sets the color mode of the new document. When you change the color mode, the elements: swatches, brushes, symbols, graphic styles of the selected new document profile are set to a new color mode.

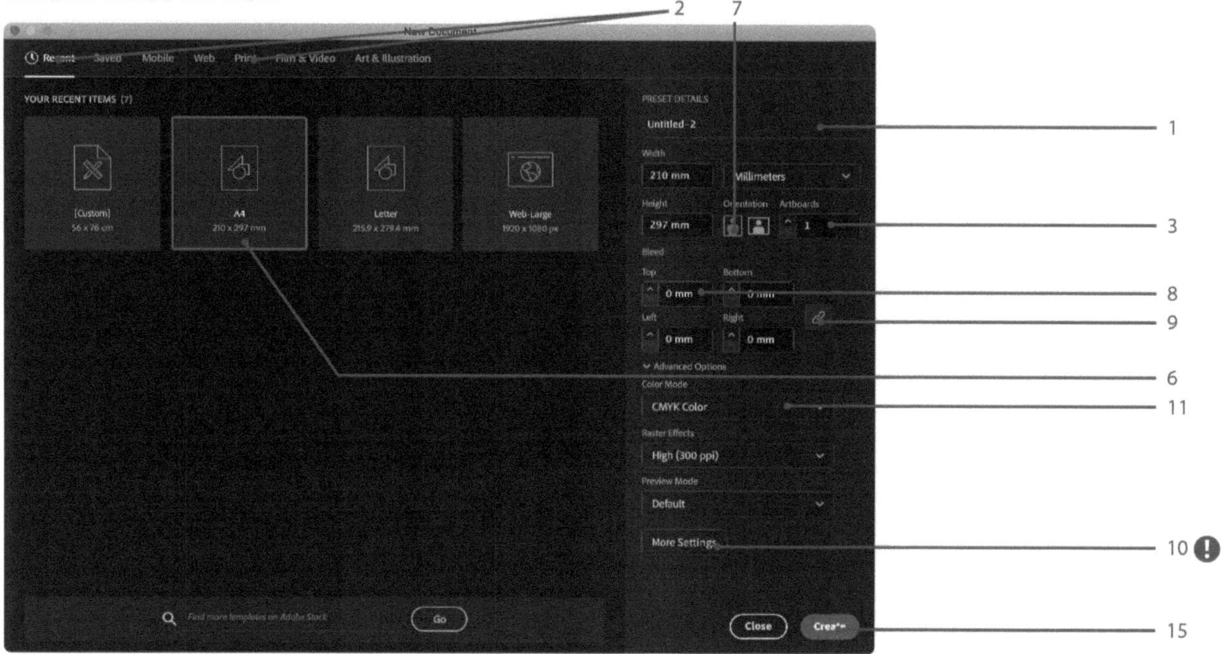

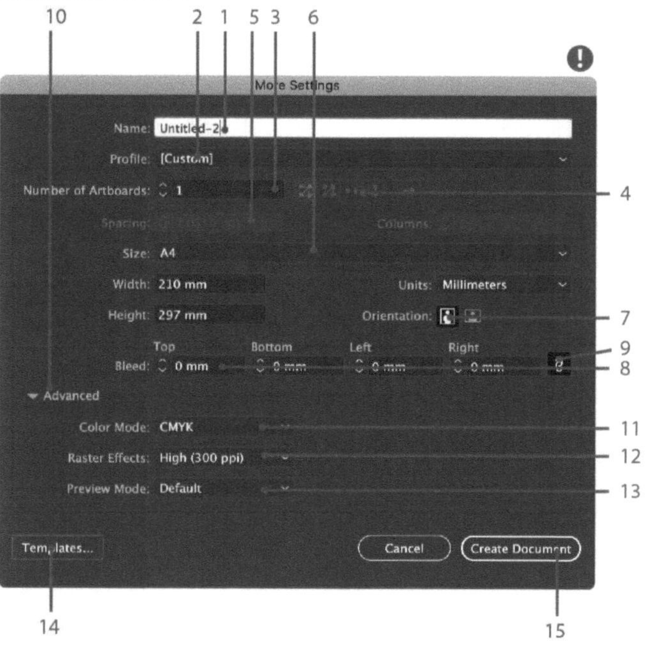

To create a new document, select **File > New**. The following window appears.

After creating the document, you can change these settings by selecting File > Document Setup > Edit Artboards and setting new preferences.

1. Type a name for the document.

2. Set the Print profile.

3.For example, set for the document artboards to 1 or 2 (for example A4 page) and the order in which you want it to appear on the screen.

4.This option is activated only at two or more artboards. **Grid by row:** Multiple artboards are arranged in the specified number of rows.

Grid by column: Multiple artboards are arranged in the specified number of columns. **Arrange by row:** Artboards are arranged in a straight row. **Arrange by column:** Artboards are arranged in a straight column. **Change from right to left in layout:** Multiple artboards are arranged in the specified row or column format, it is displayed from right to left.

5. This option is only activated with two or more artboards. Set the default spacing between artboards. This setting affects both horizontal and vertical spacing.

6.Set default size, units of measure for all artboards. You can subsequently adjust the artboards by moving and scaling as desired while you are working.

7. Specify the orientation of the document.

8. Specify the bleed location for each side of the artboard. When the lock symbol (9) is activated, the same values are automatically entered.

12.Raster effects: sets the resolution for raster effects in the document. For the profile "Print", this option is set to "High" by default.

13.Preview Mode: sets the default preview mode for the document ("Default" is optimal).

"Default" displays artwork created in the document in vector mode in color. Smoothing of curves is retained when zooming.

14. Templates allow you to create new documents with specific preferences and design elements. For example, when you design a collection, you can create a template with the desired artboard format, display settings (such as guides), and print options.

15. Use "Create" to confirm the settings.

3.2 IMPORTANT PRESETTINGS

To make changes to preferences for more convenient work with Illustrator, select (mac) **Illustrator > Preferences > General** or (windows) **Edit > Preferences > General**

Keyboard Increment: 1 pt

Set keyboard steps here: 1pt is optimal.
Note: While holding down the **Shift** key, the distance from the starting position of the object increases tenfold.

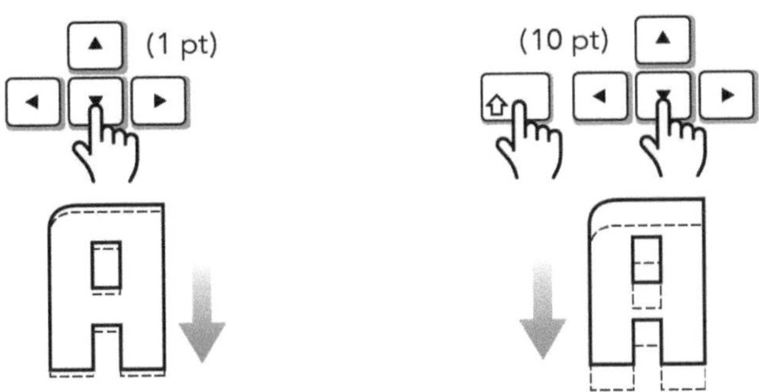

During drawing, objects are moved, among other things to gain access to fragments of an object and thereby ensure a clean selection with the direct selection tool (for example, to merge 2 endpoints to connect two paths).

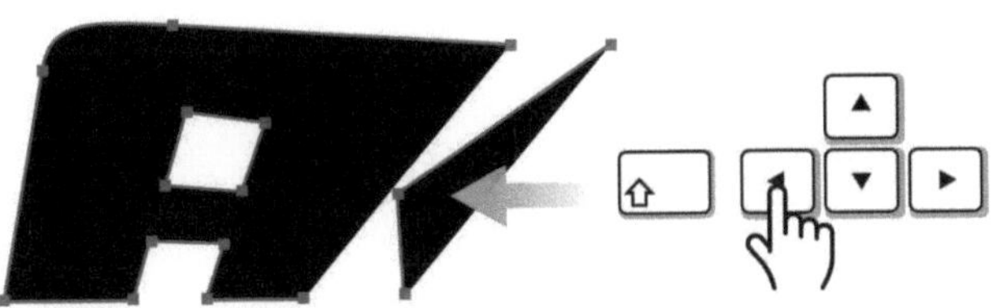

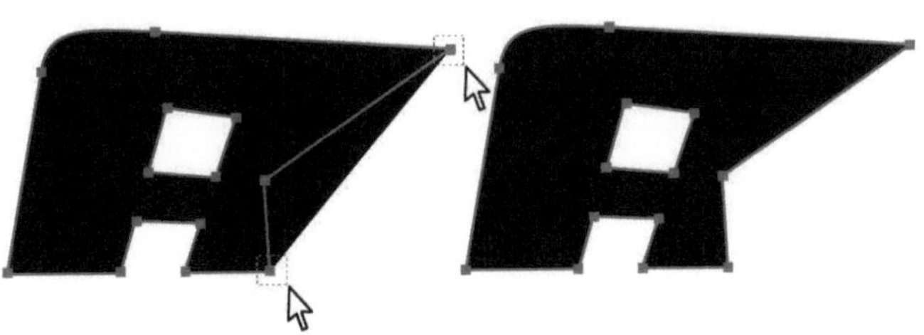

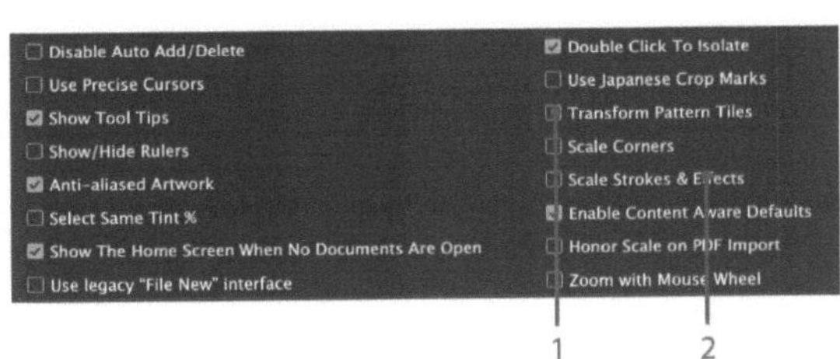

1. „Transform Pattern Tiles"
Enable "Transform Pattern Tiles" so that during the transformation of objects the patterns are also enlarged, decreased, rotated, and distorted.

2. "Scale Stroke and Effects"
Enable "Scale Strokes and Effects" to increase or decrease the strokes and effects while transforming objects.
This setting makes sense if, in retrospect, you have to reduce or enlarge the technical drawing (see example).

The stroke weight will be changed

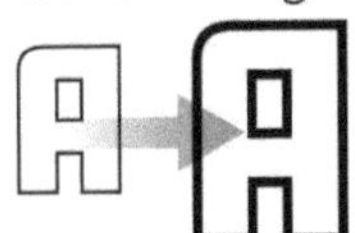

„Scale Strokes and Effects" is **activated**.

The stroke weights will stay the same.

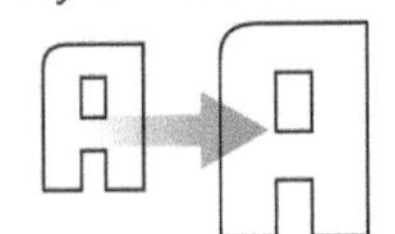

„Scale Strokes and Effects" is **deactivated**.

3.3 SELECTION & ANCHOR DISPLAY

1. Select **Illustrator > Preferences > Selection and Anchor Display** (Mac OS) or **Edit > Preferences > Selection and Anchor Display** (Windows).
2. In the "Selection" panel, set the following settings:
Tolerance: Accuracy with which a point is clicked.
Factory setting 3px is optimal.
Snap to Point: Accuracy with which an auxiliary line is magnetically attracted to a point. Factory setting 2px is optimal.
You can adjust the appearance of the anchor points and handles according to your personal needs.

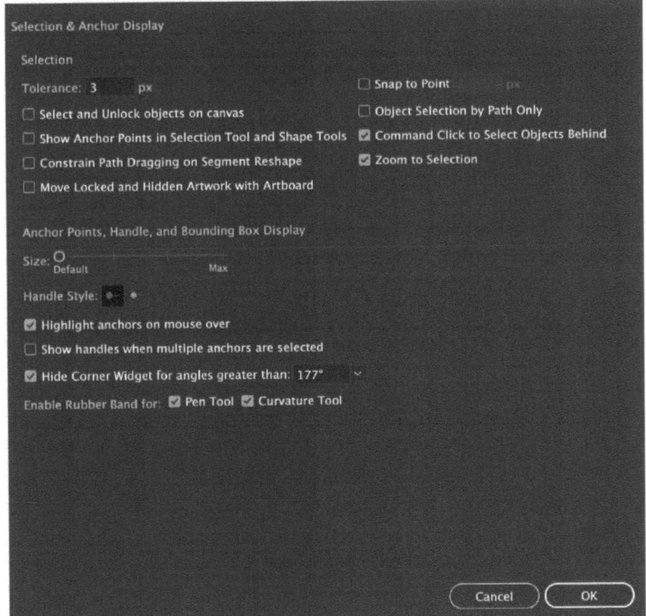

Rubber Band:
The first segment does not become visible until you click a second anchor point. It is also possible to preview path segments by selecting "Rubber Band".

3.4 ADJUSTING UNITS

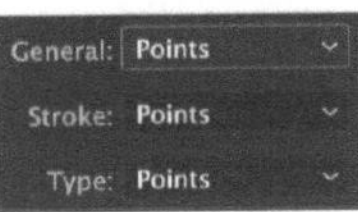

For fashion drawings in "General" it makes sense to set millimeters. For stroke and type, it makes sense to set points.

3.5 SET GUIDES AND GRID

Guides are used to align text and graphic objects.
You can create straight vertical or horizontal lines (ruler guides) and vector objects (guideline objects) converted to guides. Grids and guides are not printed.

You can choose between two helper lines - points and lines. You can also change the color of guides: Mac: **Illustrator > Preferences > Guides and Grid** / PC: **Edit > Preferences > Guides and Grid**.

While working, the guides must always be locked to ensure a faultless workflow.
Therefore, always check if the guides are locked.
View > Guides > Lock Guides must be enabled. Keyboard shortcut command "Lock/Unlock Guides": Mac alt/option + cmd + , / PC alt/option + Ctrl + ,
If guides are not locked, objects and guides are also selected (for example, if selection or direct selection tools are used). This causes problems creating allover prints or pattern brushes.
If guides do not appear, select **View > Guides > Show Guides**.
Show/Hide Guides shortcut:
Mac cmd + , / PC Ctrl + , [cmd ⌘][;] / [Ctrl][;]
To place guides on the artboard, you must first activate the rulers. Select **View > Rulers > Show Rulers**.
Show/hide ruler shortcut command:
cmd + R / PC: Ctrl + R

Place guides:
1. Place the pointer on the vertical ruler (create vertical guide), or on the horizontal ruler (create horizontal guide).
2. Drag the guide to the desired location.
You can also convert vector objects to guides if you select the object using the **Selection tool** (V) then right-click the stroke or fill color (if any) and enable Make Guides. Alternatively, select **View > Guides > Make Guides**.
3. If you want the guides to remain confined to a artboard and not extend across the entire work surface, select the **Artboard Tool** (Shift+O) and then drag the guides onto the artboard.

Delete, move, or convert guides:
1. If guides are locked, disable **View > Guides > Lock Guides**.
2. Click the guideline (or drag a selection rectangle around the guideline), then the guideline should take a different color, and then delete the guideline by pressing the **Backspace** key or by selecting **Edit > Cut or Edit > Clear**.
Delete all guides by selecting **View > Guides > Clear Guides**.
Select **View > Guides > Release Guides** to convert the helper object back to a normal graphic object.

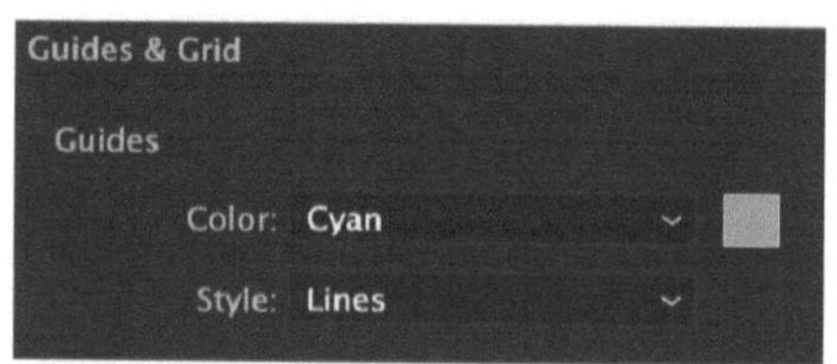

3.6 ALIGN OBJECTS ON ANCHOR POINTS AND GUIDES

1. Select **View > Snap to Point**.
2. Select the object you want to move or drag a guide and place the pointer exactly where you want to align it on an anchor point and guide.
When you enable **Snap to Point** the alignment is based on the position of the mouse pointer, not the edges of the dragged object.
3. Drag the object/guideline to the desired location.
If the pointer is 2 pixels or less apart from the anchor point or the guideline, it aligns with the point. When alignment occurs, the pointer is changed from a completed arrow to an arrow outline.

3.7 SMART GUIDES

Smart guides are temporary guides that appear when you create and edit objects or edit artboards. They automatically align with other objects when editing, aligning, and transforming objects or artboards and they also display X and Y position or delta values.

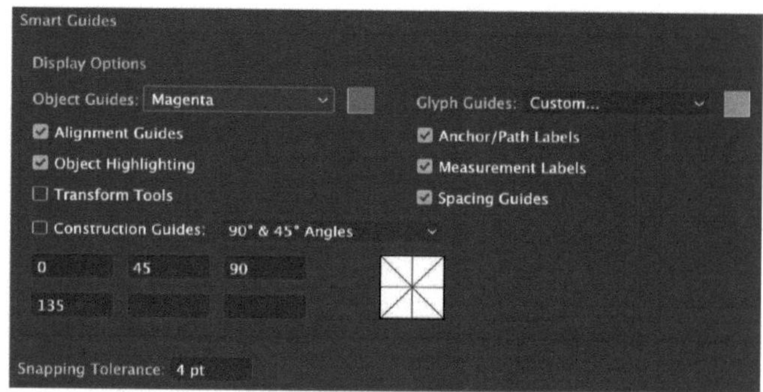

To enable Smart Guides, select **View > Smart Guides**.

Shortcut Mac cmd + U / PC Ctrl + U

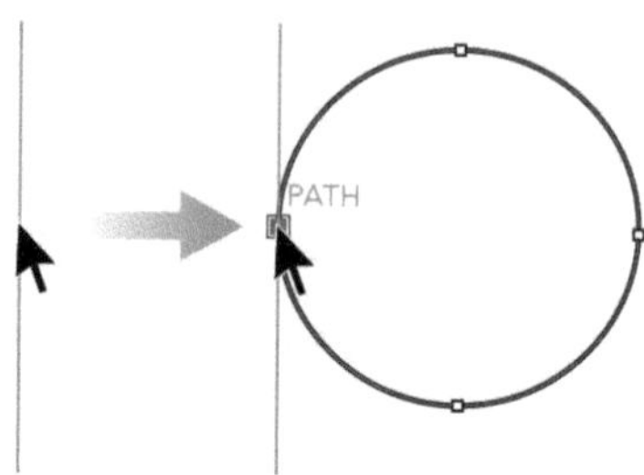

In this example, the guideline automatically aligned at an anchor point (magnetically coupled).

3.8 DOCUMENT SAVE AS

The document is always saved as .ai file (Adobe Illustrator format) to be able to open and edit it again and again. When you send technical drawings or illustrations to your customers (for example by email), the documents are in many cases also exported as **.jpg**, **.pdf** or **.tiff** files, because the **.ai** format can be easily opened only with Adobe Illustrator.

Save in adobe illustrator format (Ai):
1. Select **File > Save As...** or **File > Save as Copy...**
2. Type a file name and select a location for the file.
3. Select Illustrator **(.ai)** file format and confirm with **OK** (Mac) or **Save** (PC).
4. In the Illustrator options dialog box, specify the options you want and confirm with OK (by default you don´t have to make any changes).

1. Use the **Version** option to set the illustrator version with which you want the file to be compatible. If the document is opened in an older version, you should set the version in which the file is to be opened later (for example CS5) when saving the file in a newer version (for example CC), because older formats do not support all functions of the current version of Illustrator. So if you open a file that was saved with/for Illustrator CC (newer version) in an older version of Illustrator (for example CS5), certain types of data are changed (e.g. pattern brushes are converted and can no longer be used correctly, etc.).

2. **Create a PDF-compatible file** saves a PDF version of the document in Illustrator. Select this option if you want the Illustrator file to be compatible with other Adobe applications.

3. **Include linked files embeds files** associated with the artwork.

4. **Embed ICC profiles** creates a document with color management.

5. **Use compression** compresses PDF data in the Illustrator file.

6. **Save each artboard in a separate file** each artboard is saved in a separate file. At the same time, a separate master file is created that contains all the drawing surfaces.

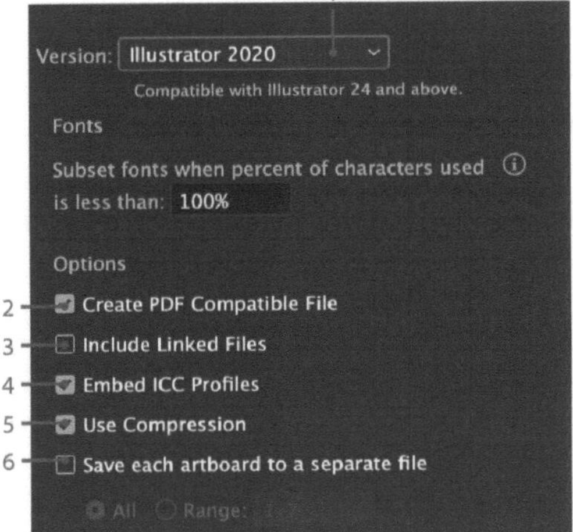

3.9 FILE EXPORT

Save in .jpg or .pdf format:

1. Select **File > Export > Export As...**
2. Type a file name and select a location for the file.
3. Select **.jpg** as the file format and click **Use Artboards**.
4. If **All** is enabled, all the artboards of the document are exported. If **Range** is enabled, you can specify which range is exported. (see example below).

If **All** is enabled, all artboards are exported.

If **range** is enabled, you can specify which range is exported. (for example 1). Then only this range is exported.

5. Select **Export**

6. Use the **Color Model** option to set the color space (set the print to CMYK, for Web, for example, if you send the exported file by email, set the RGB best).

7. The **Quality** option sets the quality of the .jpg file. I recommend adjusting the quality to 8-10.

8. Leave "Baseline" (Standard) for **compression method**.

9. The **Resolution** option sets the "pixels per inch." This is also about quality. For professional printing set 300 ppi or higher, for a "proof" 150 ppi would be sufficient, for example, if you work with a conventional printer.

3.10 DIFFERENCE BETWEEN RGB AND CMYK COLOR

Primary colors are RGB colors in additive color mixing, which is used, among other things, in computer monitors. For printing, you should save the document in the CMYK color space. Cyan, Magenta, Yellow and Black are the primary colors of the subtractive color mixture.

RGB color space includes a larger number of representable colors than the CMYK color space.

It is also possible to change the color mode later **File > Document Color Mode >** enable **CMYK** or **RGB**.
Note: After conversion to CMYK, bright colors are lost. In the fashion industry, "Textile Pantone" colors are often used to coordinate precisely the colors with the supplier.

Interesting thematically compiled color swatch libraries are located under **Windows > Swatch Libraries...**

3.11 ADDING ARTBOARDS

To add more artboards, select (**Shift + O**).

1. In the control panel, activate the icon „New artboard".
2. Place the artboard anywhere.

3.12 VECTOR AND PIXEL-ORIENTED GRAPHICS

Adobe illustrator is a vector-oriented graphics programme. Adobe Photoshop is a pixel-oriented graphics programme

With vector graphics the description of a straight line exists of a starting point and a terminator point, if necessary a fill color and line weight.

Pixel graphics exist of many small rectangles.

Pixel-oriented: have a defined size in pixel, every pixel is square and has only one color. While increasing these pixels become visible and the picture becomes blurred.

Vector-oriented: Lines, fills are defined by vectors mathematically, the objects thereby are arbitrarily scaleable without degradation (see picture).

If you find out that during the work with illustrator everything is shown in pixels, then you have activated by mistake the pixel preview:
View> Pixel Preview
Shortcut command: Mac: alt/option + cmd + Y /
PC: alt/option + Ctrl + Y

3.13 GRID AND TRANSPARENCY GRID

Grid:

1. Select **View > Show Grid.**
2. Select **View > Snap to Grid.**

Transparency grid:

1. Select **View > Show Transparency Grid.**

Grids and transparency grids are used when drawing rectangular shapes such as bags (accessories).

I personally work only with **Smart Guides (View > Smart Guides)** and (**View > Snap to Point**). I find grids and transparency grids disturbing when working with illustrations.

3.14 OTHER IMPORTANT SETTINGS

Please make sure that the following options are **always** displayed so that the work with Illustrator is not restricted.

View > Show Artboards
(Mac shortcut: Shift + cmd + H / PC: Shift + Ctrl + H).

View > Show Bounding Box
(shortcut Mac: Shift + cmd + B / PC: Shift + Ctrl + B).

View > Show Edges
(Mac shortcut: cmd + H / PC: Ctrl + H)

View > Show Corner Widget

Under Mac: **Illustrator > Preferences > User Interface** / PC: **Edit > Preferences > User Interface** you can adjust the brightness of your user interface.

3.15 WORKING WITH RULERS

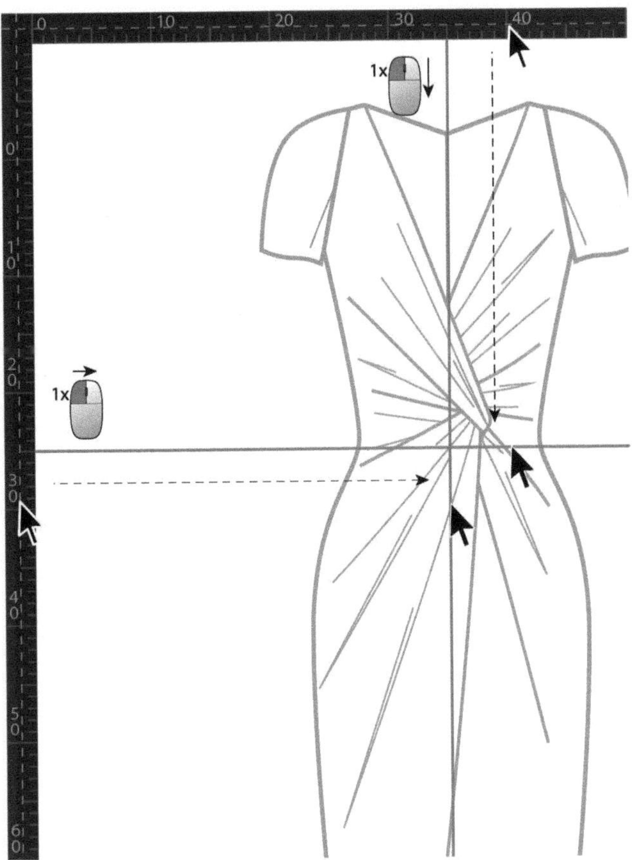

To place objects exact in the work surface and to do measurements, you can use for it rulers. Activate **View > Rulers > Show Rulers** (shortcut command Mac: cmd + R / PC: Ctrl + R). The place in the upper left corner of the sign window on which "0" stand is called ruler zero.

In Adobe Illustrator there are separate rulers for documents and artboards.

„Global Rulers": **View > Rulers > Show Rulers**
are window rulers that appear on the top and left sides of the drawing window. The default ruler zero is located at the top left of the drawing window.

„Artboard Rulers": **View > Rulers > Change to Artboard Rulers** appears on the top and left sides of the active artboard. The standard artboard ruler zero point is located at the top left of the artboard.

The difference between the artboard rulers and the global rulers is that the origin point depends on the active artboard when the artboard rulers are selected. It is also possible to specify different origin points for artboard rulers.

3.16 CONTROL PANEL

Different panels can be found under **Window**.
In the panels, you can set and change different settings for objects and for different Illustrator functions.
e.g.:
- In the **stroke** panel, among other things, you can set the stroke weight for a path or "Dashed Line" for a quilting seam.
- In the swatch panel, among other things, you can set the stroke color of an object (for example, fill a dress with a color, pattern, or gradient).

- In the **Layers** panel, you can change the arrangement of objects within the document, lock them, and so on.

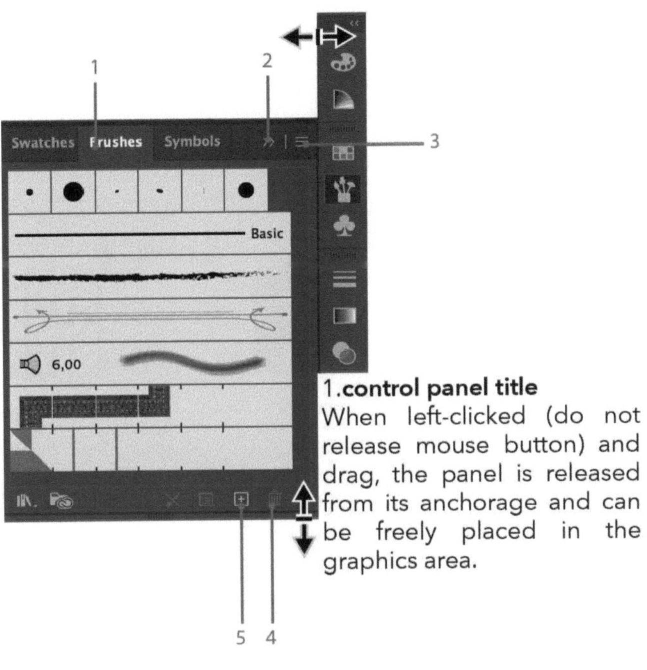

1.control panel title
When left-clicked (do not release mouse button) and drag, the panel is released from its anchorage and can be freely placed in the graphics area.

2.Extend control panel
By clicking on the double arrow, the control panel group is reduced or enlarged.

3. Here you can show **more options** for the respective control panel. 

4. Control panel specific **delete** command (for example, in the brush panel, this will delete a specific brush rapport).

5. Panel specific command **new** (for example, a new color is created in the Swatches panel).

You can adjust the window size by dragging the mouse pointer to the right or left bottom to resize the window.

3.17 MENU COMMANDS

Menu commands are used to activate various program functions, instructions (e.g. Object > Path > Offset Path), open panels, change workspace. Many shortcuts in this book refer to program functions that can be found under menu commands.

If the menu command bar is not visible, press the F key (this will change the screen mode).

3.18 FILL AND STROKE COLOR

In fashion design, mostly technical drawings and fashion illustrations are created with Adobe Illustrator. An object can be assigned a stroke without **fill** color (for example, a black/white technical drawing) or a pattern with a **fill** color but without **stroke** color (for examplea rapport for a check pattern). However, an object can also be assigned both **stroke** and **fill** color (for example, a colored technical drawing/illustration).

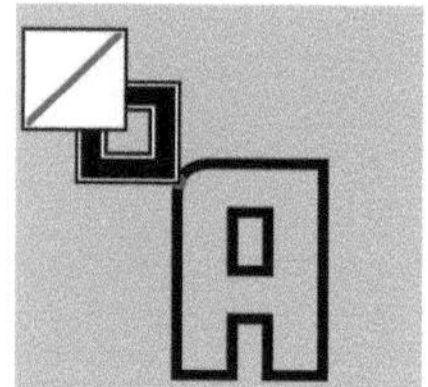

Stroke: „black"
fill:
„None"

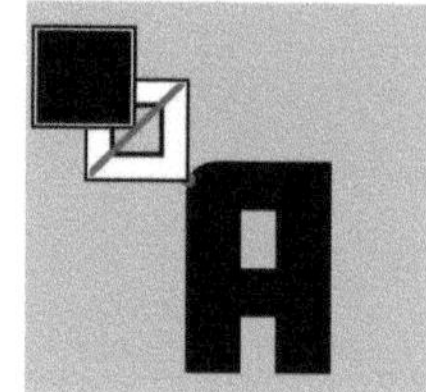

Stroke: „None"
fill:
„black"

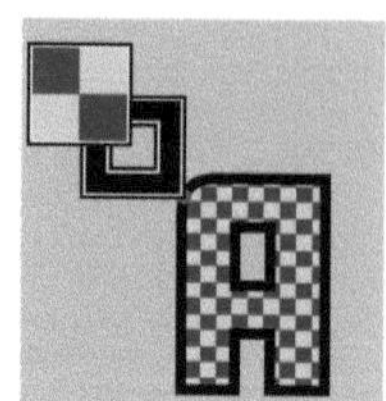

Stroke: „black"
fill:
filled with
„pattern"

A fill in an object can be either a color, a pattern, or a gradient. The visible outline of an object is a stroke. However, stroke can also be the edge of an live painting group or a path.

Different weights, colors, and patterns can be assigned to a stroke. You can also apply different pattern brushes (e.g. overlock seam, blind stitch, etc.)

fills (color, pattern, gradient) can be applied to both open and closed objects, as well as to closed objects of live painting groups.

Fill is activated   **Stroke is activated**

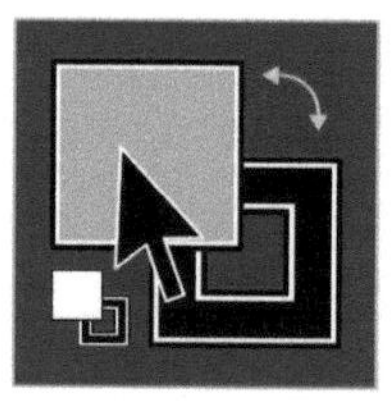

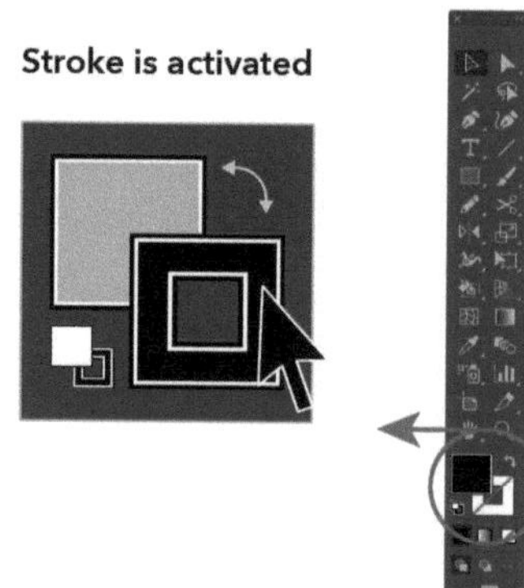

Option 1:

To set a fill or stroke color
Double-click in the **tools panel** either on a fill or stroke.

Option 2:

To set colors or patterns for a fill or stroke, select **Window > Swatches**.

Always make sure that the fill or stroke is enabled (placed in the foreground) when changing a color while working. Because if you plan to change stroke color, but the "fill" is in the foreground, then the fill color and not the stroke color, is changed. **The X button places fill or stroke in the foreground.**

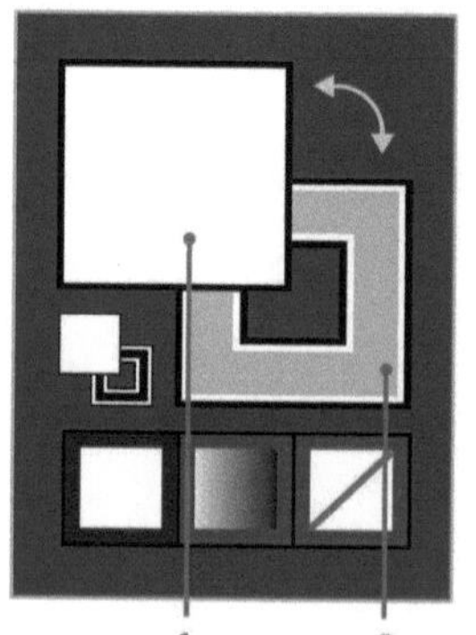

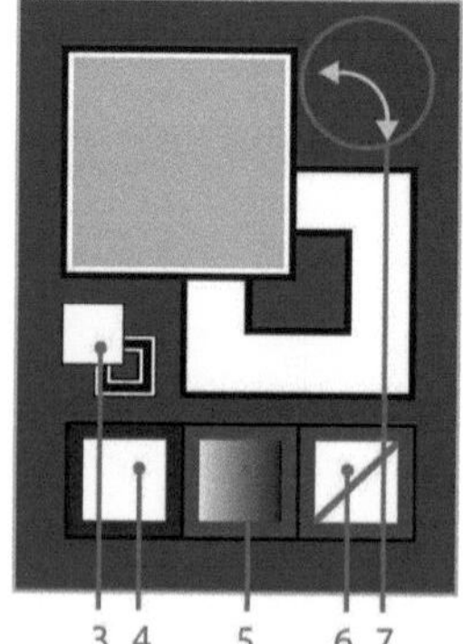

1. A *Single click* (left mouse button) bring the fill to the foreground, then open **Window > Swatches** and select a color/pattern. With a *double click* the **Color Picker** is opened, here you can mix colors individually.

2. A *single click* (left mouse button) brings the stroke to the foreground, then opens **Window > Swatches** and selects a color/pattern. With a *double click* **Color Picker** is opened, here you can mix colors individually.

Under **Window > Swatch Libraries >...** you can find many interesting color libraries (compiled by topic). The selected color from one of these swatches is automatically copied to the swatch panel of the document.

3. The default fill and stroke (S/W) setting is enabled (D).

4. Activates the most recently selected fill color on an object with a gradient fill or an object with no fill color or stroke color (,) .

5. Activates the B&W gradient (.) .

6. Deselects the fill color or stroke color of the selected object (#) .

7. Fill and stroke color are exchanged (Shift + X).

3.19 DIFFERENT FILL AND STROKE COLORATION SETTINGS

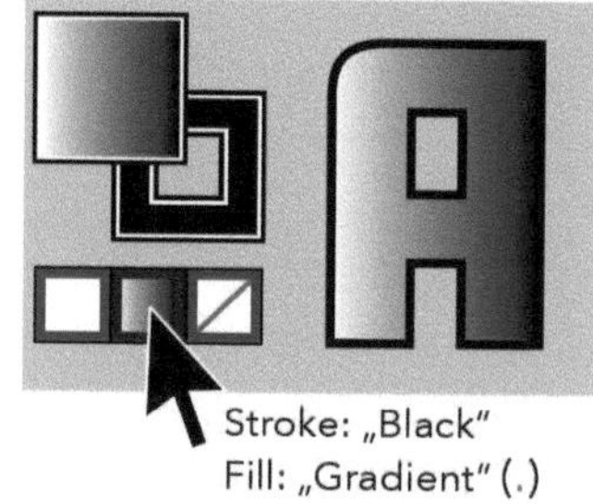

Stroke: „Black"
Fill: „Gradient" (.)

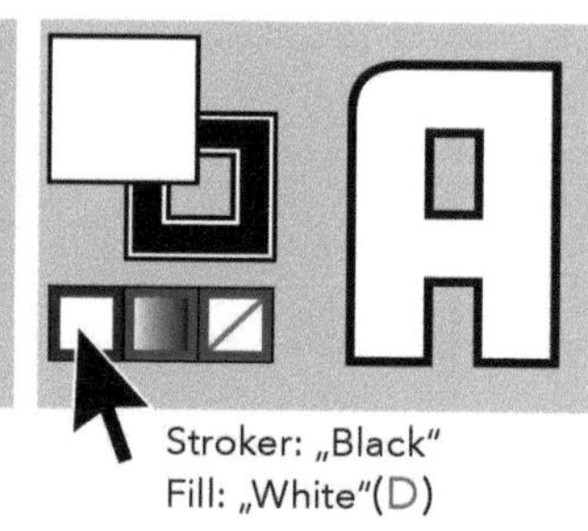

Stroker: „Black"
Fill: „White"(D)

Stroke: „None" (#)
Fill: „None" (#)

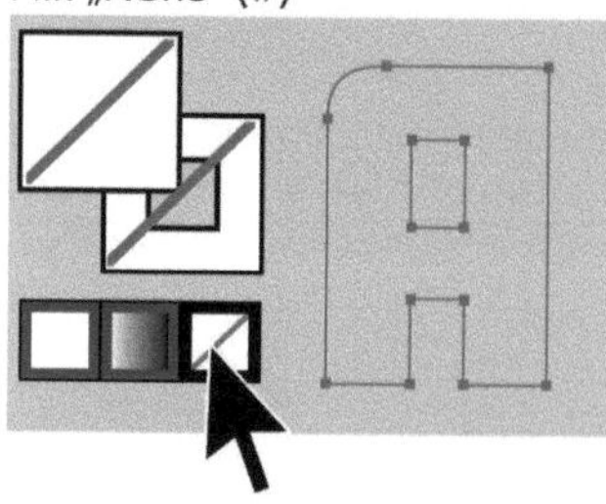

Stroke: filled with a Pattern"
Fill: „White"

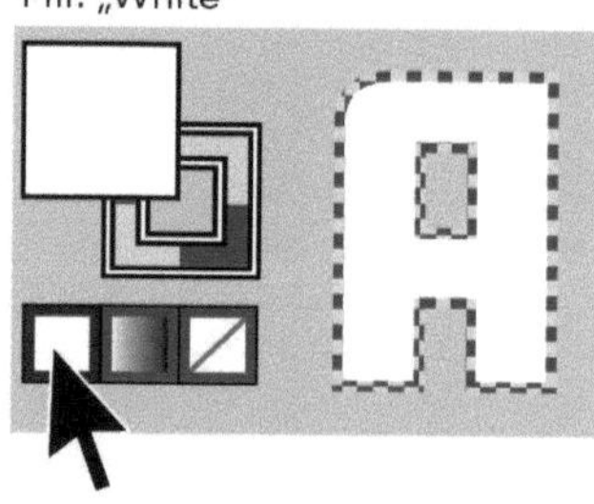

3.20 COLOR PICKER

 To select a color, double-click the fill or stroke to select a color using the Color Picker.

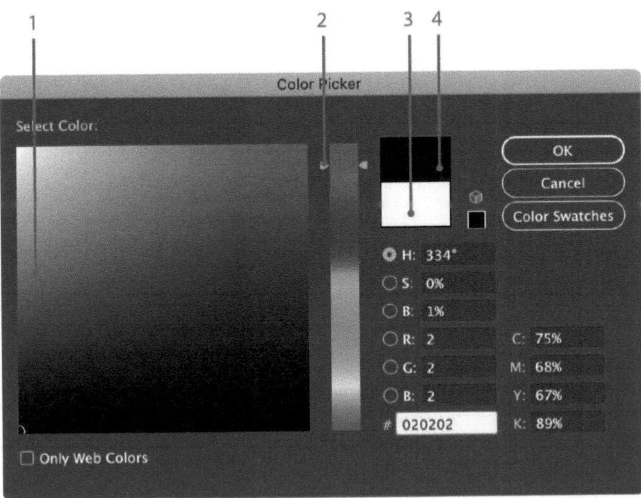

- You can mix colors or enter them numerically in the color picker.

Mix colors:
1. Click in the color spectrum (1) and use the mouse pointer to drag within the color spectrum.
2. Drag along the color slider at the triangles (2).
4. Then confirm with "OK."

Note: (3) is the original color and
(4) the new color (preview).

3.21 SWATCHES

Swatches include colors, gradients, and patterns. The swatches stored in Illustrator file appear in the Swatches panel. Color fields can be stored individually or arranged in groups (4) (**important for summerizing the season collection colors**).
An interesting way that is often used at work is to import color field libraries from other Illustrator documents:

1. **Window > Swatches** (opens swatches).
2. Click on the icon
3. **Open Swatch Library > Other Library...**
4. Select an Illustrator (.ai) document with a swatch library and confirm with "Open."

This allows you to import colors/patterns/gradients from other documents.

This is especially important when designing a fashion collection, because a collection contains a certain number of colors and patterns. Therefore, you only need to create your swatches once, and then you can import this library into a new document again and again from an Illustrator document.

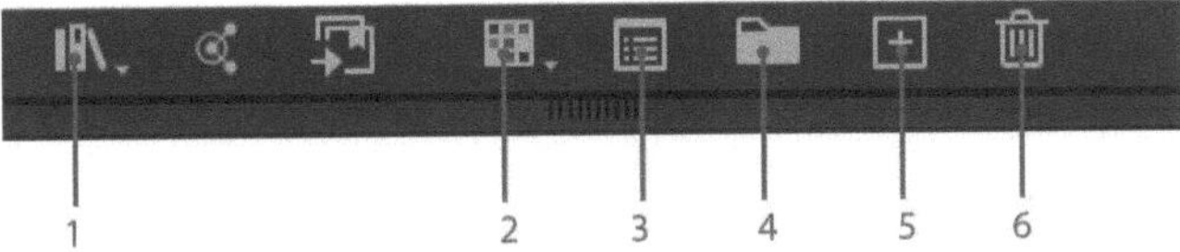

1. "Swatch Libraries menu" menu: Here are different swatch libraries arranged by topics.
2. Show Swatch Kinds menu: Here you can define which swatch types are displayed. For example, when you click Show Pattern Swatches, only patterns that are in your document are displayed.
3. For a selected color, you can click Swatch Options, which displays the swatch name, color style, and color mode.
4. New Color Group: A new color group is created. You can click a specific swatch (left-click) and drag into the new swatch. You can also select and drag multiple swatches with **Shift** key.
5. Create a new swatch.
6. Delete swatch.

3.22 COLOR
Window > Color (F6)
You can also enable "fill" and "stroke" and assign colors here.

3.23 GRADIENT

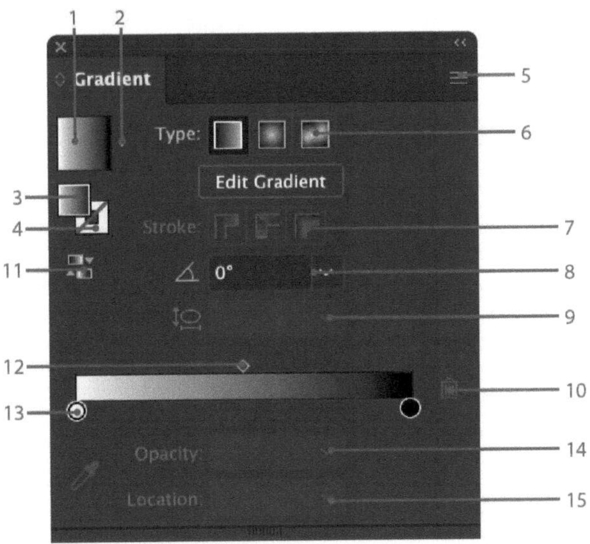

Gradient is a gradual adjustment from at least two colours. Gradient fills are stored as swatches and can be opened from the swatch window.
In a fashion illustration or technical drawings gradients are used in different ways, e.g. for metal elements like chains, push buttons etc. You can apply a gradient to a technical drawing to let it look more three-dimensional.
Open **Window > Gradient**

1. **Gradient** box: Selected gradient.
2. Menu **Gradient**: More gradients.
3. Apply Gradient to "**Fill**".
4. Apply Gradient to "**Stroke**"
5. **Panel Menu** (show options)
6. **Type of gradient** (linear or radial)
7. **Stroke gradient type** (see "chain" example)
8. **Angle** (set angle for gradient)
9. **Aspect Ratio**
10. **Delete stop**
11. **Reverse Gradient** (reverse gradient for stroke or fill)
12. **Midpoint** (determines the transition density of colors)
13. **Gradient slider** (gradient consists of at least 2 swatches, more can be added). By double-clicking a color slider ⬘ , the swatches are opened, here you can change the color. When you move the pointer to the gradient slider, you can create additional color sliders:
14. **Opacity** (Transparency of the gradient is set)
15. **Location**

Example:

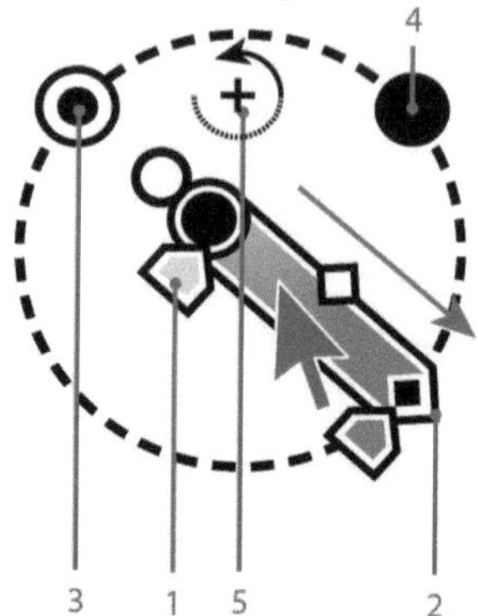

Gradient Optimizer

Appears when the mouse pointer is moved over the gradient tool (gradient must already exist).

1. Colour regulator
2. Gradient direction
3. Expansion
4. Aspect ratio (only for type: "Radial Gradient")
5. Drag and rotate the „spin icon" to reposition the angle.

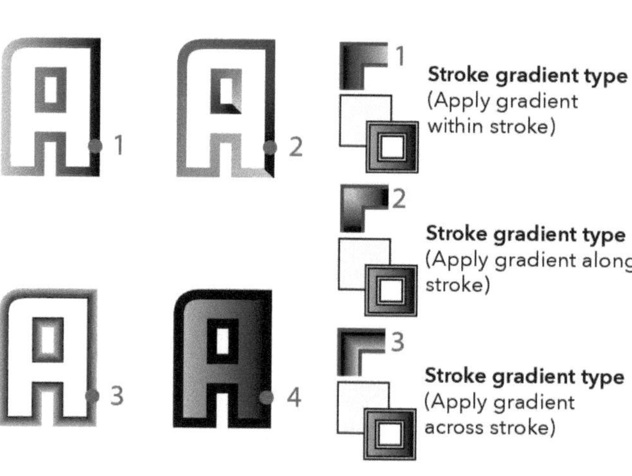

3.24 GRADIENT TOOL

Activate the **Gradient Tool** (G) in the Tools panel

Gradients can be added or edited using the Gradient tool. When you click in an object with a fill color using the Gradient tool, the object is filled with a gradient. The Gradient Optimizer lets you specify the angle, position, extent of a linear gradient, or focus, origin, and extent of a circular gradient for an object.

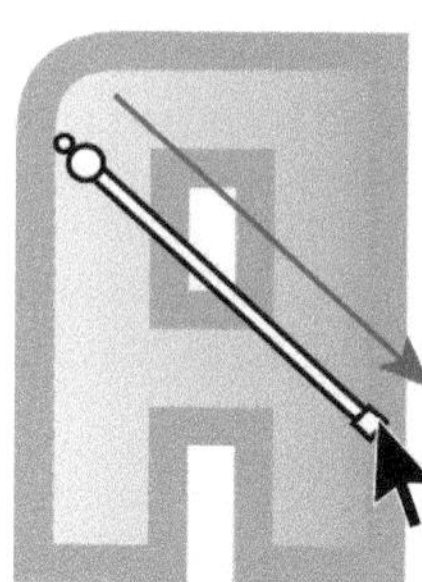

Gradient Tool

3.25 LAYERS

To keep track of all objects in the document, "Layers" panel is used. For example, each document can contain hundreds of objects such as paths, shapes, anchor points, etc., and each object automatically creates a new "Sublayer" in the "Layer" panel.

Since the selection of certain artwork becomes more difficult, for example when several copies lie on top of each other or smaller elements are hidden by larger ones, it is recommended to work with several layers. This allows you to control the order of the image material much more easily and change the stacking order of the objects.

You can also move objects between layers later. Use the Layers panel to select, hide, lock, and modify the objects.

Open **Windows > Layers**

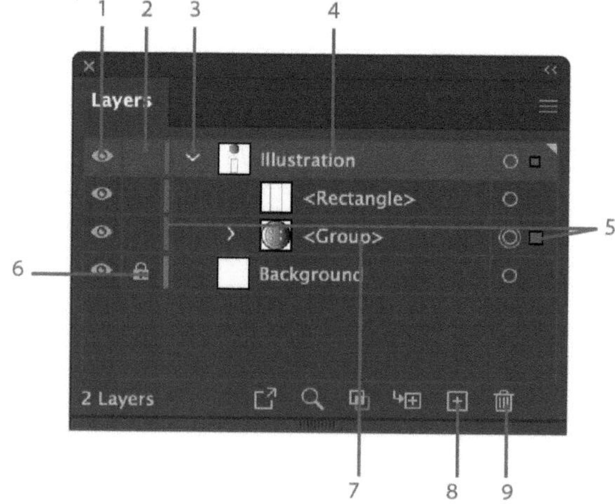

1. **Visibility column:** Indicates whether items in the layers are visible or hidden.
2. **Edit column:** Indicates whether elements are locked (lock icon is displayed) or unlocked.
3. Fold up (sublayers become visible) or close.
4. Layer name or sublayer name.
5. Layer color.
6. Layer is locked.
7. Grouped objects.
8. Create a new layer.
9. Delete layer or sublayer.

3.26 VECTOR GRAPHICS

Lines and curves in Illustrator are vector objects defined by mathematical calculations. A vector graphic is resolution independent, so you can move, resize, enlarge, copy, and change all objects as desired and the quality of the graphic is not changed. The quality of the graphic remains unchanged also when the document is saved as a PDF file.

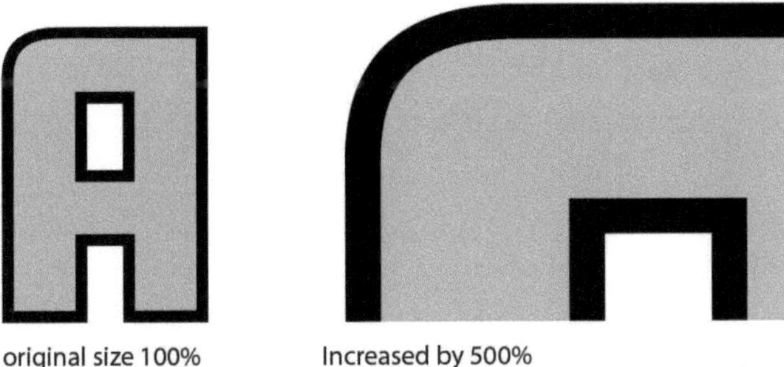

original size 100%   Increased by 500%

3.27 PATHS

Lines are predominantly created in Illustrator using the **Pen Tool** (P) . Lines are called paths and have curved or straight segments. Segments consist of points, which are called anchor points.

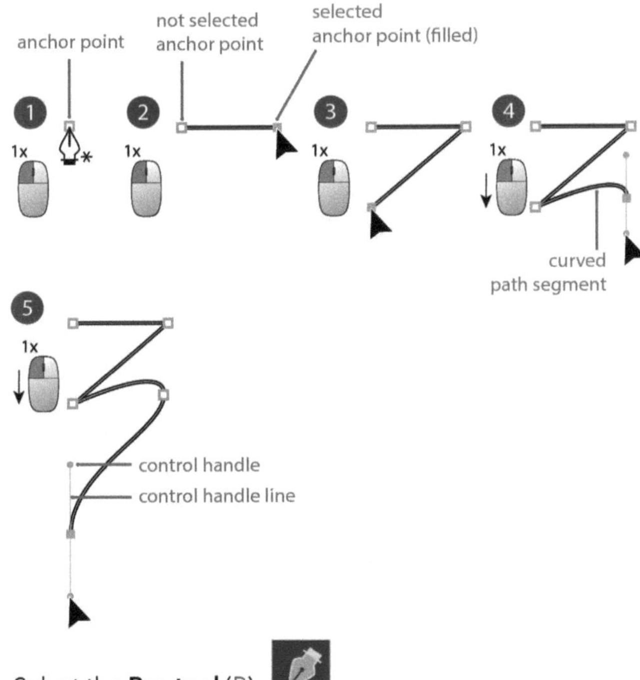

Select the **Pen tool** (P).

Step 1. Place the **Pen Tool** (P) anywhere in the artboard where you want the line to begin, and left-click (do not drag!) to define the first anchor point. The path does not become visible until you create a second anchor point by clicking.

Step 2. Click again where you want the line to end. **Shift** key will limit the angle of the path to 45 °.

Step 3. Set an anchor point by another click.

Step 4. Position the tool where you want the curve to begin, hold down the left mouse button, and drag the pointer (release only when you are satisfied with the curve). **Shift** key constrains the angle of the path to 45 °.

The pointer of the **Pen Tool** becomes an arrowhead.

You can also adjust the control handle line from both sides by dragging the control handle.

Step 5. Position the tool where you want the curve to continue and hold down the left mouse button. Hold down **Shift** key to limit the angle of the path to 45 °.

Paths can be open or closed (see example).

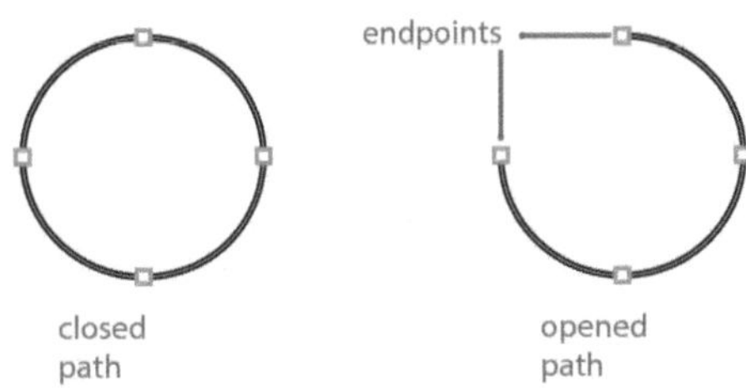

When you drag, rotate, or drag the path segment with the **Direct Selection Tool** (A) at the control handle of the control handle line, the shape of the path is changed. The shape and size of the curve segments determines the angle and length of a direction line.

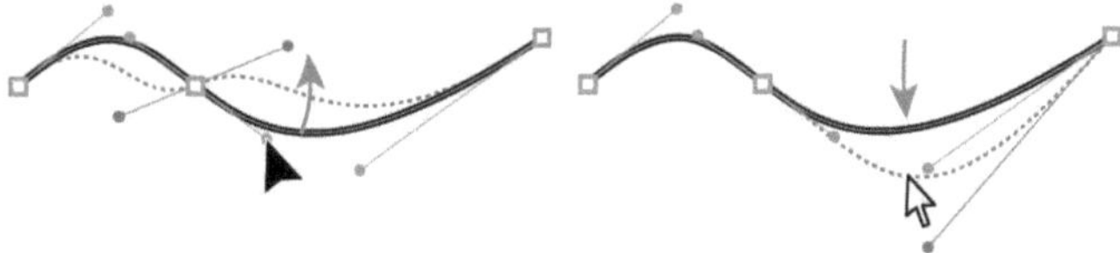

Paths have two types of anchor points: **smooth points** and **corner points** (see example below). At a smooth point, path segments are connected to a continuous curve, and at a corner point, the direction of a path is changed. A smooth point connects only curve segments. A corner point connects both straight segments and curve segments, or both in combination. A smooth point always has two direction lines, they are moved together as a straight unit.

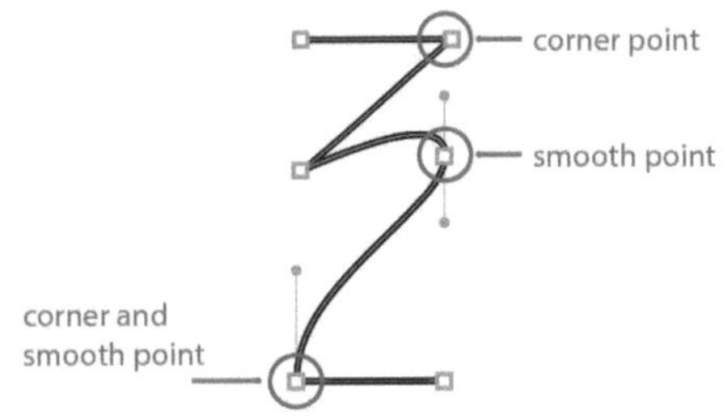

Use the **Anchor Point Tool** (Shift + C) to create a smooth point (curve) from a corner point or vice versa. If there are errors while drawing with the **Pen Tool** (P), you can correct them at any time with the **Direct Selection Tool** (A) and in some difficult cases with the **Anchor Point Tool** (Shift + C).

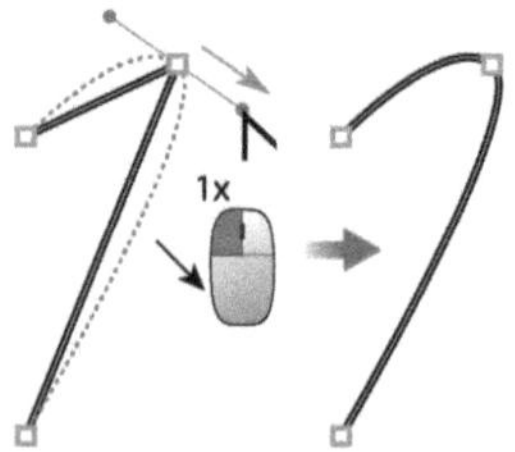
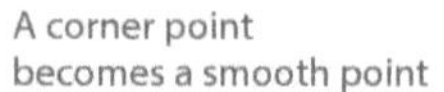
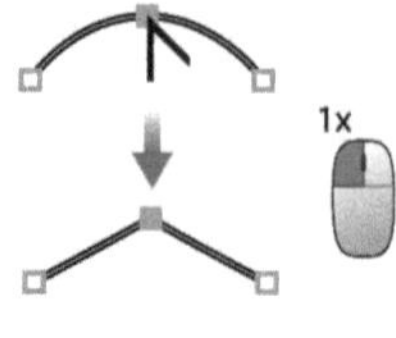

A corner point
becomes a smooth point

A smooth point
becomes a corner point

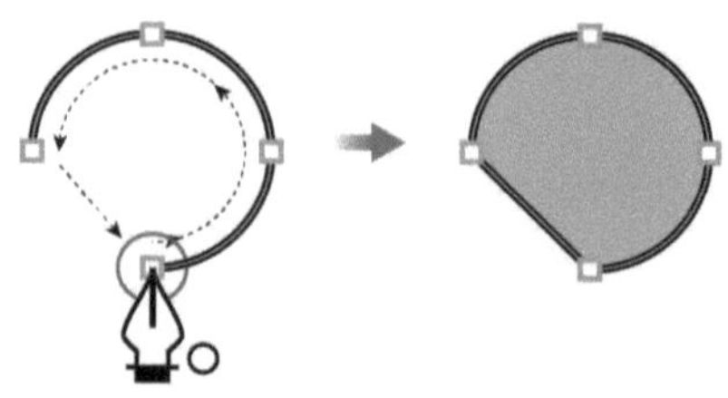

The line of a path is called a **Stroke**. Paths can contain patterns, colors, or gradients on their interior, this area is called a **Fill**. A stroke can be applied to a path, the stroke can have a width, color, or pattern.

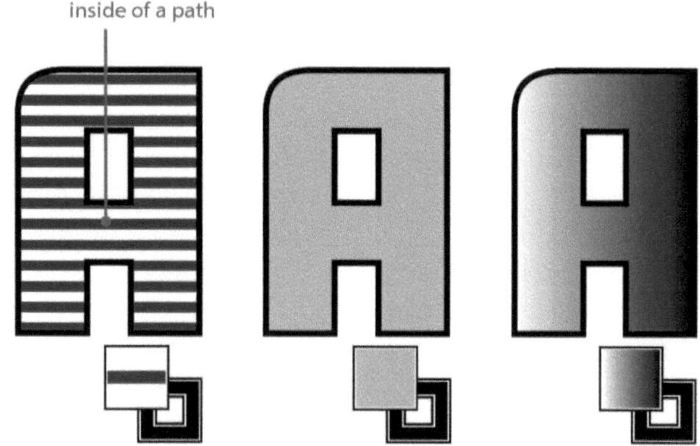

inside of a path

When you click an anchor point with the **Direct Selection Tool** (A), the control handle line appear on all connected curve segments.

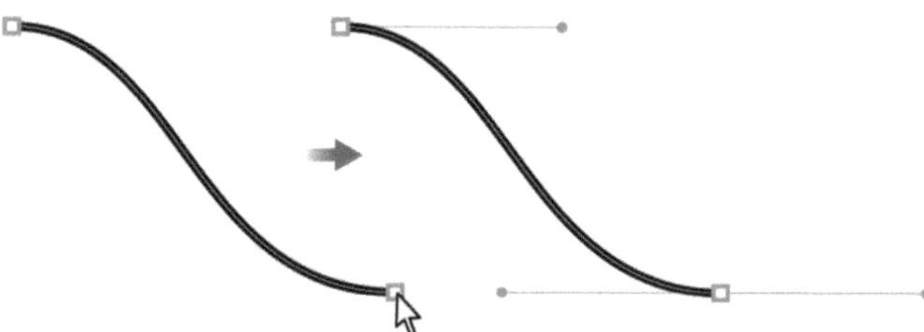

If you place the **Pen Tool** (P) over a start or end point of a previously *unselected* path (do not click), the tool appears with a slash, which means that the path can be drawn further from that anchor point.

When the existing path is connected to a current path at the start or end point, the **Pen Tool** (P) appears with a rectangle.

PATH B   *PATH A*

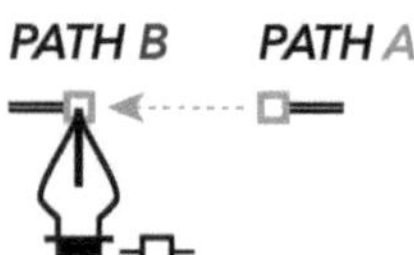

When the **Pen Tool** (P) is moved to the starting point when drawing a path, a small circle symbol appears, which means that the shape can be closed with a click (left click).

Add Anchor Point Tool (+)

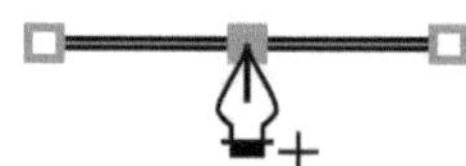

Using **Add Anchor Point Tool** (+), you can add new anchor points on a path.

Note: Pen Tool (P) is automatically replaced by **Anchor Point Adding Tool** when you move the pointer over a path.

Delete Anchor Point Tool (-)

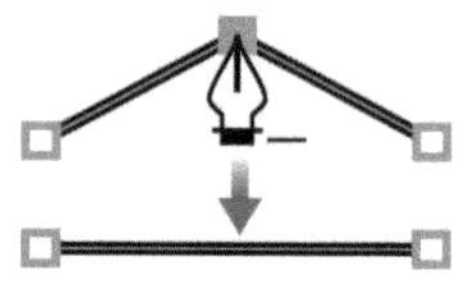

Use the **Anchor Point Delete Tool** (-) to delete anchor points on a path.

Note: Pen tool (P) is automatically replaced by **Anchor Point Delete Tool** when you place the mouse pointer over an anchor point. However, it **does not** work at a start or end point of the path!

3.28 CONTROL PANEL OPTIONS

Select **Window > Control** (Default is always enabled).

When anchor points are selected using the **Direct Selection Tool** (A), the control panel appears at the top. Here you can set different settings for anchor points, this panel fulfills a quick access to functions e.g. from the pen tool group.

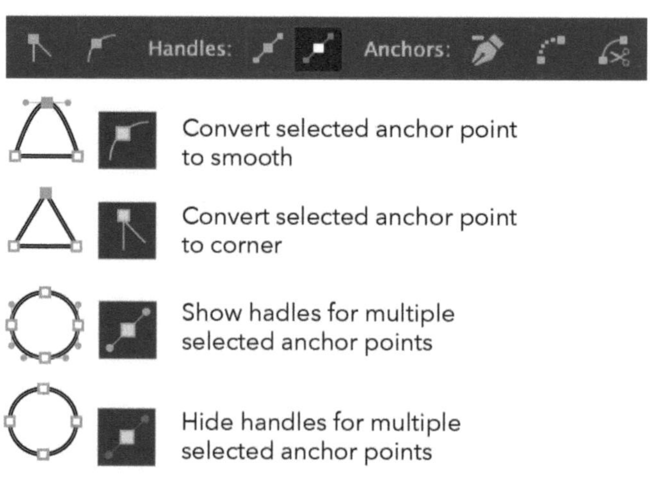

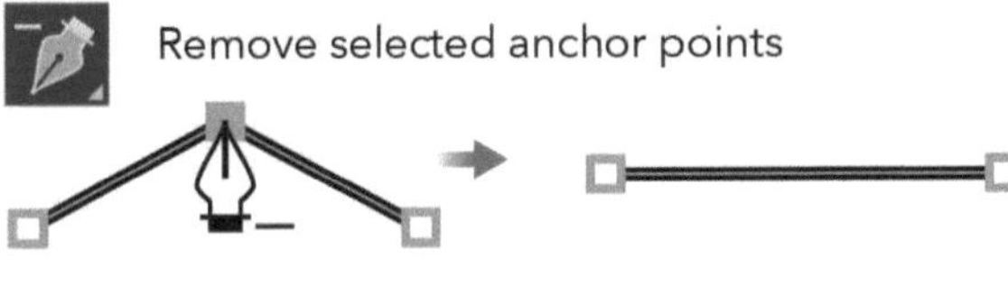

Remove selected anchor points

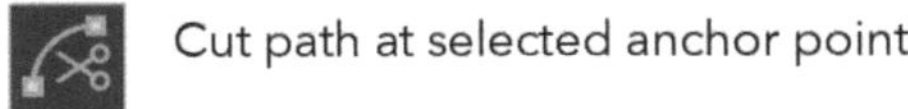

Cut path at selected anchor points

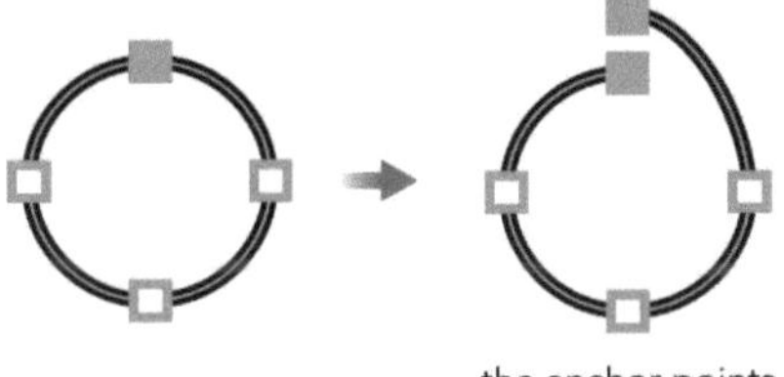

the anchor points
were separated

Connect selected anchor points

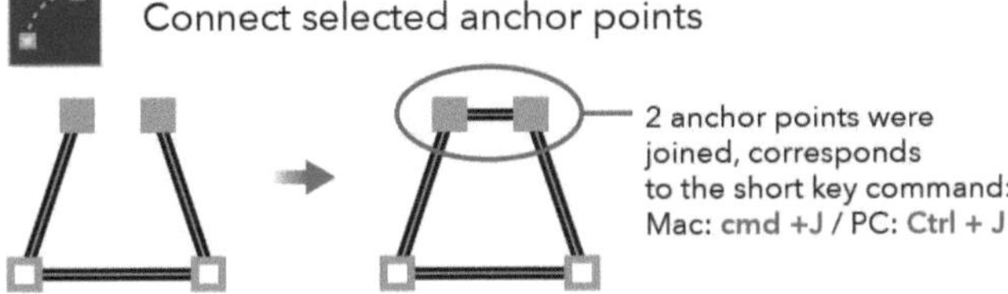

2 anchor points were
joined, corresponds
to the short key command:
Mac: cmd +J / PC: Ctrl + J

Using the **Line Segment tool** (\) straight line segments are drawn. Basically, straight line segments are almost always created with the **Pen Tool** (P). Only in rare cases **line segment tool** is used.
The same applies to the **Arc Tool** , because the **Pen Tool** (P) already fulfills the functions of these two tools.

You can use the **Pencil Tool** (N) to draw and edit paths with your free hand. You can use this tool to edit arbitrary paths, for example, to expand, connect two paths, change the shape of paths.

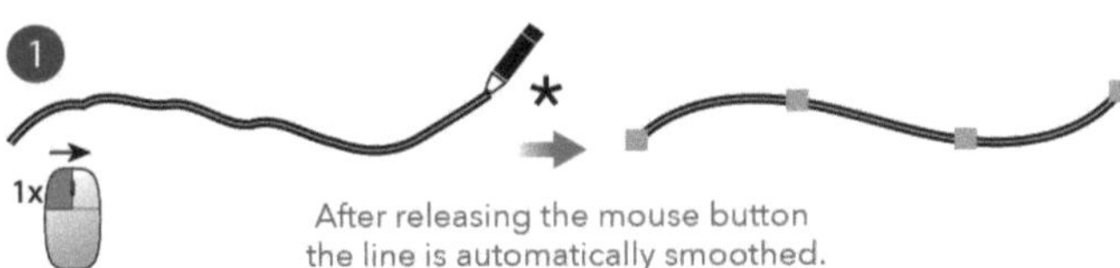

Step 1. Draw Line: Place the **Pencil Tool** (N) anywhere in the artboard where you want the line to start, press the left mouse button (do not release!) and move the mouse pointer, only then release.

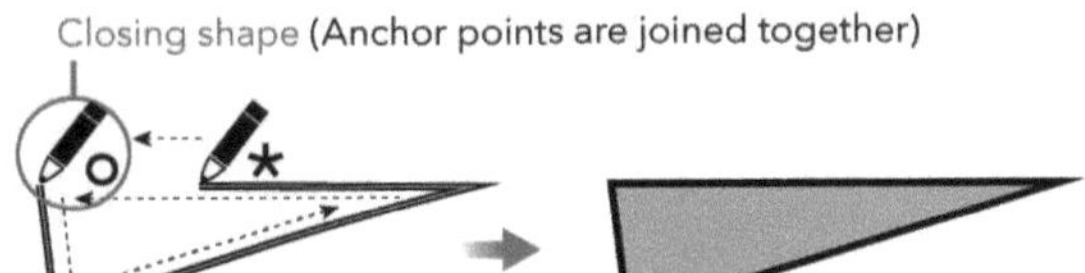

Step 2. Draw closed shape: Place the **Pencil Tool** (N) anywhere in the artboard where you want the line to start, press the left mouse button (do not release!) and move the mouse pointer, arriving at the starting point, a small circle symbol appears, now release the mouse button.

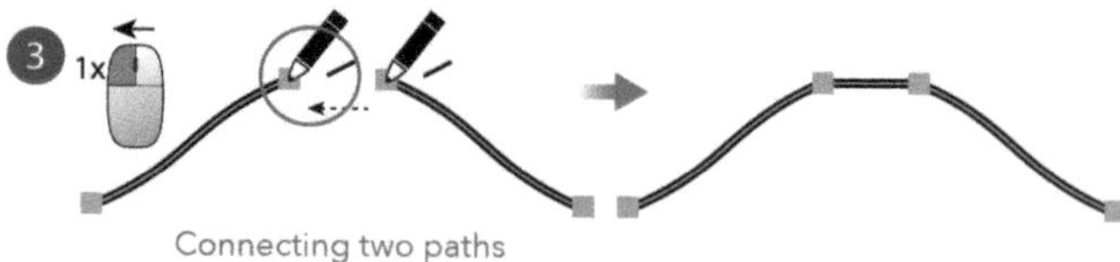

Connecting two paths

Step 3. Connecting two paths: To connect two paths, use the **Selection Tool** (V) to select both paths (see working with the selection tool). Place the pointer of the pencil tool on the start or end point (press left mouse button, do not release) and drag to the other path (start or end point), then release.

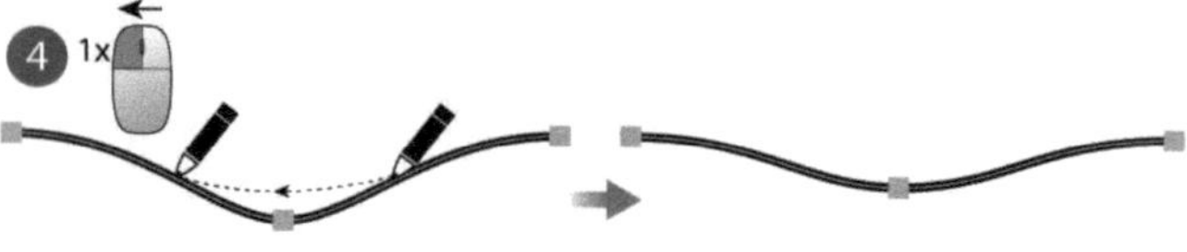

Change the shape of paths

Step 4. Changing the shape of paths: To change the shape of a path, first select the path using the **Selection Tool** (V) Place the pointer of the pencil tool on the path (X symbol on the tool should disappear, then they are close enough to the path). Then press the left mouse button (do not release) and drag to the desired place, then release the mouse button.

You can use the options for the pencil tool to set different settings for the pencil tool.

Double-click the pencil tool to set the following options:

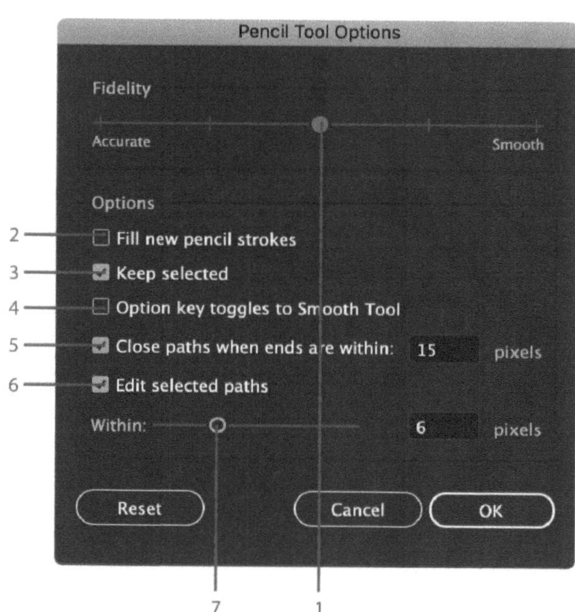

1.Fidelity: The higher the value, the smoother and less complex the path is.
2.Fill new pencil strokes: Applies a filling to a pencil stroke.
3.Keep selected: After drawing, the path remains selected.
4.Option key toggles to Smooth Tool: When the Shift button is activated, it is switched to smooth tool.
5.Close paths when ends are within: Determines whether you can change a selected path or not.

6/7.Edit selected paths: Determines how close the mouse (pixel spacing) must be to a path in order to edit a path using the Pencil tool.

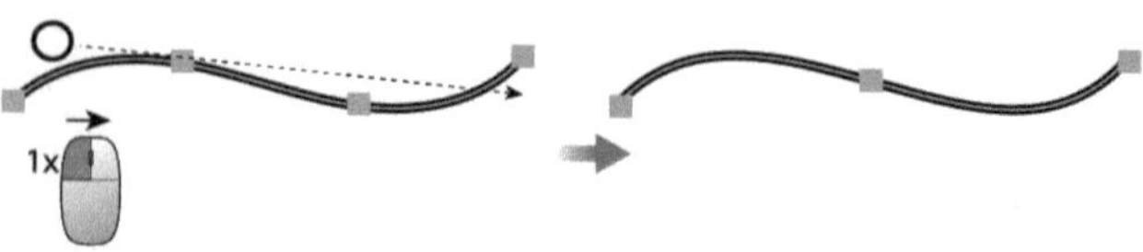

With the **smooth tool** you can smooth paths.

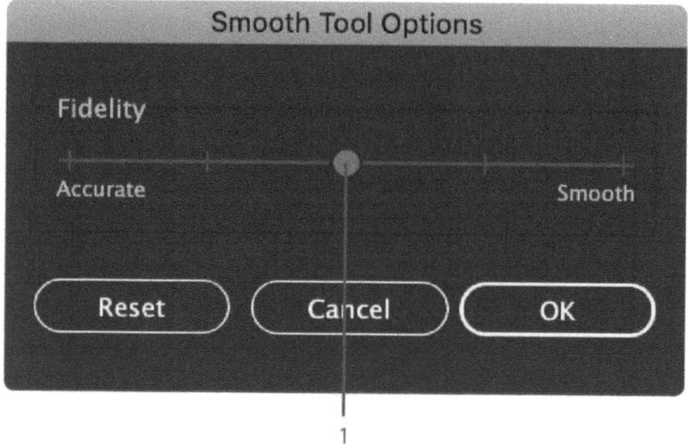

First, select the path with **Selection Tool** (V). Then drag the tool along the entire path segment.

Double-click the **Smooth Tool** to change the degree of smoothing.

1.Fidelity: The higher the value, the smoother and less complex is the path.

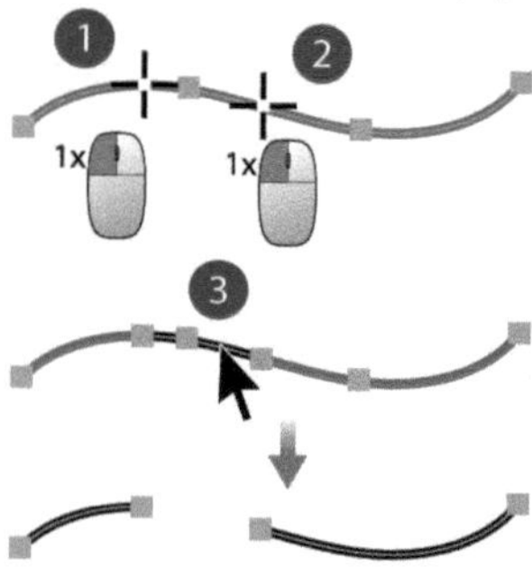

Use the **Scissors Tool** (C) to split paths.

Step 1 and 2. To split a path, click in two places on the path.

Step 3. Use the **Selection Tool** (V) or **Direct Selection Tool** (A) to click the segment between the two new anchor points.

Step 4. Press the Backstep button to delete the selected segment. 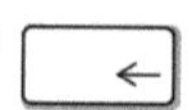

The **Scissors Tool** (C) is better suited for separating paths and deleting segments than the **Eraser Tool** (Shift+E), because eraser tool change the shape of the path so that precise separation is not possible. Eraser Tool is used to delete fills inside an objects.

3.29 STROKE SETTINGS

In the stroke panel you can adjust the strock weight, for technical drawings different stroke weights are used to make a technical fashion drawing look more aesthetic.

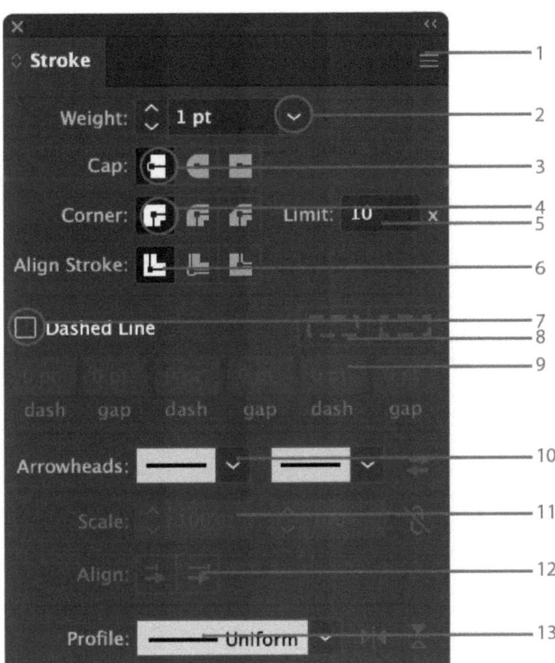

Step 1. Select an object using the selection tool **Selection Tool** (V).

Step 2. Open the stroke panel:
Window > Stroke

1. Show options
2. Stroke weight corresponds to the thickness of the stroke (see example)

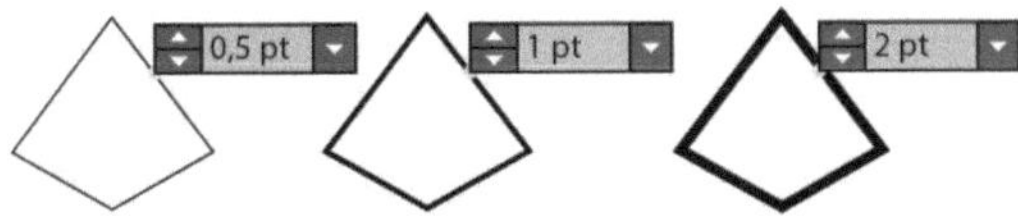

3. "Cap" determines how you want the path to look at the start or end point. You have three options: "Butt Cap" "Round Cap" "Projecting Cap".

When the dashed line (point 9) are activated, the set "Cap" is automatically applied to the line. If "Cap" is set to "Round Cap" and the distance between stroke and gap is too small, there is a risk that after exporting the drawing (e.g. jpg format) "dashed line" will no longer be clearly distinguishable from a normal line. Which can lead to misunderstanding, because "dashed line" is used in the technical fashion drawing, among other things, to represent a simple quilting seam. Therefore, better is to set the "Cap" to "Butt Cap".

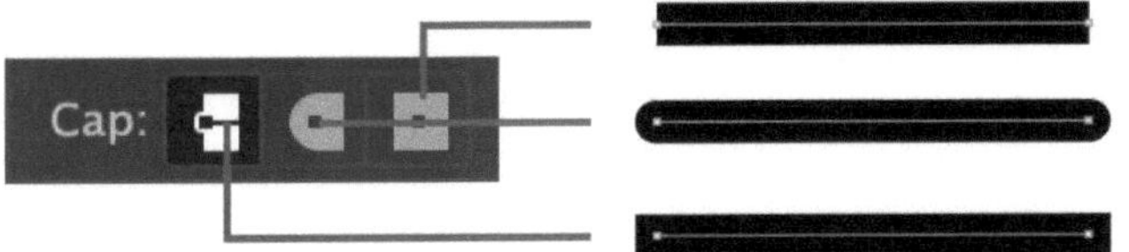

4. Corner determines how corners of a previously selected path should look. You have three options: "Miter Join" "Rounded Join" "Bevel Join".

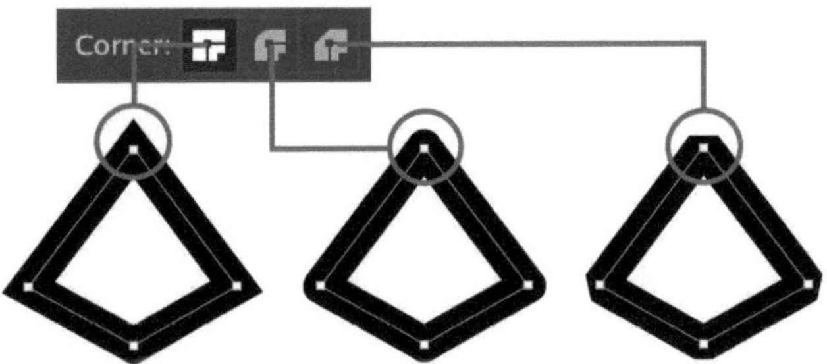

5. The miter limit determines (between 1 and 500) when the program switches from a pointed to a flattened corner. The standard miter limit is 10.

6. With „align stroke" you can align the stroke along the path (possible only for closed objects). You have again three options: „Align Stroke to Center", „Align Stroke to Inside", „Align Stroke to Outside".

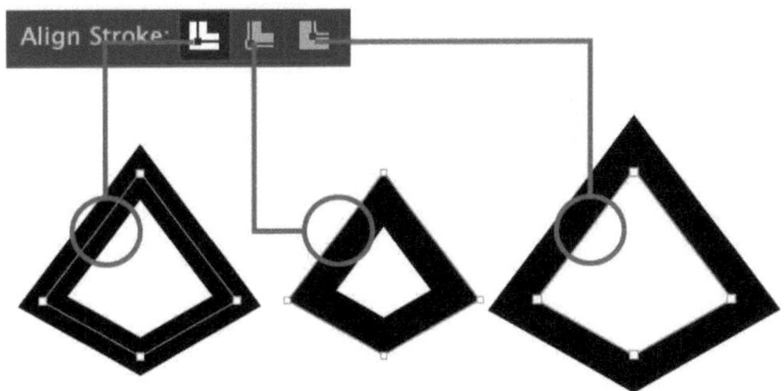

7. Dashed line setting is predominantly used to represent a simple quilting seam in technical fashion drawings.

8. The setting „Preserves exact dash and gap lengths" and „Aligns dashes to corners and path ends, adjusting lengths to fit"

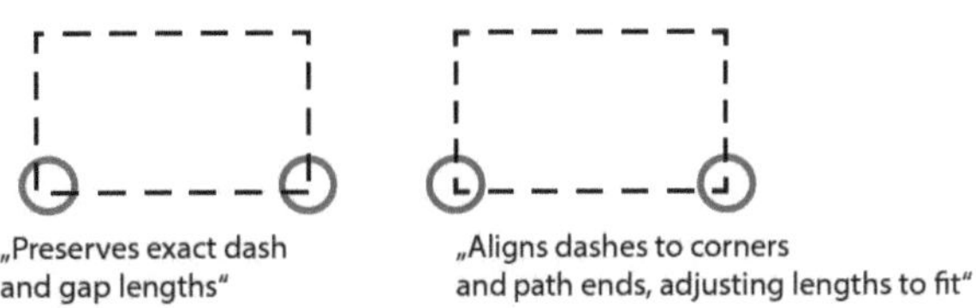

Both settings are used for technical fashion drawings.

9. Entering the line length and gap length in the corresponding fields defines a line pattern (for example quilting seam).

Depending on the size of the drawing, use the following settings:
- dash: **5**/gap: **3,5**, dash: **3**/gap: **2**, dash: **2**/gap: **1,5**.

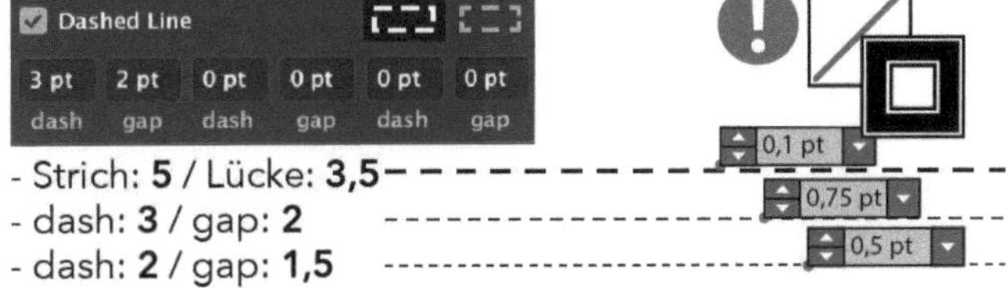

10. „Arrowheads" can be used for dimensioning of technical drawings.

11. You can scale the beginning and end of the arrowheads independently.

12. You can place arrowhead at the end of the path.

13. With the "Profile" setting, you can set different stroke profiles for the stroke, for example, to make a line look graphically more interesting.

4.0 SHAPE TOOLS

With the shape tools you can create for example angular and rounded pockets, buttons, various accessories.

These tools are summarized in the tools panel. The following tools are available for selection:

- **Rectangle Tool** (M)

- **Rounded Reactangle Tool**

- **Ellipse Tool** (L)

- **Polygon Tool**

- **Star Tool**

- **Flare Tool**

The tools are grouped together, click the group with the left mouse button and hold down the button for about 1 second, then the group opens and you have access to other tools (or click the right mouse button). It applies to all tools with a small triangle at the bottom right.

4.1 RECTANGLE TOOL

The **Rectangle Tool** (M) draws squares and rectangles.

Select the Rectangle tool and set the stroke color to "black" and fill color to "None". 

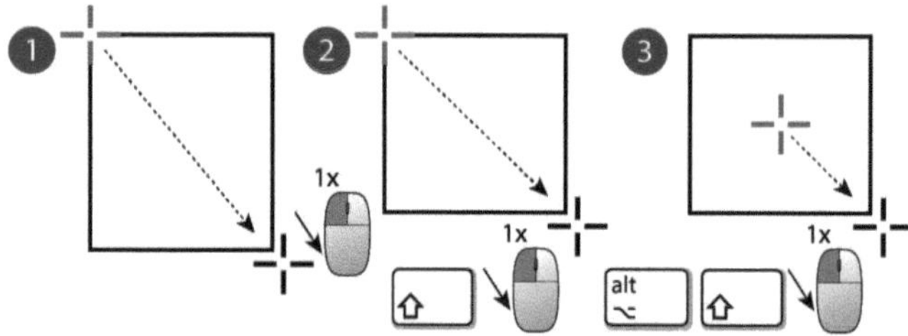

Step 1. To draw a rectangle, drag the mouse pointer (displayed as a cross) in the diagonal direction while holding the left mouse button until the rectangle assumes the desired shape and size.

Step 2. To draw a square, press and hold the **Shift** key and pull the cursor by holding the left mouse button in diagonal direction, until the square assumes the desired size.

Step 3. To draw a square from the center, press and hold the **alt/option + Shift key** and drag the mouse pointer in the diagonal direction while holding the left mouse button until the square assumes the desired size.

To create a rectangle by entering values, click anywhere in the document, set the width and height in the options window, then click OK.
Starting with **Illustrator CC**, you can create a rounded rectangle or circle from a rectangle.

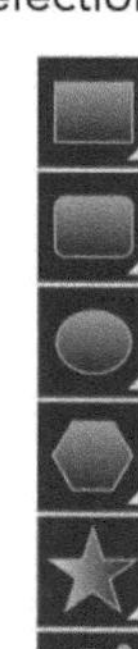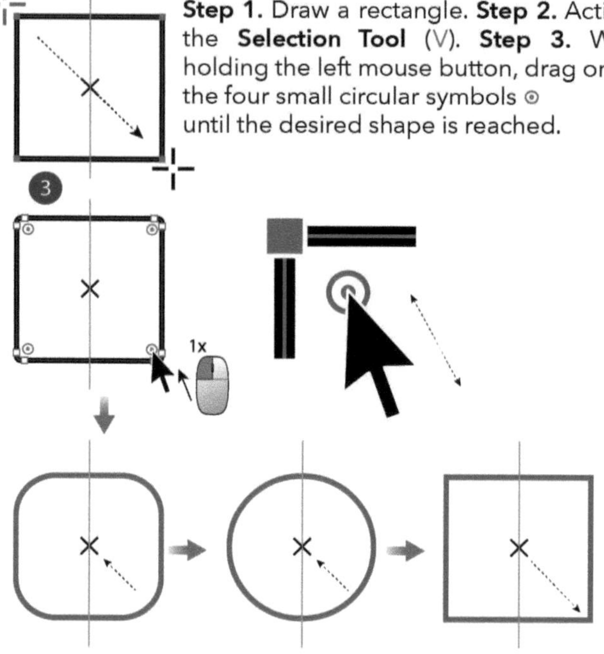

Step 1. Draw a rectangle. **Step 2.** Activate the **Selection Tool** (V). **Step 3.** While holding the left mouse button, drag one of the four small circular symbols ⊚ until the desired shape is reached.

4.2 ROUNDED RECTANGLE TOOL

The **Rounded Rectangle Tool** is used to draw rounded pocket forms, belt buckles etc.
Select rounded reactangle tool and put the stroke color to "Black" and fill color to "None". 

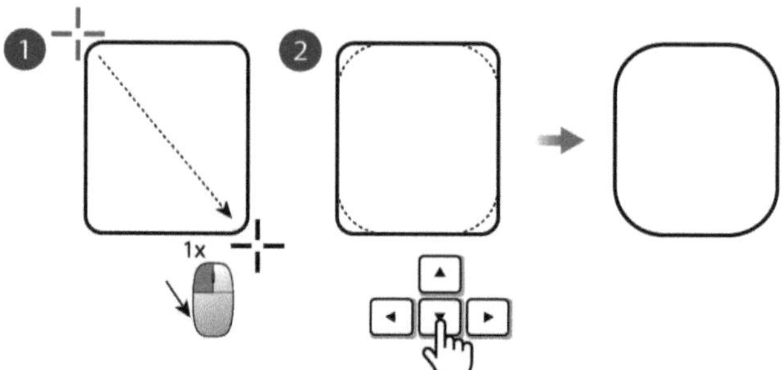

Step 1. To draw a rounded rectangle, drag the mouse pointer in the diagonal direction while holding the left mouse button until the rectangle assumes the desired shape and size.
Step 2. Do not release the left mouse button and click the keyboard arrow keys (▲ increases the round, ▼ decreases the round).
When the **Shift** key is additionally pressed, an isosceles square is drawn and by holding down the **alt/option** key the square is drawn from the center. With **alt/option + Shift** key, an isosceles square is drawn from the center.

You can also round each corner individually.

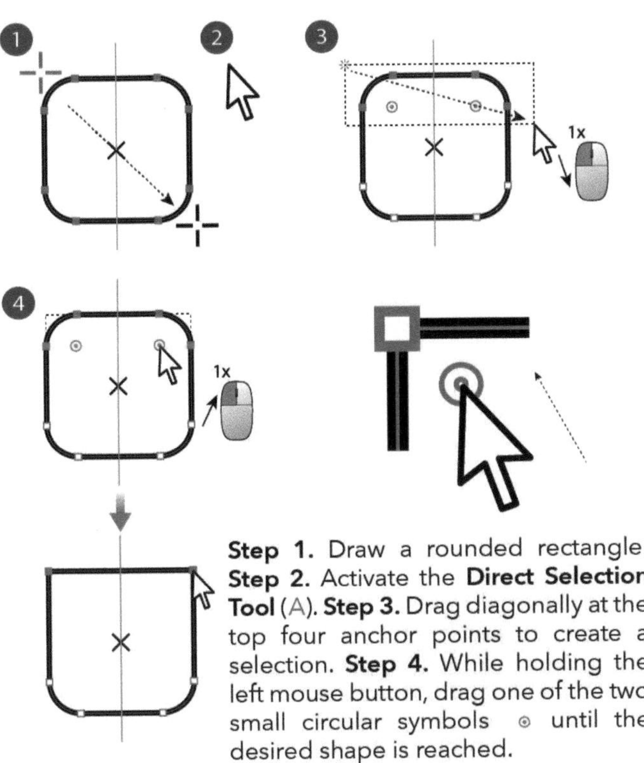

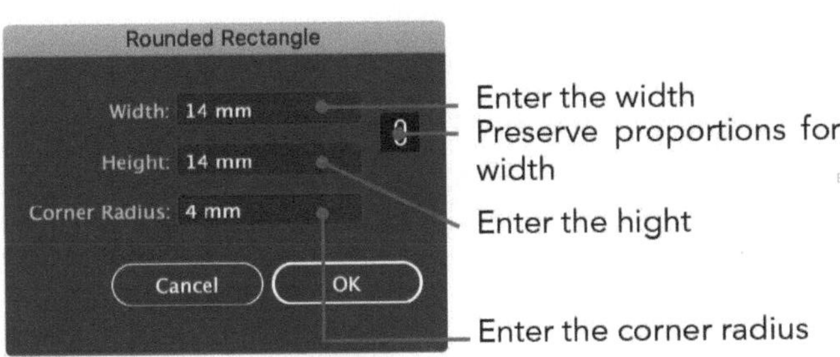

Step 1. Draw a rounded rectangle. **Step 2.** Activate the **Direct Selection Tool** (A). **Step 3.** Drag diagonally at the top four anchor points to create a selection. **Step 4.** While holding the left mouse button, drag one of the two small circular symbols ⊙ until the desired shape is reached.

To create a rounded rectangle by entering values, use the **rounded rectangle tool** and click anywhere in the document, set the width, height, and corner radius in the options window, then confirm with OK.

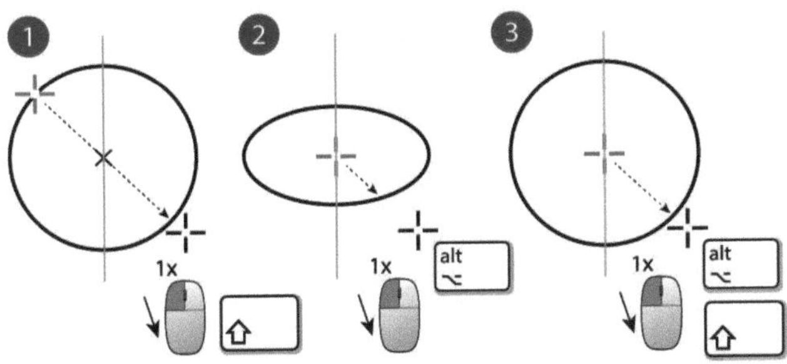

4.3 ELLIPSE TOOL

The **Ellipse Tool** (L) creates circles and ellipses. The ellipse tool is used to draw buttons, various metal elements, etc.

Select the ellipse tool and set the stroke color to "black" and "fill" color to „None".

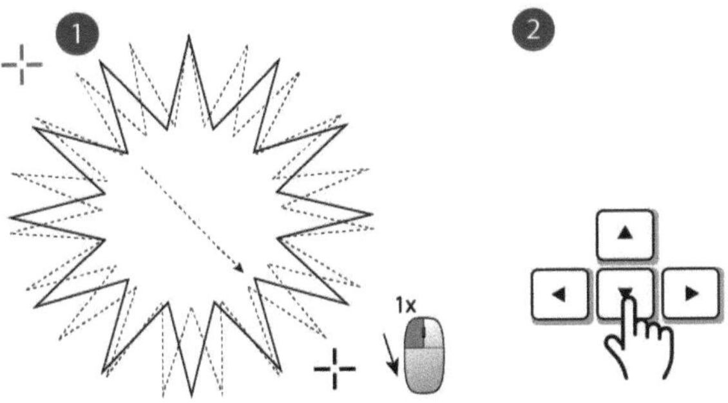

Step 1. To draw an ellipse, press and hold the left mouse button and drag the pointer in the diagonal direction until the ellipse becomes the desired shape and size. To draw a circle, press and hold the **Shift** key and drag the pointer in the diagonal direction while holding the left mouse button.
Step 2. When the **alt/option** key is activated, the ellipse is pulled from the center.
Step 3. To draw an ellipse proportionally from the center, hold the **alt/option** + **Shift** button and drag the mouse pointer in the diagonal direction while holding ^the left mouse button until the ellipse assumes the desired size.

4.4 POLYGON TOOL

Select the **Polygon Tool** and set the stroke color to "black" and fill color to "None".

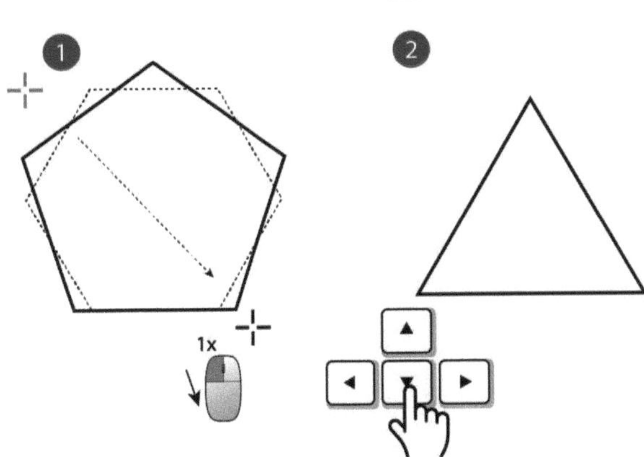

Step 1. While holding the left mouse button, drag the pointer clockwise or counterclockwise until the polygon assumes the desired shape and size.
Step 2. *Do not* release the left mouse button and click the keyboard arrow keys (▲ increase the number of sides, ▼ decrease the number of sides).
When the **Shift** button is additionally pressed, the object is aligned at a 90 ° angle and by holding the **alt/option** key the object is drawn from the center.

You can also create a polygon by entering values. Click anywhere in the document, select the radius and number of sides for the polygon, and click OK.

4.5 STAR TOOL

Select the **Star tool** and set the stroke color to "black" and fill color to "None".

Step 1. While holding the left mouse button, drag the pointer clockwise or counterclockwise until the star assumes the desired shape and size.

Step 2. *Do not* release the left mouse button and click the keyboard arrow keys (⬆ increase the number of points of the star, decrease the number of points of the star ⬇). When the **Shift** button is additionally pressed, the object is aligned at a 90 ° angle.

You can also create a star by entering values. Click anywhere in the document, **Radius 1** enters the distance between the center and the inner points of the star, and **Radius 2** enters the distance between the center and the outer points of the star. Under "Points" you can enter the desired number of points. Confirm your entries with "OK".

4.6 DEFORMATION TOOLS

With the deformation tools, you can deform strokes and fills in different ways to create, for example, fur optics, pleated optics, etc. (see examples). By double-clicking on one of these tools in the toolbar, the dialog box is opened, where you can make further settings.

There are three important settings in the dialog box. **Width and height**: Tool size is set, **Angle**: Tool angle is set, **Intensity**: Tool intensity is set (see example ② , here the setting was set between 10% -15% to keep precise control over the tool).

Apply: Place the tool over an selected object, press and hold the left mouse button and move the mouse pointer.

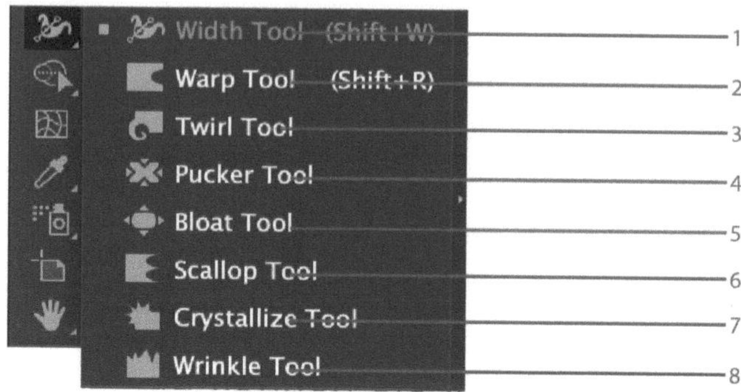

① 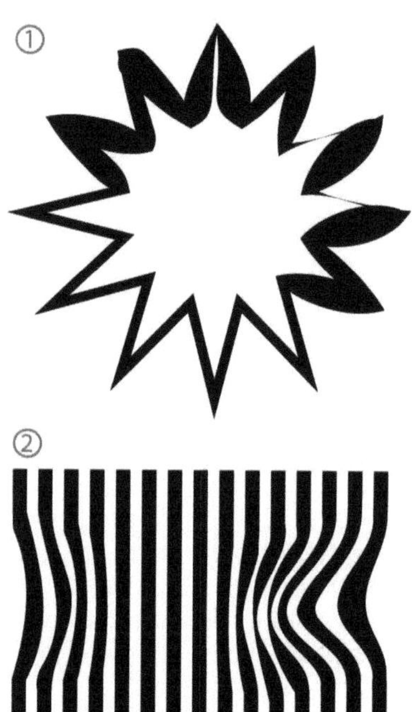

② 

③ 

④

⑤ 

⑥ 

⑦ 

⑧ 

5.0 SELECTION TOOLS

To modify an object (shape, stroke, color, anchor point etc.) in Adobe Illustrator, it must be selected first.

Various selection techniques are available for this purpose.

Under menu View, the following options must always be activated: **View > Show Edges** and **View > Show Bounding Box**.

Selection Tools

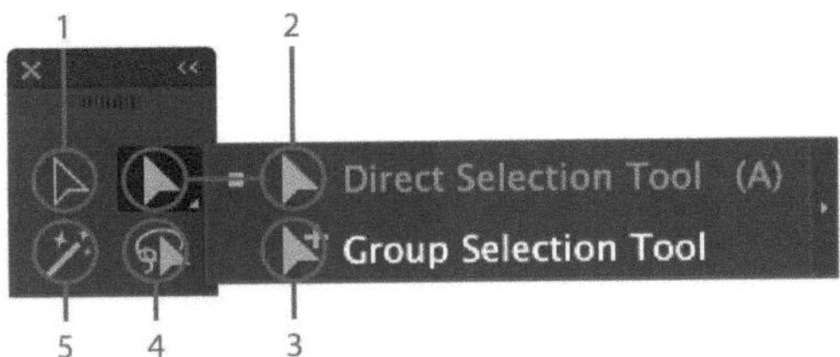

There are five selection tools available:

1. Selection Tool (V)

2. Direct Selection Tool (A)

3. Group Selection Tool

4. Lasso Tool (Q)

5. Magic Wand Tool (Y)

Predominantly is used the
selection tool 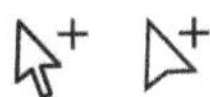 and the direct selection tool

1. Selection Tool (V)
The Selection tool allows you to select only the entire object or group of objects. All anchor points of the object are selected.
Selection tool is mostly used to transform, move, and delete entire objects.

2. Direct Selection Tool (A)
You can use the direct selection tool to precisely select individual anchor points of an object or group of objects. Thus, individual anchor points of the object can be selected.
Direct selection tool is mostly used to make corrections to objects (paths), delete individual anchor points, or copy fragments of a path.

3. Group Selection Tool
Use the group selection tool to select individual objects in an object group. All anchor points of an object are always selected.

4. Lasso Tool (Q)
The lasso tool allows you to precisely select individual anchor points of an object or group of objects. Lasso tool performs the same functions as the direct selection tool. This tool is mostly used for very complicated objects if it is to difficult to make a selection with a rectangle (direct selection tool).

5. Magic Wand Tool (Y)

With the magic wand tools you can select objects with similar surface color, stroke color, stroke weight. Double-click the tool to set the tolerance for selection in the options window.

5.1 SELECTION TECHNIQUES

Select entire objects using the **Selection Tool** (V).

Step 1. To select the entire object, left-click the fill color of the object (press and release the left mouse button).

Step 2. To select the entire object, left-click the stroke color of the object (press and release the left mouse button).

Step 3. To select the entire object, click on the path of the object if there is no stroke or fill color, activate the outline view: **View > Outline** (cmd + Y / Ctrl + Y)

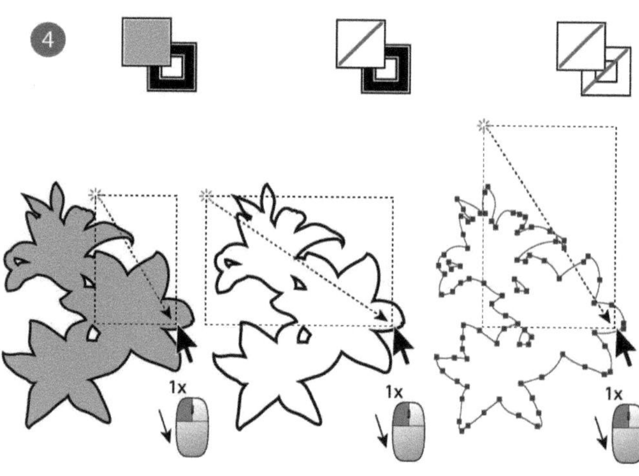

How the selection box with the selection tool is drawn, does not matter. In the end result the entire object is selected.

Step 4. Use the selection tool to drag a selection rectangle around the object while holding the left mouse button. The selection rectangle can only touch the object in one place, so it does not have to be dragged over the entire object. (Press, drag, and release the mouse button).

Select individual anchor points using the **Direct Selection Tool** (A).

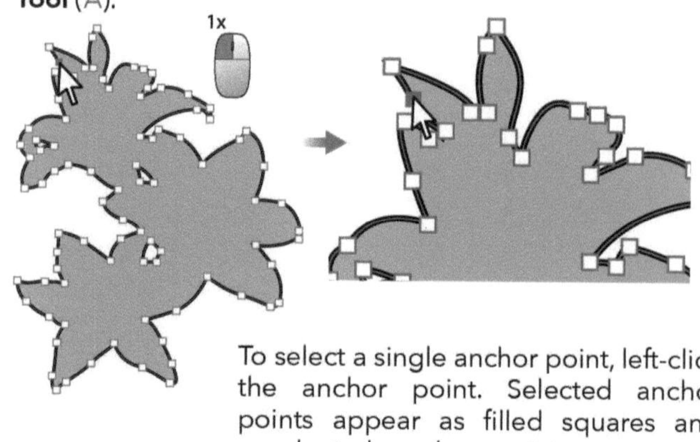

To select a single anchor point, left-click the anchor point. Selected anchor points appear as filled squares and unselected anchor points appear as filled white squares.

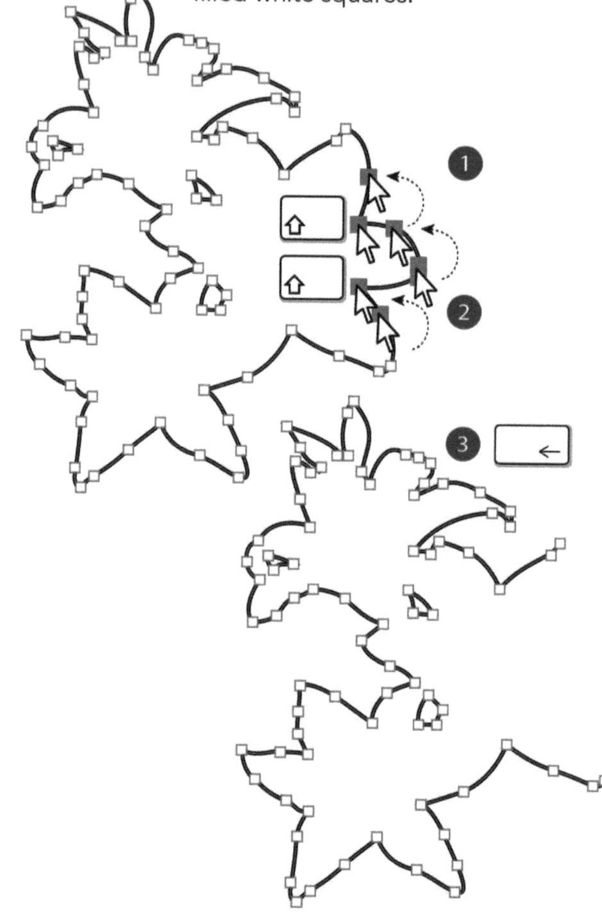

Step 1. To select the first anchor point, left-click an anchor point.

Step 2. Activate **Shift** key (do not release) and select another anchor point.

Step 3. Do not release **Shift** key and select another anchor point.

Step 4. Click the **Backspace** key (or **delete** button) to delete selected anchor points (the path created by connecting anchor points is deleted).

Select individual anchor points using the **Lasso Tool** (Q)

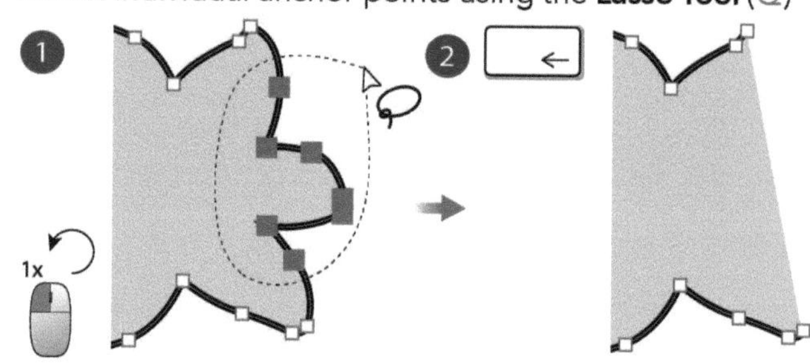

Step 1. To select a single or multiple anchor points, press and hold the left mouse button and move around the anchor points you want to select.
Step 2. Click the **Backspace** key to delete selected anchor points (the path created by the anchor point connection is deleted).

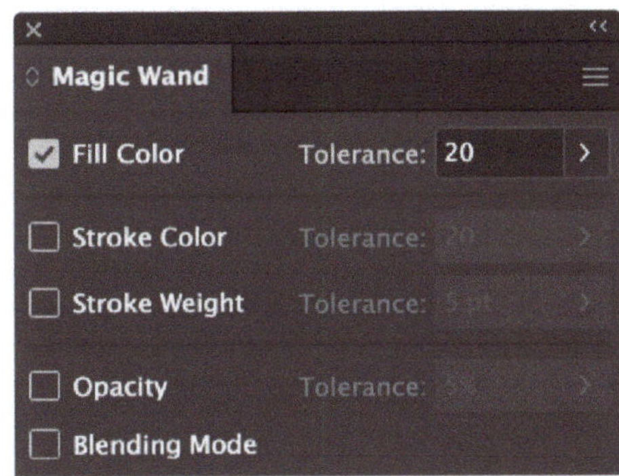

The higher the tolerance value, the more objects with a similar, for example, fill color are selected.

Select objects in the Layers panel.

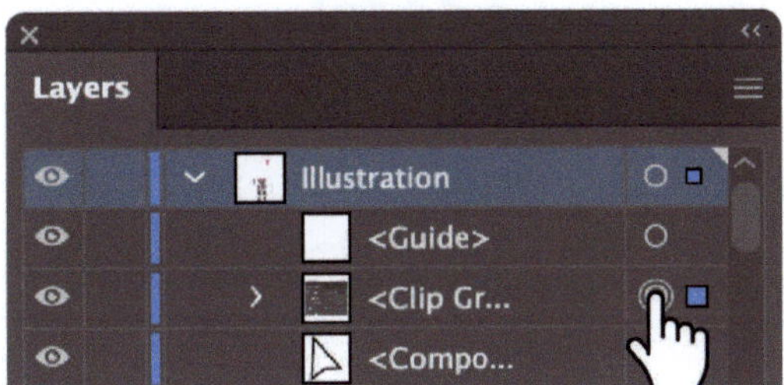

Open Layers panel: **Window > Layers**
Clicking the circle next to the layer or sublayer name, than all objects on that layer or sublayer will be selected.

If you additionally hold the **Shift** key and click more circles when selecting in the layers panel, you can add more layers and sublayers to the existing selection.

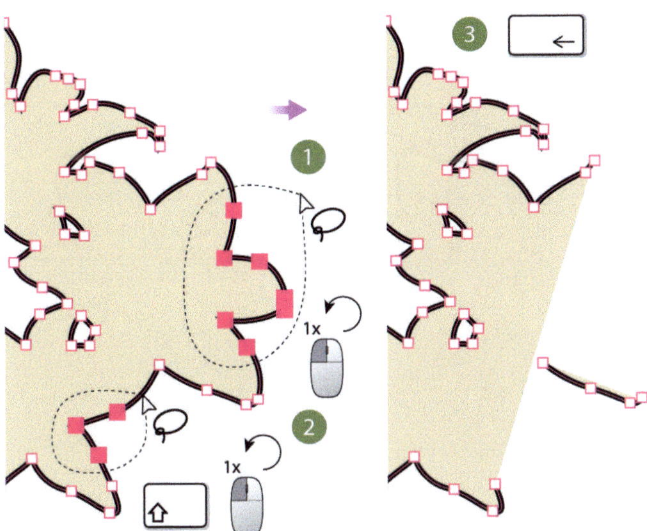

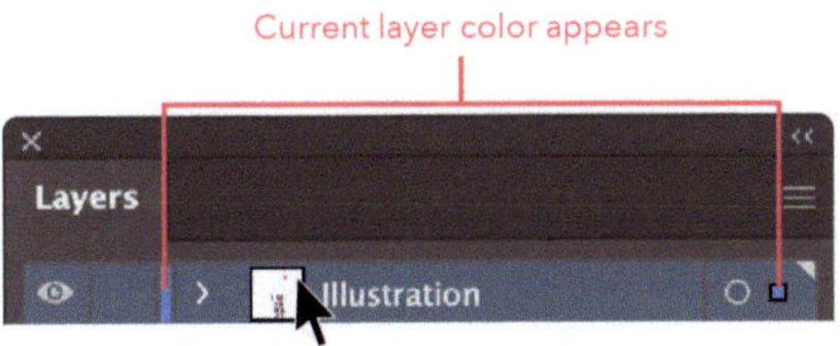

Double-click the layer preview to change the selection color of this layer.

Step 1. To select a single or multiple anchor points, press and hold the left mouse button and move the pointer around the anchor points you want to select.
Step 2. Activate **Shift** key (do not release) and select another anchor point.
Step 3. Activate **backspace** key to delete selected anchor points (the path created by connected anchor points is deleted).

If the **Shift** key is not pressed, the previous selection is disabled.

Use the **Magic Wand tool** (Y) to select similar objects.

Other selection techniques.

Use the Magic Wand tool to click an object if there are objects with similar fill color in the document, then they will be selected.
To select the objects with the same stroke color, stroke width, opacity, or blending method, double-click the magic wand tool (options window opens).

Select > Same... and **Select > Object...**
Here, various possibilities are offered to select objects, e.g. by brush strokes, clipping masks etc.
These choices are very precise (there is no tolerance setting as with the magic wand tool).

When selecting objects that have different fill or stroke colors, a question mark appears to highlight the inconsistency of colors (see example).

Move objects and individual anchor points.

Use the **Selection Tool** (V) to move entire objects: Press and hold the left mouse button and drag the object in any direction.

Alternatively, you can use the arrow keys (but the object must be selected first with the selection tool).

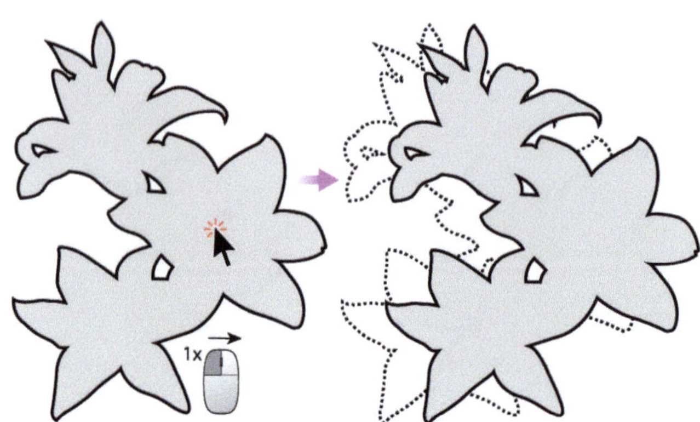

Use the **Direct Selection tool** (A) to move individual anchor points: Place the tool over an anchor point, click on the point, do not release the left mouse button, and drag.

Alternatively, you can use the arrow keys (the anchor points must be selected first using the Direct selection tool).

Deselect

Option 1:
To deselect, use the **Selection tool** (V) or **Direct Selection tool** (A) (left mouse button) and click in the blank drawing area.

Option 2:
Select the following shortcut key command:
Mac: command + Shift + A key / PC: Ctrl + Shift + A key

Option 3:
Select > Deselect.

 Before you start drawing a new object (path), it is always better to deselect the previous object!

5.2 COPY OBJECTS

Adobe Illustrator has a variety of ways to duplicate objects (copy and paste).

Option 1:

Mostly, the "create a copy on the same place" command is used. In this case, the duplicate is created above the original object.

The object must be selected first.
Then activate the following shortcut command:
command + C / Ctrl + C (**Edit > Copy)**

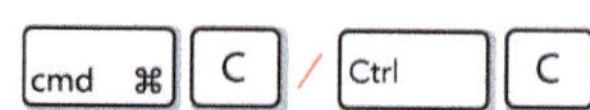

Than **Edit > Paste in Front**: cmd + F / Ctrl + F

The duplicate is placed on the original object, which does not clearly indicate whether a duplicate is present.

However, it is visible in the **Layers panel** because a new sublayer is created for each duplicate.

original object

two duplicates lie
above one another

Duplicate

Option 2:

You can also insert the duplicate behind the original object.
Edit > Copy: cmd + C / Ctrl + C
Edit > Paste in Back: cmd + B / Ctrl + B

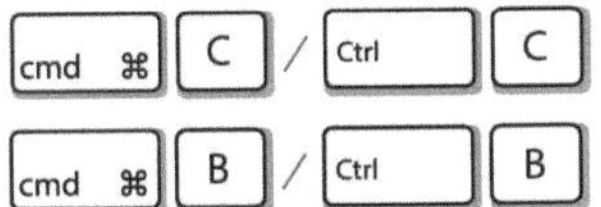

Duplicate

two duplicates lie
above one another

original object

Option 3:

You can paste the duplicate in an offset location (but it is rarely used because this copy method is inaccurate).
Edit > Copy: cmd + C / Ctrl + C
Edit > Paste: cmd + V / Ctrl + V

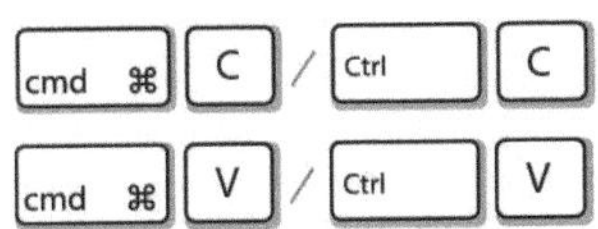

Option 4:

You can insert the duplicate at the original location. This copying method is identical to "Paste in Front".
Edit > Copy: cmd + C / Ctrl + C
Edit > Paste in Place:
Shift + cmd + V / Shift + Ctrl + V

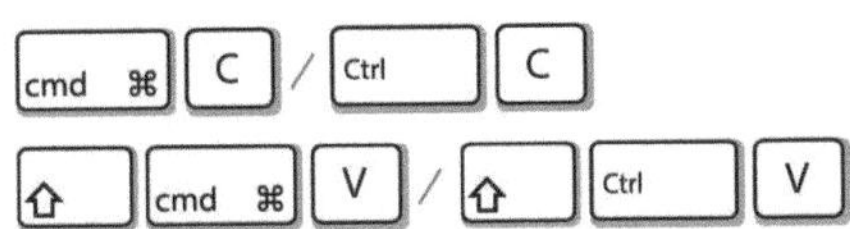

Option 5:

You have the option by dragging with the mouse cursor to create a duplicate (drag&drop method)

To do this, press the **alt/option** key (do not release the mouse button) and drag the object with the **Selection Tool** (V) while holding the left mouse button. At a possible destination, first release the mouse button and then release the **alt/option** key (see Example A).

If you also hold the **Shift** key, the duplicate is aligned vertically or horizontally with the original object (see Example B).

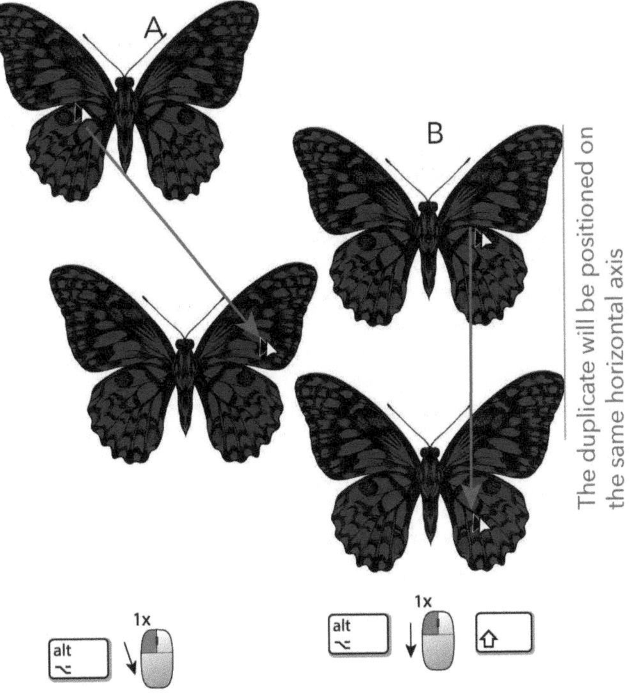

The duplicate will be positioned on the same horizontal axis

When copying, the selection tool arrow is replaced by a double arrow .

Option 6:

You can use arrow keys to create a duplicate.

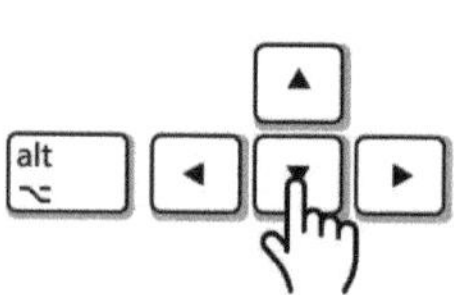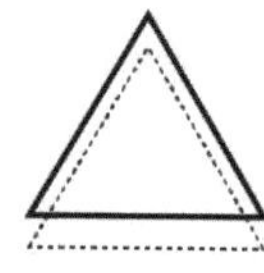

Select an object, press the **alt/option** key (do not release the mouse button), press the arrow key and release, then release the **alt/option** key.

Option 7:

You can create duplicates from the Layers panel.
Open the Layers panel **Window > Layers**
The object should not be selected.

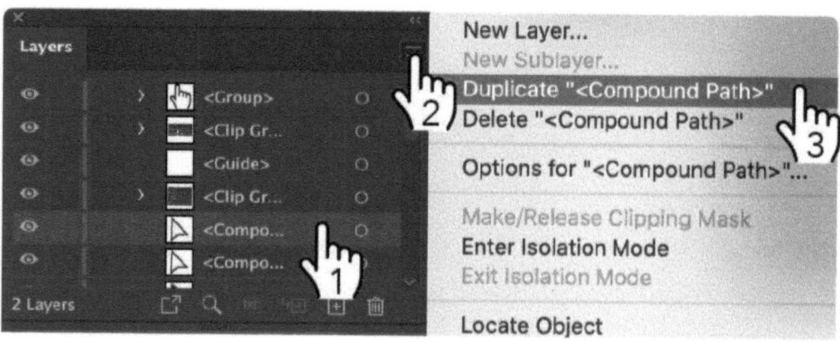

Step 1. Select layer or sublayer.
Step 2. Select layer or sublayer menu.
Step 3. Click on „..." duplicate.

5.3 ROTATE TOOL

With the **Rotate Tool** (R) the objects will be rotated around a fixed point. You can also rotate and copy objects simultaneously.

Step 1. Use the **Selection Tool** (V) to select one or more objects.
Step 2. Activate the **Rotate Tool** (R) (it is in a common group with the Reflect Tool). The cursor is replaced by a crosshairs. Press the **alt/option** key (do not release) and left-click where you want the axis of rotation to be (a dialog box opens), then release the **alt/option** key and mouse button.
Step 3. In the dialog box, type 30° for the "Angle" option and click "Copy". Always activate the "Preview" to see the preview of the result.
Step 4. Now you can generate an other copy with the same settings, activate the following short key command: cmd + D / Ctrl + D or **Object > Transform > Transform Again.**

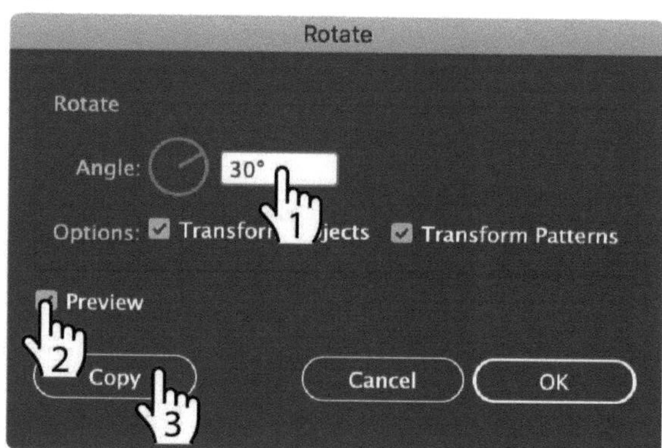

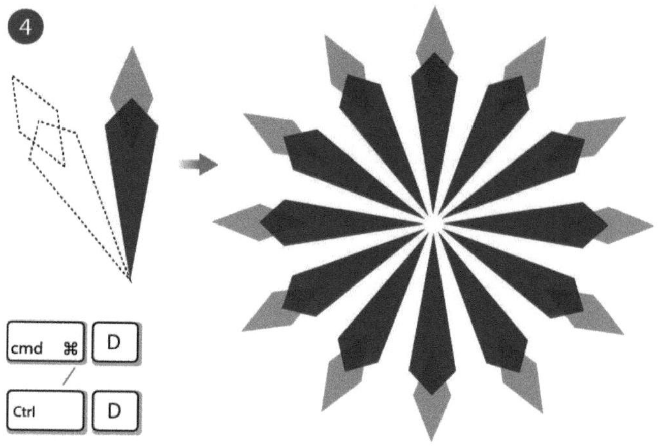

Further possibilities to work with the rotate tool:

- You can also rotate the object around its center point by dragging the pointer in a circular motion anywhere in the document window.

- If you want to set a new origin for the rotation, click anywhere in the document window once, then move the pointer away from the origin and drag it in a circular motion.

Objects can also be rotated with the bounding box.

1. Use the **Selection tool** (V) to select one or more objects.
2. Place the pointer outside the bounding box near a handle so that the pointer appears as a double arrow, and then move the pointer.

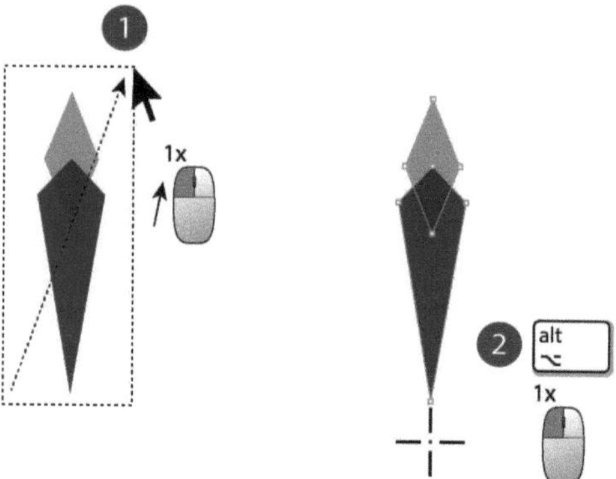

6.0 TUTORIAL: POLKA DOT PATTERN

First, create a new A4 page in Adobe Illustrator **File > New > A4**.

Step 1. Set in the tools panel the fill color for example „beige" and the stroke color „None".

Step 2. Activate **Ellipse Tool** (L), press and hold **alt/option** and **Shift** key, then create a circle. First release the mouse button and then the alt and Shift keys.

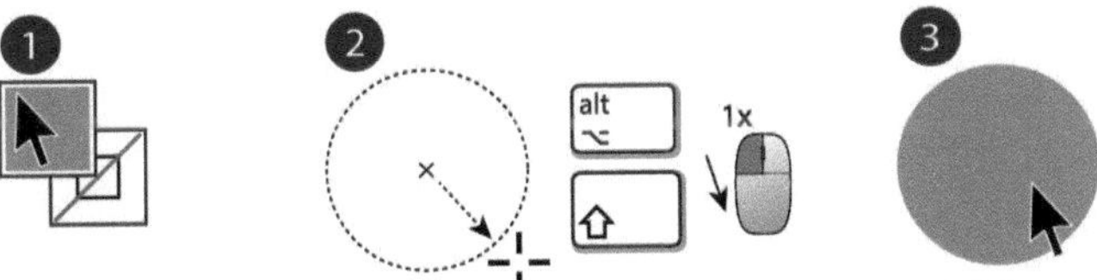

Step 3. Select the object with the **Selection Tool** (V) and activate the command **Object > Pattern > Make**.

Step 4. Set the following settings (see figure) and change the distance (3) between objects, to adjust the distance proportionally, set "maintain proportions" (2).

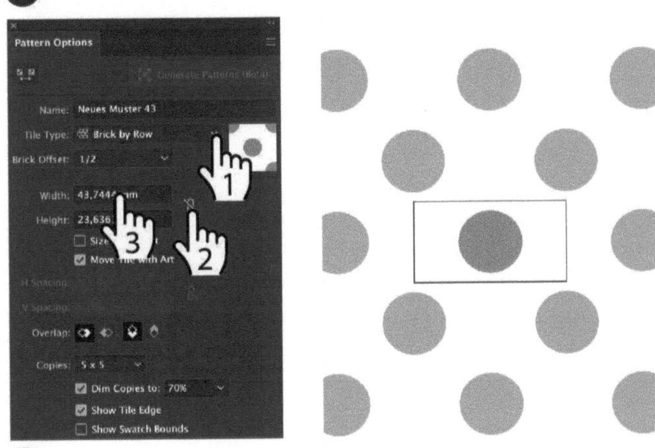

Step 5. Confirm the settings with "Done" in the control panel (at the top). Now you can find the pattern in the Swatches window **Window > Swatches**.

Step 6. Select the **Rectangle Tool** (M) and create a rectangle.

Step 7. And fill in the rectangle with your pattern from the swatches window **Window > Swatches**.

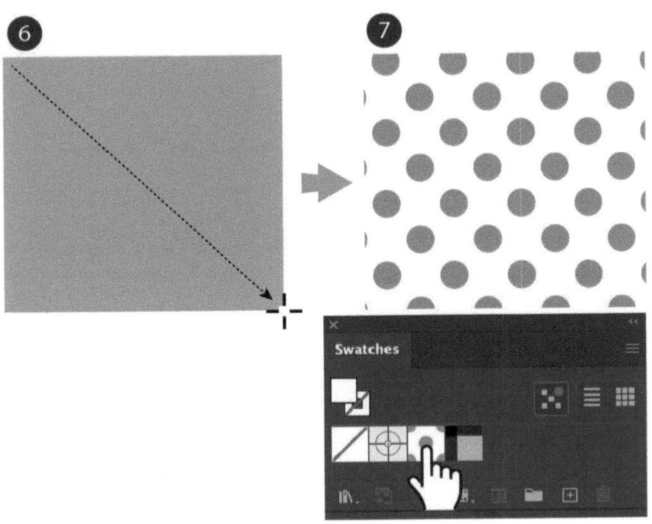

Step 8. Create a rectangle in the background by simply copy&paste the rectangle with the pattern Cmd+C/Crtl+C and Cmd+F/Ctrl+F, then apply a fill color. Place the rectangle in the background **Object > Arrange > Send to Back**. When designing patterns, the idea of adding an extra rectangle to the background for an all-over print is frequently applied. This method is simple to use. Another method to add a background can be found in tutorial 6.23 on page 82.

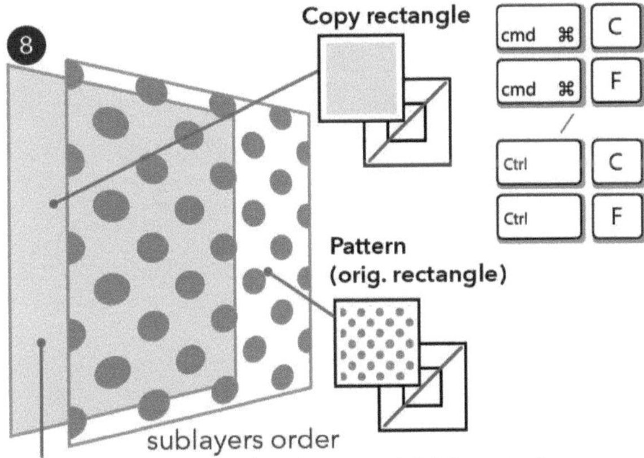

Put the copy in the background **Object > Arrange > Send to Back** and apply a fill color.

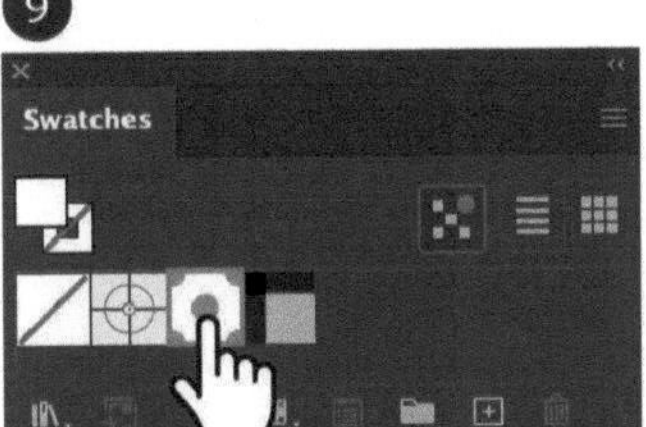

Step 9. If you want to rework your pattern, first select it with the **Selection Tool** (V) and double-click on the pattern in the **Window > Swatches** or go to **Edit > Pattern > Edit Pattern**.

Step 10. To change the colors, click the **Recolor artwork** button in the control panel or activate the **Edit > Edit Colors > Recolor Artwork** command. In the window that appears, click on the „Advanced Options". Now you can set the colors for multiple objects at the same time.

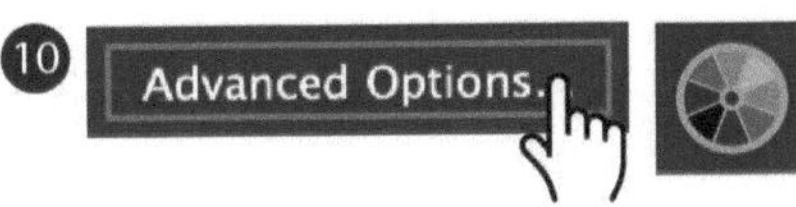

Here you have the opportunity to set specific colors (1). If you click on this button (2) this window will appear immediately the next time you recolor it.

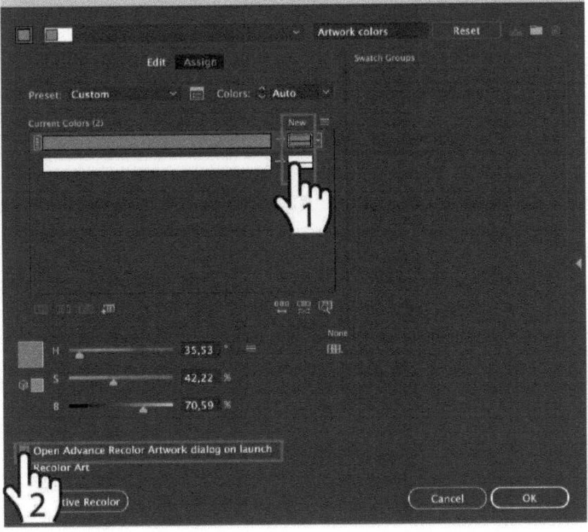

Step 11. If you want to resize your pattern, first select it with the **Selection Tool** (V), then right click on the object and go to **Transform > Scale...**

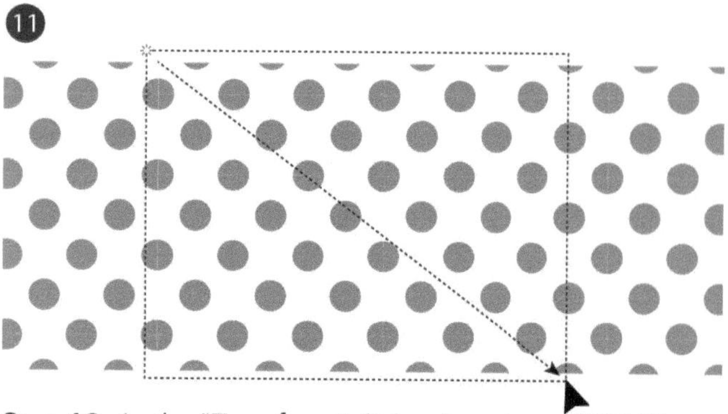

Step 12. In the "Transform" dialog box, turn off (1) "Transform Objects" so that only the pattern is transformed. To change the size, set a value in "Uniform".

Make sure that 100% is the current size of the pattern, meaning if you want to make the pattern 80% smaller, enter **20%**. If you want to enlarge the pattern by 80%, set it to **180%**.

Sometimes you have to deactivate and activate the preview to see the result.

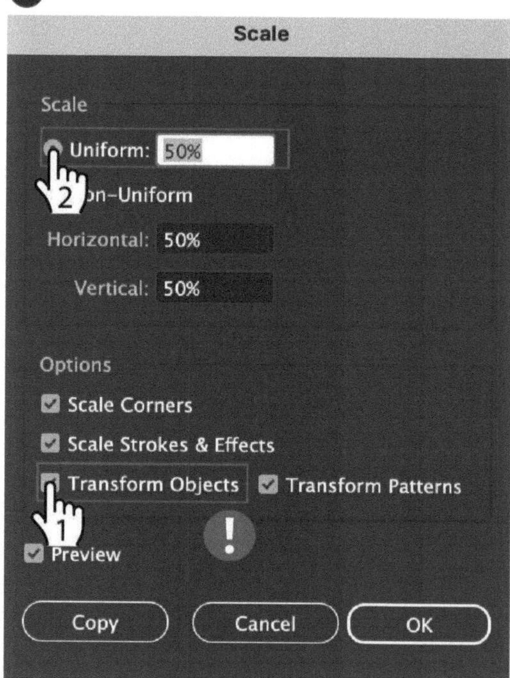

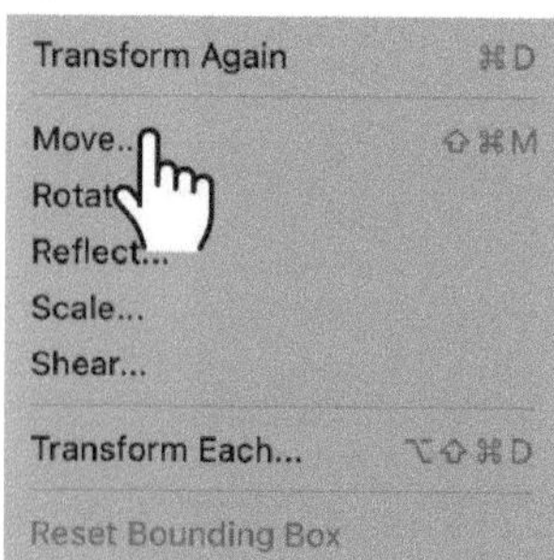

You also follow the same steps if you want to move or rotate the pattern, right click on the object and go to **Transform > Move...**

6.1 TUTORIAL: PINCHECK PATTERN

First, create a new A4 page in Adobe Illustrator **File > New > A4**.

Set: **View > Rules >Show Rules, View > Guides > Lock Guides, View > Guides > Show Guides, View > Smart Guides, View > Snap to Point.**

Step 1. Set in the tools panel the fill color „blue" and the stroke color „None".
Step 2. Activate the **Rectangle Tool** (M) and draw a rectangle.
Step 3. Copy this rectangle with the shortcuts Cmd+C/Crtl+C (Copy) and Cmd+F/Ctrl+F (Paste in Front).

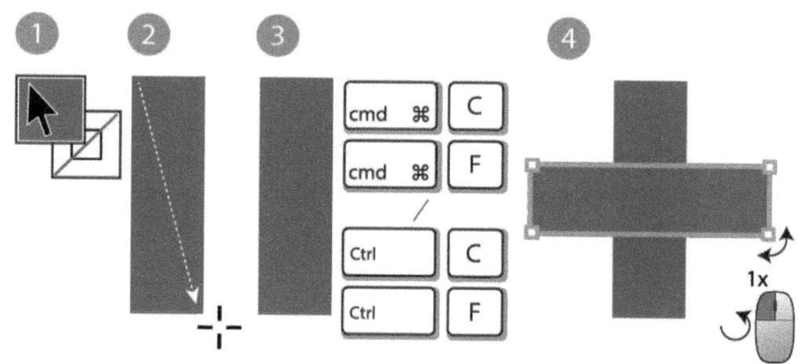

Step 4. Press and hold the **Shift** key and rotate the objects clockwise (90°). First release the mouse button and then the Shift key.

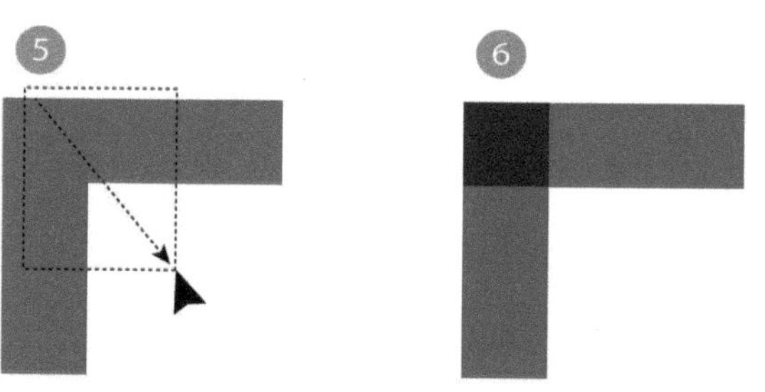

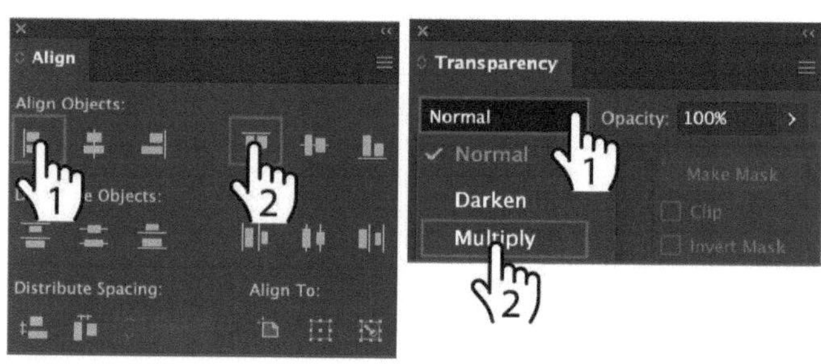

Step 5. One way to align objects in Illustrator is the „Align" window **Window > Align**. First select both objects with the **Selection Tool** (V) and set the following settings (see figure).
Step 6. Now open the „Transparency" window **Window > Transparency** and change the settings to "Multiply" (see figure).

The various filter settings in the "Transparency" window are often used when creating prints, "Multiply" occurs very often.

Step 7. The two objects are still selected. Place four guides on each side.

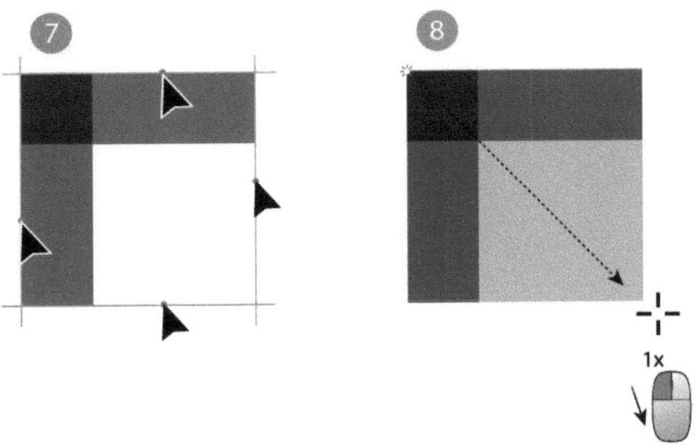

Step 8. Create a rectangle with the **Rectangle Tool** (M) along the guides and move it to the background **Object > Arange > Send to Back**.

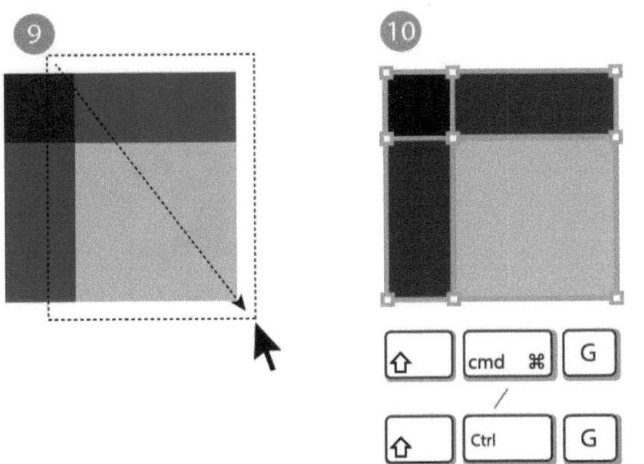

Step 9. Now select all objects with the **Selection Tool** (V) and activate the command **Object > Flatten Transparency...**

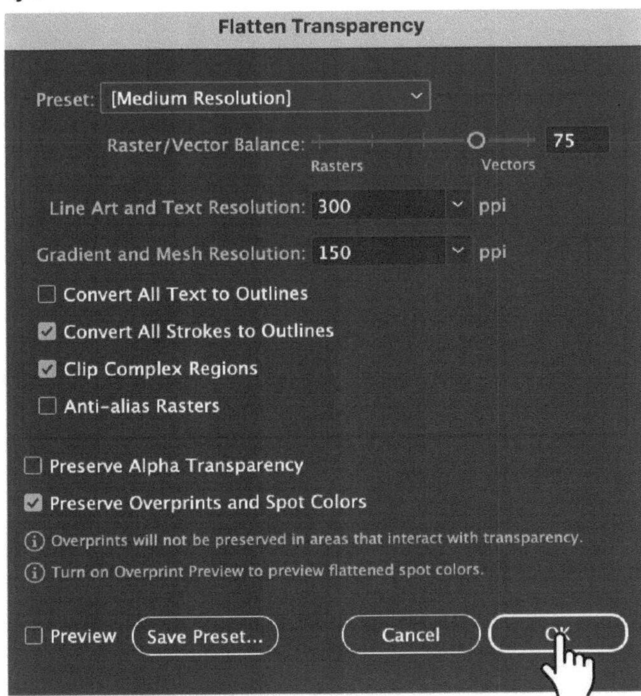

In the window that appears, keep the settings as they are and confirm them with "OK".

Step 10. Ungroup the objects with the shortcut Shift+command+J / Shift+Ctrl+J (Ungroup) or activate **Object > Ungroup.**

After applying the "Flatten Transparency" command, the objects will be converted into individual objects on the basis of color separation.

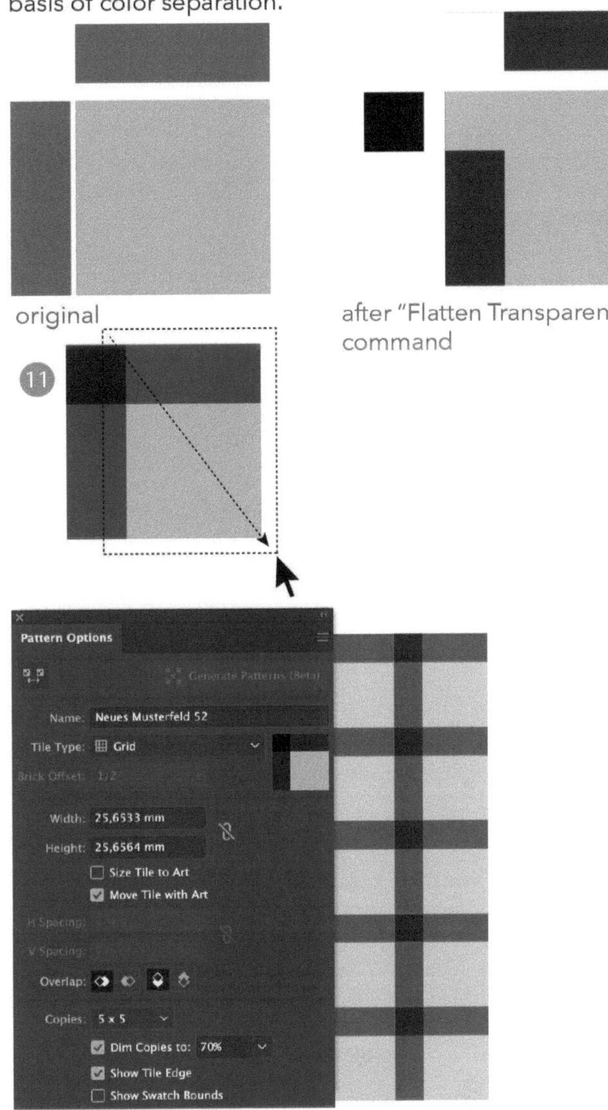

original

after "Flatten Transparency" command

Step 11. Select all objects with the **Selection Tool** (V) and activate the command **Object > Pattern > Make**.
If you have a rectangular repeat, you don't need to make any further settings. Confirm the settings with "Done" in the control panel (at the top). Now you can find the pattern in the Swatches window **Window > Swatches**.

Step 12. Select the **Rectangle Tool** (M) and create a rectangle. And fill in the rectangle with your pattern from the swatches window **Window > Swatches**.

How to recolor and transform the pattern see previous tutorial.

6.2 TUTORIAL: RASTER

When creating graphic content such as logos, symbols, various corporate design products, the grid setting is very important.

You can adjust the grid's settings under **Illustrator > Preferences > Guides & Grid...** (Mac) and **Edit > Preferences > Guides & Grid...** (Windows).

Here you will find two important settings so that you can determine the size of the grid and the subdivisions.

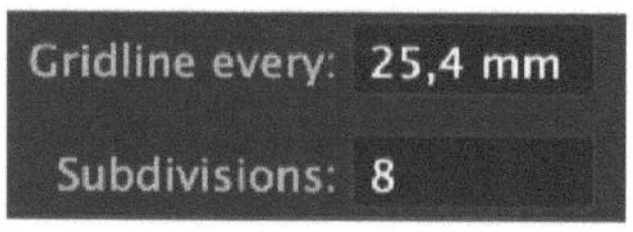

Gridline every:	25,4 mm
Subdivisions:	8

Once you have set the grid size, it is important to activate the grid **View > Show Grid** and **View > Snap to Grid**.

With this setting, the objects are magnetically coupled to the grid when drawing.

First, create a new A4 page in Adobe Illustrator **File > New > A4**.

Step 1. Create with the **Rectangle Tool** (M) the first object. You will notice that the object will automatically snap to the grid.
Step 2. With the **Direct Selection Tool** (A) you can select an anchor point, the „corner widget" will appears, now you can drag with the **Direct Selection Tool** (A) on this corner widget to make the corners round.
Step 3. Create additional objects as you wish. You will notice that the objects are snap to each other and this makes it much easier to align the objects neatly with each other.

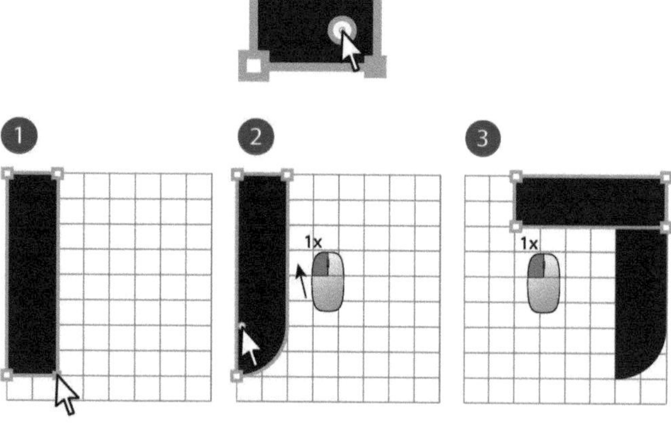

6.3 TUTORIAL: SIMPLE GEOMETRIC PATTERN

First, create a new A4 page in Adobe Illustrator **File > New > A4.**

Step 1. Set in the tools panel the fill color to „black" and the stroke color to „None".

Step 2. Right click on the **Rectangle Tool** (M) in the tools panel to open additional tools. Activate now the **Polygone Tool**, click in the empty drawing area to open the tool settings. Reduce the corners to three to get a triangle and confirm it with „OK".

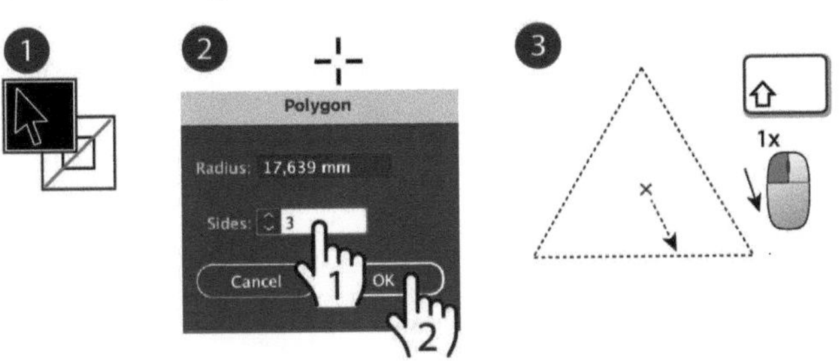

Step 3. Hold down the left mouse button and drag the cursor down to create a triangle, additionally hold down the **shift** key to align the object at a 90° angle. First release the mouse button and then the Shift key.

Step 4. To create a geometric pattern, activate the command "**Object > Pattern > Make**".

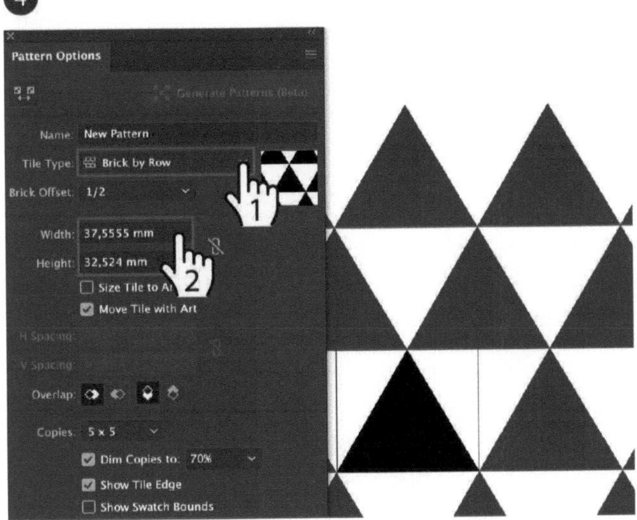

Set the following settings (see figure) and change the distance (width&height) between objects so that gaps are no longer visible.

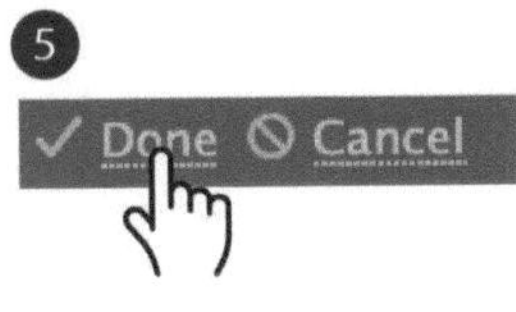

Step 5. Confirm the settings with "Done" in the control panel (at the top). Now you can find the pattern in the Swatches window **Window > Swatches**.

6.4 TUTORIAL: SERPENTINE STRIPES PATTERN

First, create a new A4 page in Adobe Illustrator **File > New > A4.**

Step 1. Activate the **Pen Tool** (P), press and hold the left mouse button and drag the direction point to the right, additionally press and hold the **Shift** key to align the object at a 90° angle. First release the mouse button and then the Shift key.

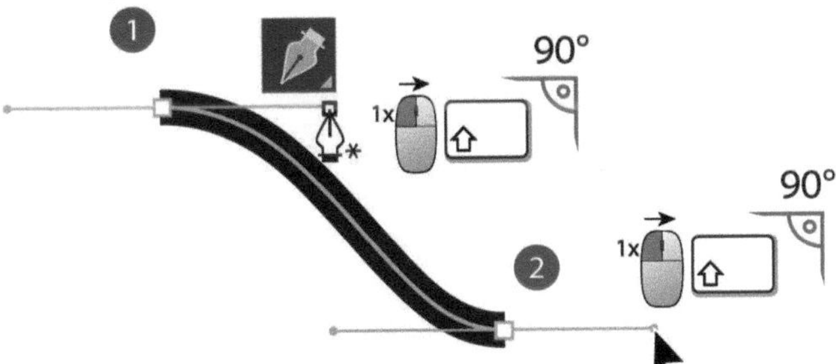

Step 2. Place now the mouse cursor on a new position and repeat the process as in step 1.

Step 3. Click on V key (Selection Tool) and click on an empty drawing area to deselect the object. Alternatively you can activate the shortcut command+Shift+A / Ctrl+Shift+A. Now select with the **Selection Tool** (V) the object to create a clean selection.

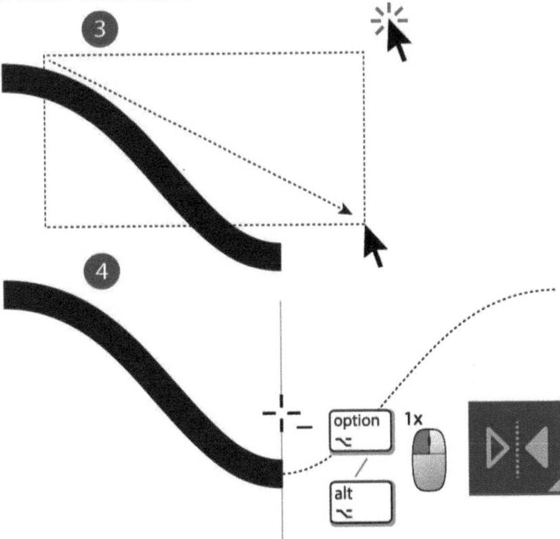

Step 4. Select the **Reflect Tool** (O), position the mouse cursor on the vertical guide, press and hold the **alt/option** key (do not release the alt/option key) and click the left mouse button. The Reflect dialog box appears, then release the **alt** key.

Turn on "Vertical," "Preview," make sure everything is in order, and then click "Copy." A mirrored duplicate is created.

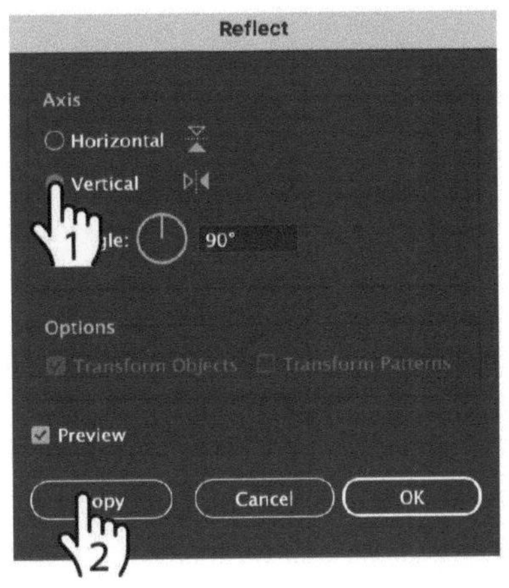

Step 5. Press and hold the left mouse button and drag with the **Direct Selection Tool** (A) a selection around two anchor points (one endpoint for every half). Activate the shortcut option+command+J /alt+Ctrl+J (Average...). Select "Both" and "OK" in the dialog box, then press the shortcut command+J / Ctrl+J (Join).

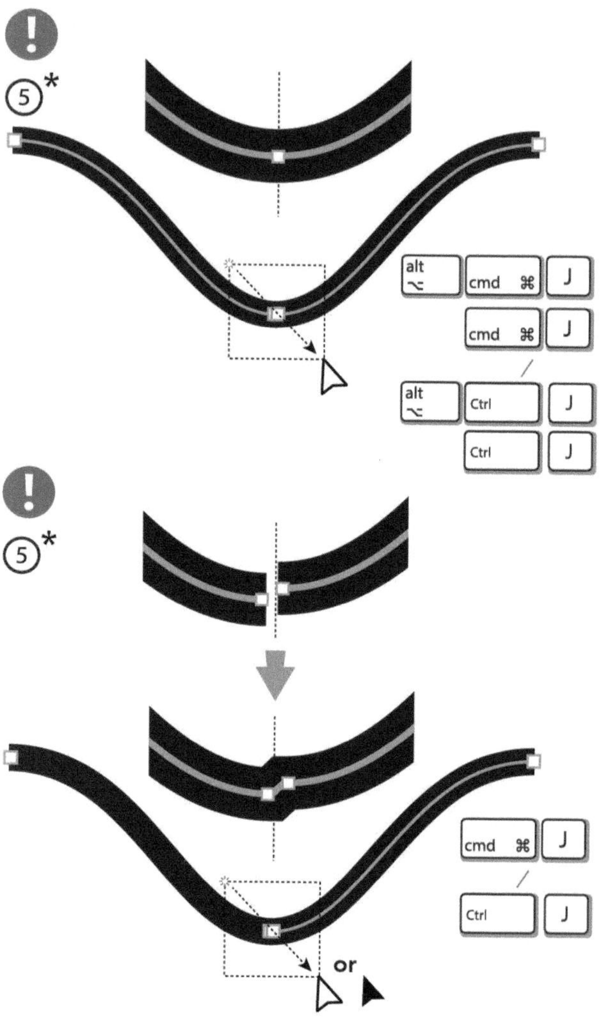

It is important to note that if you only use the shortcut command+J / Ctrl+J (Join) and the copy of the object is not exactly mirrored, the anchor point will be connected by a line. This indicates that the drawing is not entirely clean because the two anchor points are not connected to a single anchor point.

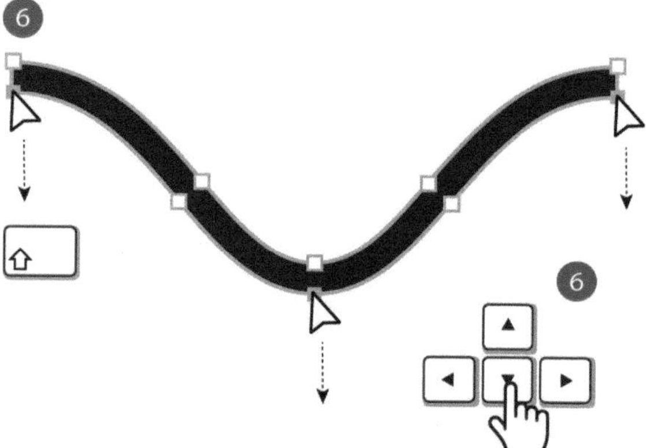

Step 6. Activate the command "**Object > Expand**" and confirm the settings with "OK". Press and hold the **Shift** key and select with the **Direct Selection Tool** (A) three bottom anchor points.
Press the bottom arrow key down to move the anchor points.

Step 7. With the **Selection Tool** (V) select the entire object. Activate then the shortcut command+C / Ctrl+C (Copy) and the shortcut command+F / Ctrl+F (Paste in Front). Drag the copy down.

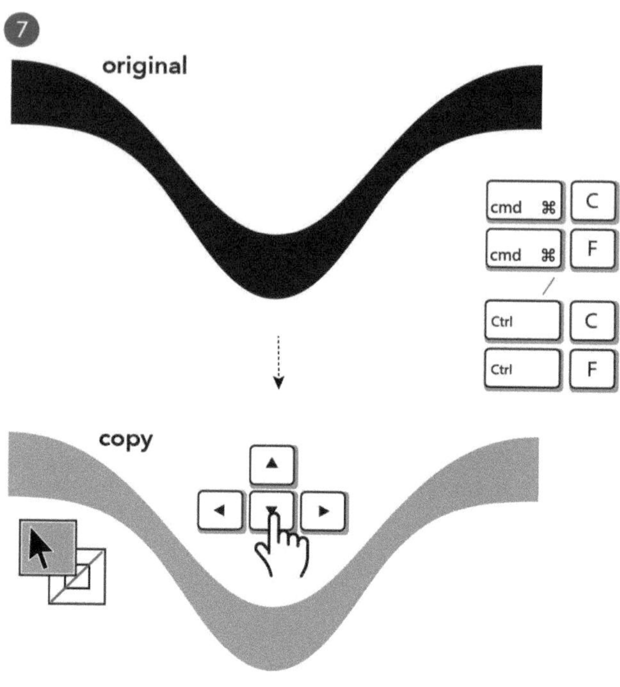

Step 8. Activate the **Blend Tool** (W), click on the first object (original) to define the „initial object" and click then on the second object (copy) to create an alignment between this two objects.

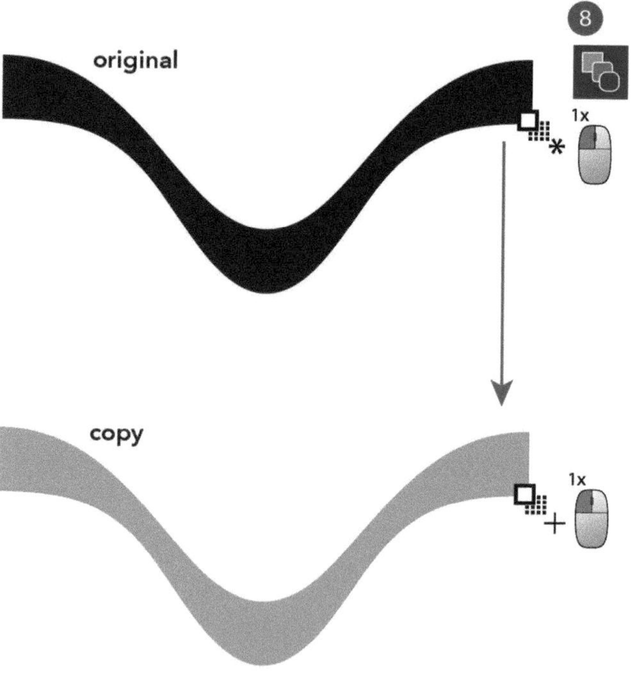

Step 9. Double-click on the **Blend Tool** (W) in the tools panel or activate the **Object > Blend > Blend Options** command to set the number of intermediate objects.

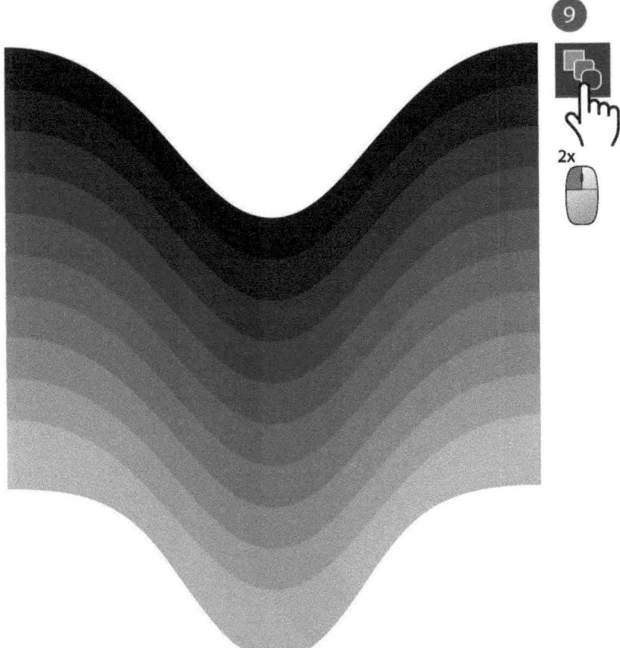

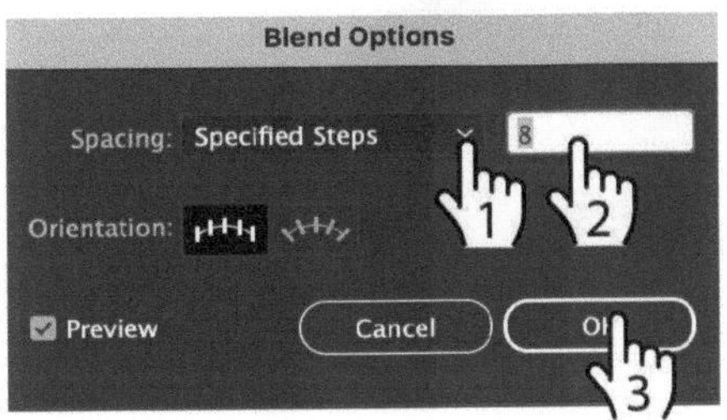

Change settings to "Specified Steps" (1), enter the number of intermediate objects (2) and confirm it with „OK"(3).

Step 10. To change the order of the colors, click the **Recolor artwork** button in the control panel or activate the **Edit > Edit Colors > Recolor Artwork** command. In the window that appears, click on the „Advanced Options".

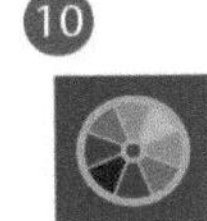

Step 11. In the next window click on the button „Randomly change color order".

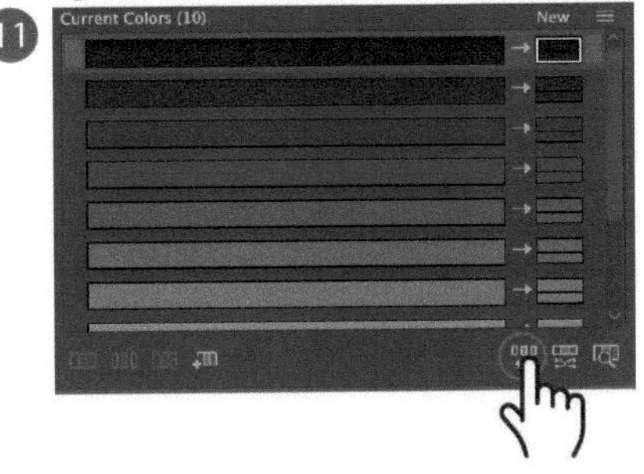

This indicates that the colors can be switched around as needed. Then confirm the settings with „OK".

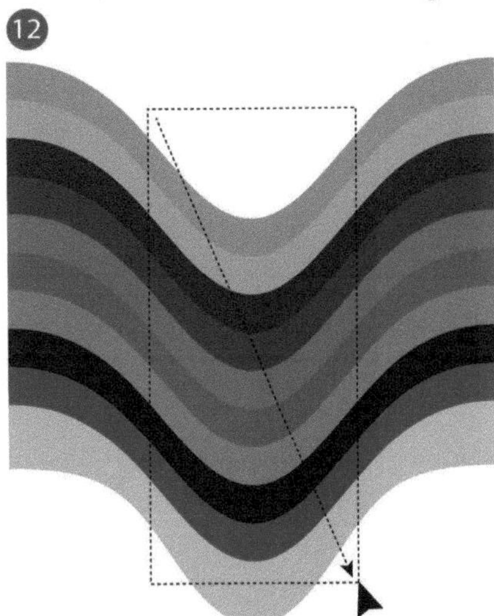

Step 12. Drag with the **Selection Tool** (V) a selection around the objects and activate the command **Object > Pattern > Make**.

Step 13. Set the following settings (see figure). Since it depends on the size of the object, the distance (height &width) between each object is set separately for each pattern.

Step 14. Confirm the settings with "Done" in the control panel (at the top). Now you can find the pattern in the Swatches window **Window > Swatches**.

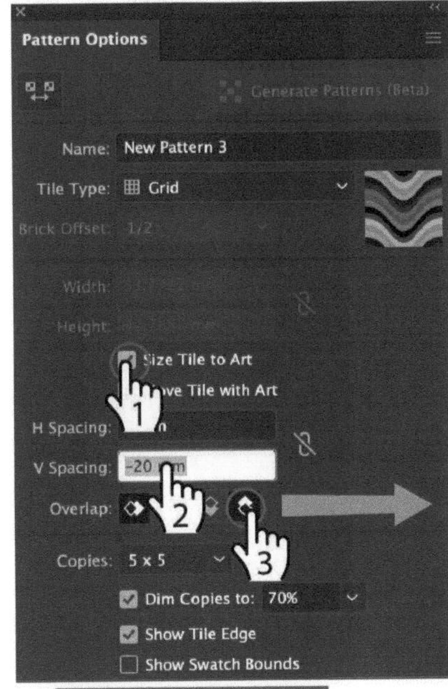

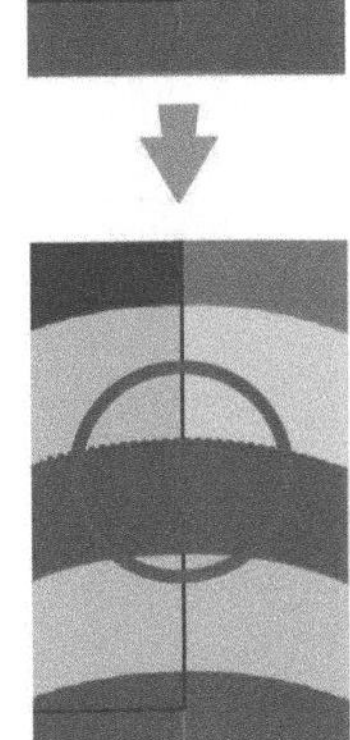

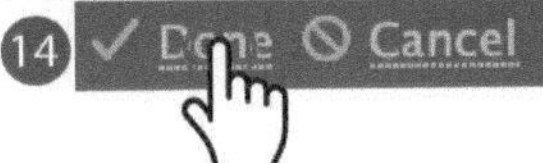

6.5 TUTORIAL: DISTORT OBJECTS

First, create a new A4 page in Adobe Illustrator **File > New > A4.**

Step 1. Create a new A4 document in Illustrator **File > New... >A4.** Open the font dialog box **Window > Type > Character.** Click with the **Text Tool** (T) in the empty drawing area, set the size of the text to 200pt or bigger, choose font that you like and type a series of numbers. Confirm the text rectangle with the **Esc** key.

Step 2. Activate now the **Free Transform Tool** (P).
Step 3. Another toolbar appears, here you have access to two additional tools **Perspective Distort** (1) and **Free Distort** (2).
Step 4. Now you can distort the object however you want using these two tools.

Perspective Distort (1)

Free Distort (2)

6.6 TUTORIAL: DISTORTION AND TRANSFORMATION FILTER TECHNIQUE

First, create a new A4 page in Adobe Illustrator **File > New > A4**.

Step 1. Select the **Text Tool** (T), click in the empty drawing area with the left mouse button and write a word. Confirm the textbox with **Esc** key or with **Selection Tool**

Step 2. Change the fill and stroke color in the tools panel. Then activate the command **Object>Expand..** to convert the object to outlines.

Step 3. Now select the object with the **Selection Tool** (V) and create 3 copies of this object with the shortcut command+C / Ctrl+C (Copy) and the shortcut command+F / Ctrl+F (Paste in Front). After positioning the copies, rotate them to the appropriate angle in 90° angle with the **Shift** key.

Step 4. Left click the mouse button and drag with the **Selection Tool** (V) around all objects to select them. Use the shortcut cmd+G / Ctrl+G (or choose **Object > Group**) to group the objects.

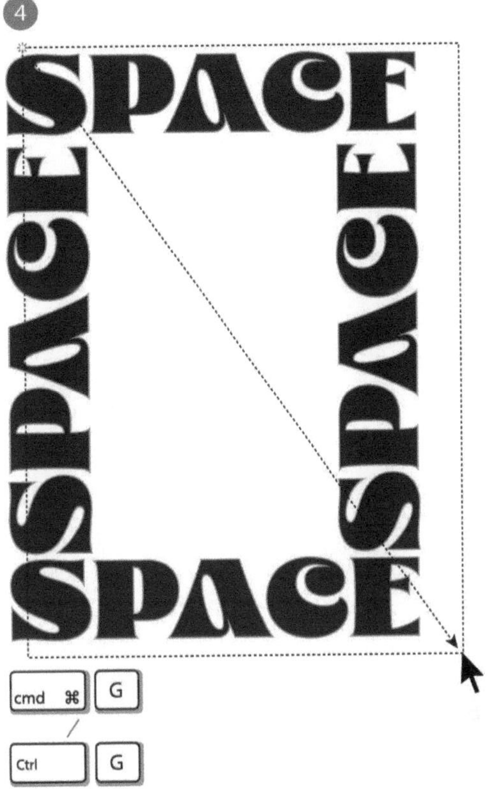

Step 5. Now open the panel **Transform (Effect > Distort&Transform > Transform...)** and apply the following settings (see figure) , then confirm the settings with „OK".

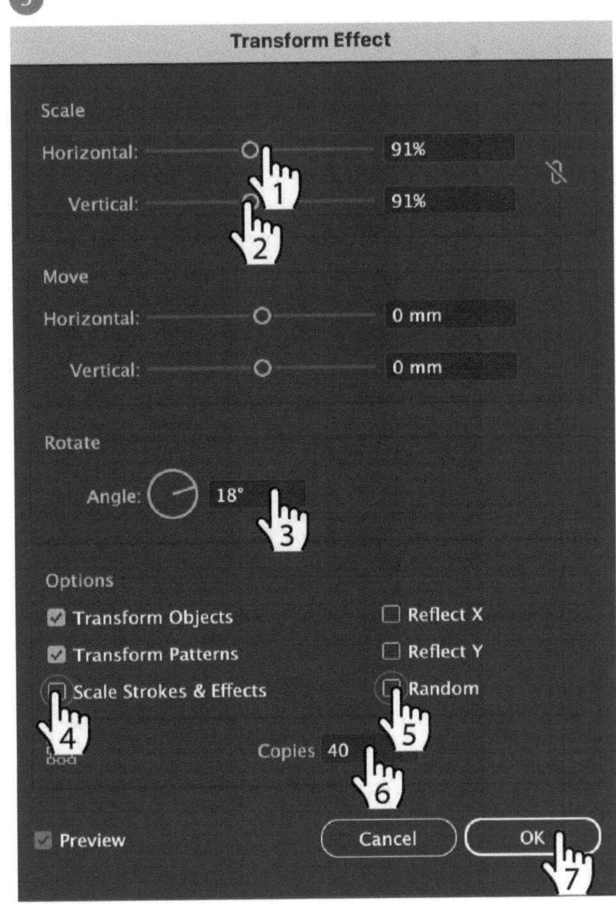

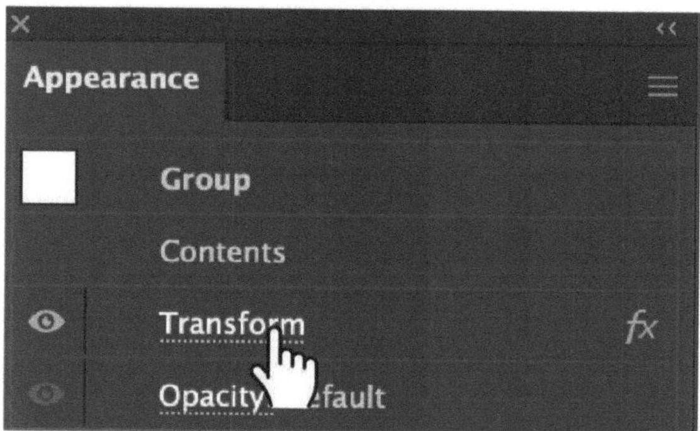

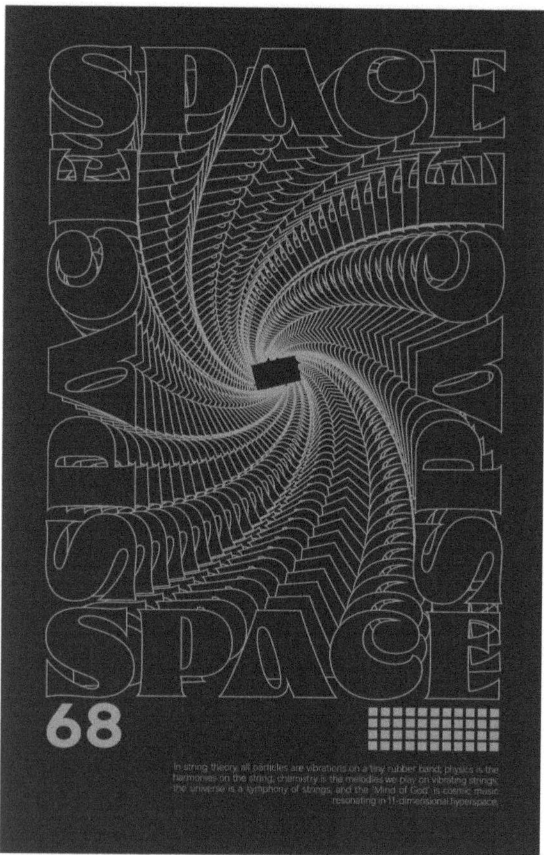

Step 6. You can change the artwork's settings in the **Appearance panel** if needed, go to **Window>Appearance.**

6.7 TUTORIAL: WARP FILTERS

First, create a new A4 page in Adobe Illustrator **File > New > A4.**

Step 1. For this placement print create multiple graphics. You can use various tools for this, e.g. the **Text Tool** (T), **Pen Tool** (P) or different basic shapes like **Rectangle Tool** (M).

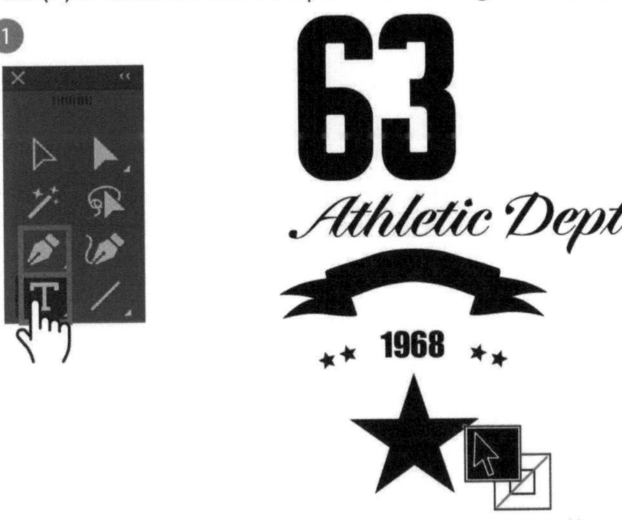

Step 2. For some tools in Illustrator you can apply different settings. For these two tools **Polygone Tool** and **Star Tool**, there are two ways to do this.

A. Activate the **Polygone Tool**, press and hold the left mouse button and drag the direction point clockwise or counterclockwise, additionally press the arrow keys to add or delete corners (▲ increase the number of corners, decrease the number of corners ▼). If you hold addittionaly the **Shift** key the object will be aligned at a 90° angle. Then first release the mouse button and then the Shift and arrow keys. This way you can draw for example a triangle.

You can apply the same technique for the **Star Tool**.

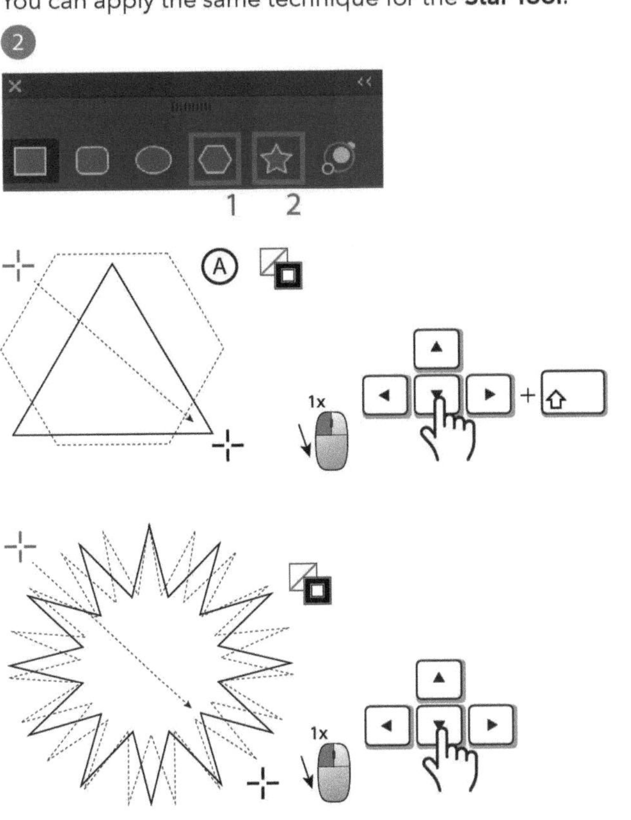

"

B. The second technique is to click in the document with one of this two tools. For example if you klick with the **Star Tool**, **Radius 1** enters the distance between the center and the inner points of the star, and **Radius 2** enters the distance between the center and the outer points of the star. Under "Points" you can enter the desired number of points. Confirm your entries with "OK."

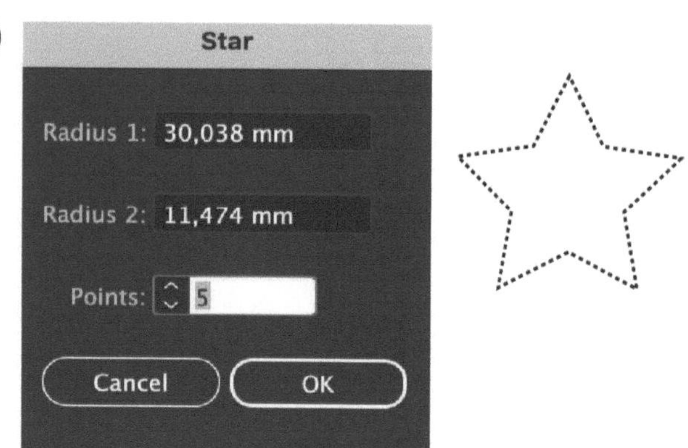

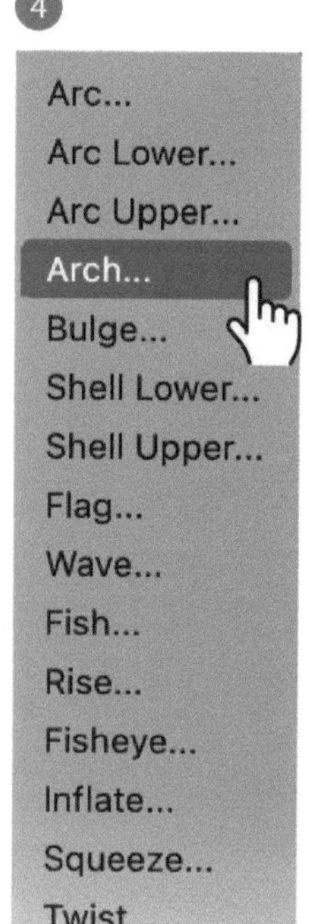

Step 3. Open the font dialog box **Window > Type > Character**. Click with the **Text Tool** (T) in the empty drawing area, set the size of the text to 200pt or bigger, choose font that you like and type a word. Confirm the text rectangle with the **Esc** key.

Step 4. Activate the filter **Effect › Warp › Arch**. Change the „bend" settings as you wish and confirm it with „OK".

Step 5. Try out other filters from this group. You can also combine several filters from this filter group.

Step 6. You can also access the settings you made in the Appearance window **Window › Appearance**. There you have the opportunity, for example to change or delete the filter settings.

Step 7. Additionally if you want to create a simple texture, find a photo of the desired template (for example surface structure) and see exercise 6.25 (page 88) on how to create bitmap images.

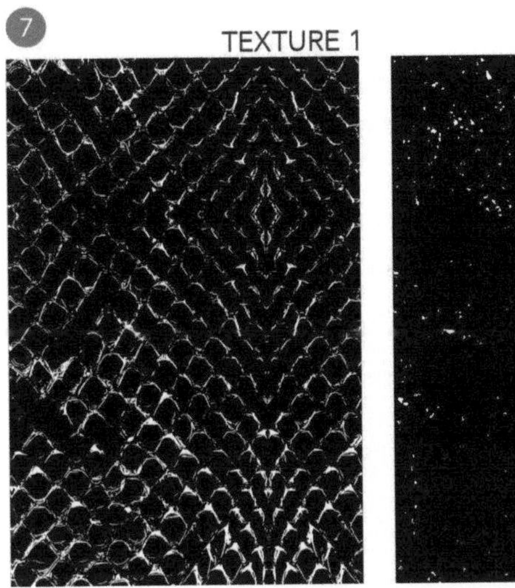

TEXTURE 1

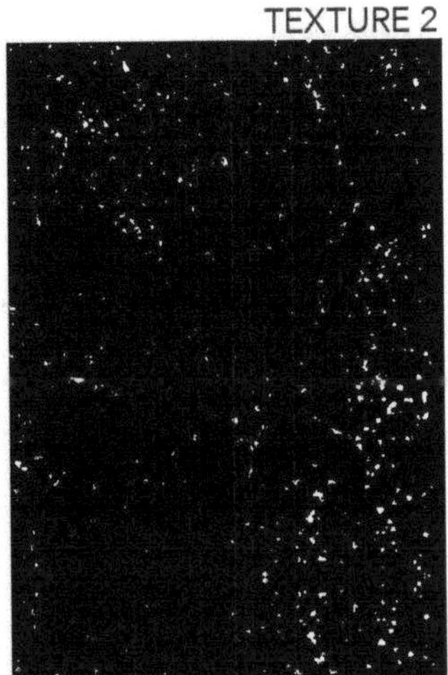

TEXTURE 2

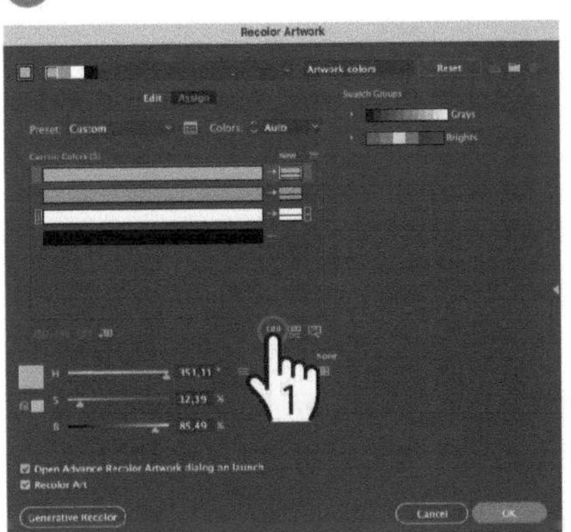

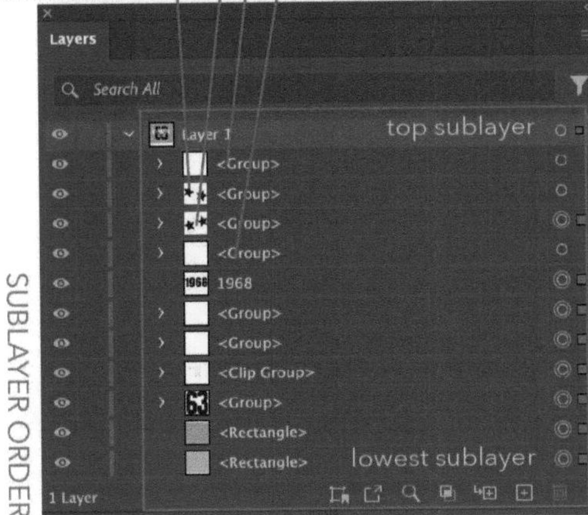

SUBLAYER ORDER

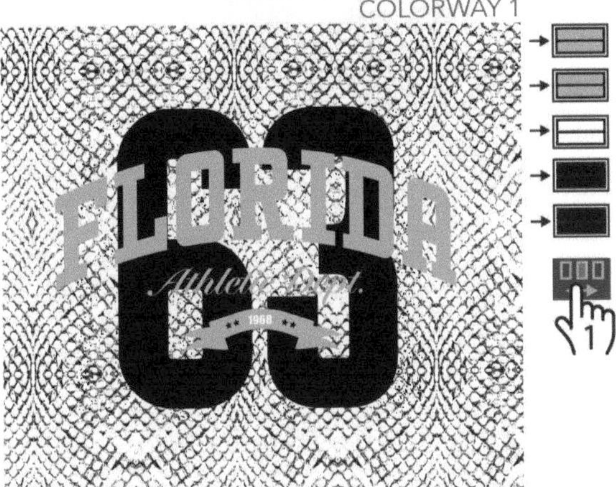

COLORWAY 1

COLORWAY 2

COLORWAY 3

Step 8. Now place the objects in the correct order. To change the order of the objects, work with the sublayers in the Layers panel **Window › Layers** or select the individual objects and activate the command **Object › Arrange › Send to Back** or **Object › Arrange › Send to Front**.

Step 9. To recolor the artwork, open the command **Edit › Edit Colors › Recolor Artwork…**

To play creatively with colors, click on the "Randomly change color order" (1) button. This reorders the objects' colors and creates interesting colorways.

6.8 TUTORIAL: BITMAP&RASTERIZE TECHNIQUE

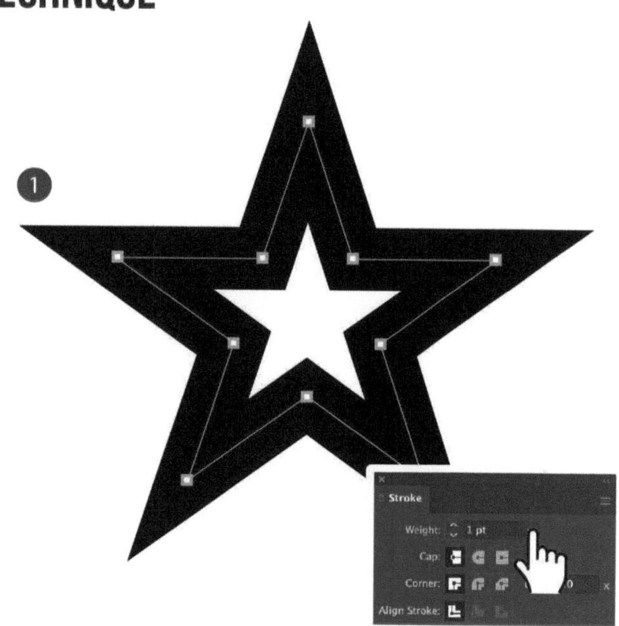

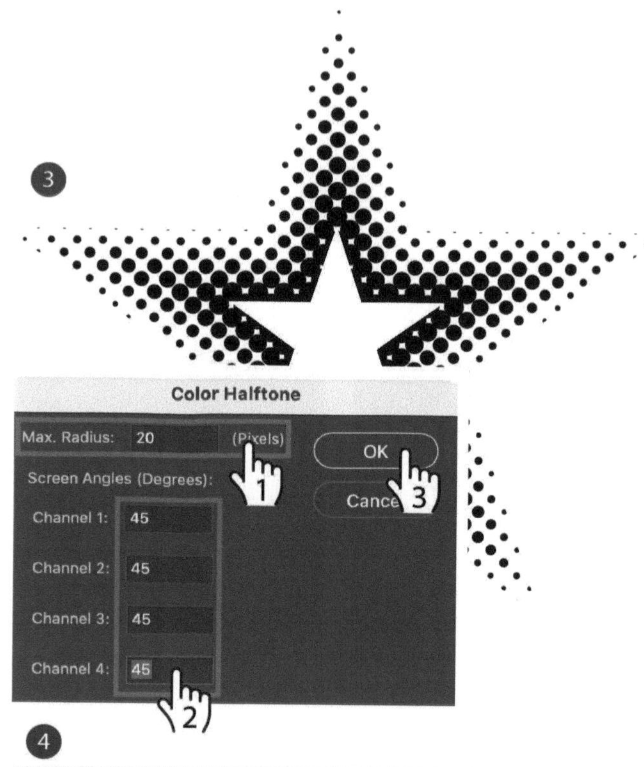

First, create a new A4 page in Adobe Illustrator **File > New > A4.**

Step 1. Set in the tools panel the fill color „None" and the stroke color „black" and change the stroke „Weight" for example to 60 pt **Window > Stroke.**

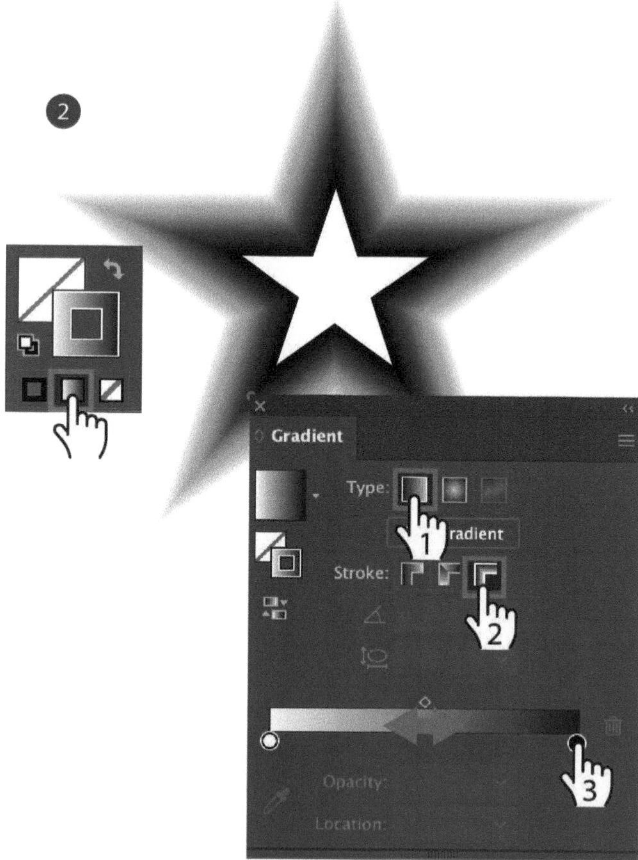

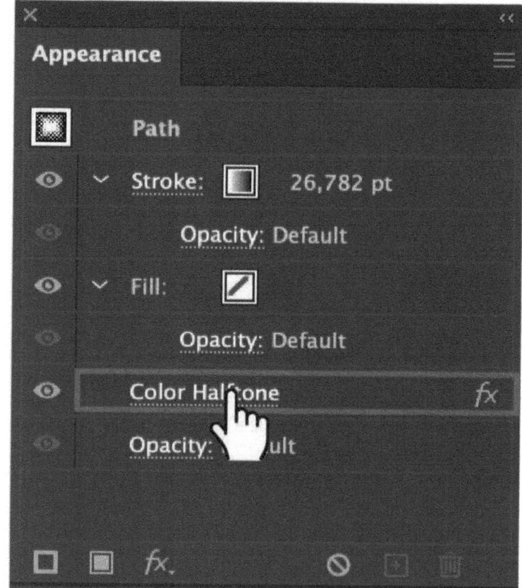

Step 4. The effect settings can be changed at any time in the **Window > Appearance** menu.

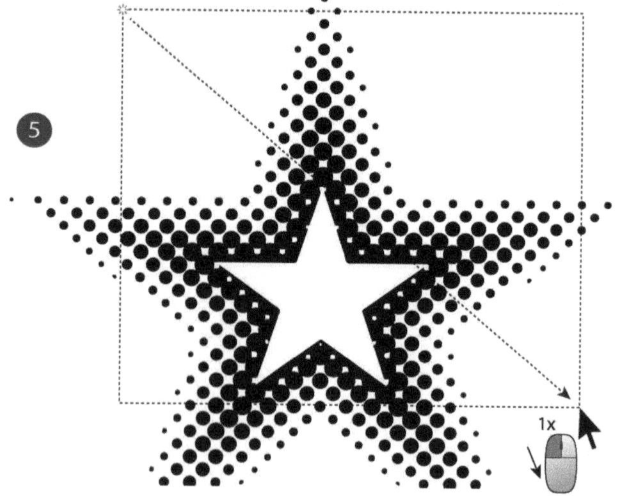

Step 2. Set in the tools panel the stroke to „Gradient", open the gradient window **Window > Gradient**, change the settings (see figure). With the value "3" you can adjust the gradient individually.

Step 3. Apply to the object **Effect > Pixelate > Color Halftone...** Set the following values in the dialog box.
The smaller the value for "Max. Radius" (1), the finer the dots are. You can set this value between 4-127.

Step 5. It is now necessary to vectorize the object in order to recolor it. Select the object first with the **Selection Tool** (V) and activate the command **Object > Expand Appearance**. Confirm the settings with "OK".

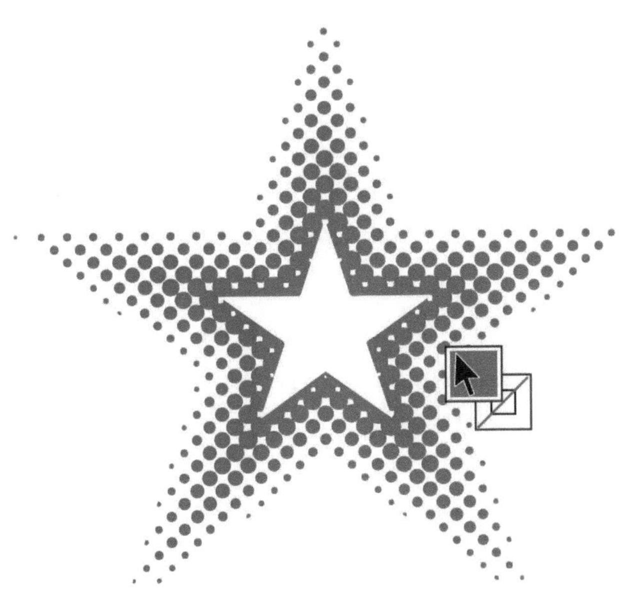

Step 6. In the control panel click on the „Tracing Presets" button ⌄ , select „Sketched Art" and click at the end on „Expand". Expand

Now the object is vectorized and can be recolored.

6.9 TUTORIAL: QUATREFOIL PATTERN

First, create a new A4 page in Adobe Illustrator **File > New > A4.**

Set: **View > Rules >Show Rules, View > Guides > Lock Guides, View > Guides > Show Guides, View > Smart Guides, View > Snap to Point.**

Step 1. Set in the tools panel the fill color „black" and the stroke color „None". Activate **Ellipse Tool** (L), press and hold **alt/option** and **Shift** key, then create a circle. First release the mouse button and then the option/alt and Shift keys.

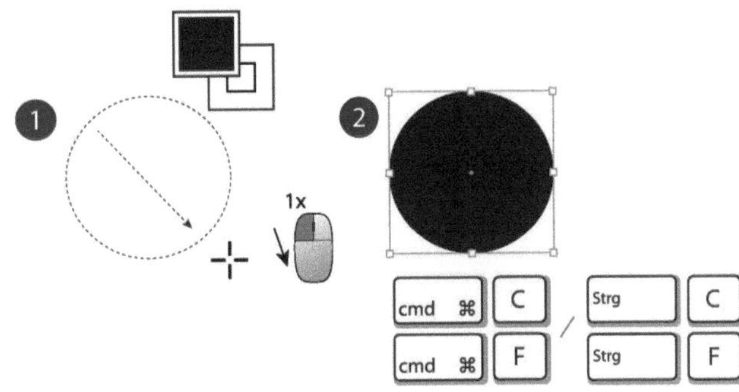

Step 2. While the object is still selected, copy it with the shortcut Cmd+C/Crtl+C and Cmd+F/Ctrl+F.
Step 3. Move the copy with the keyboard arrow keys ▾ down.

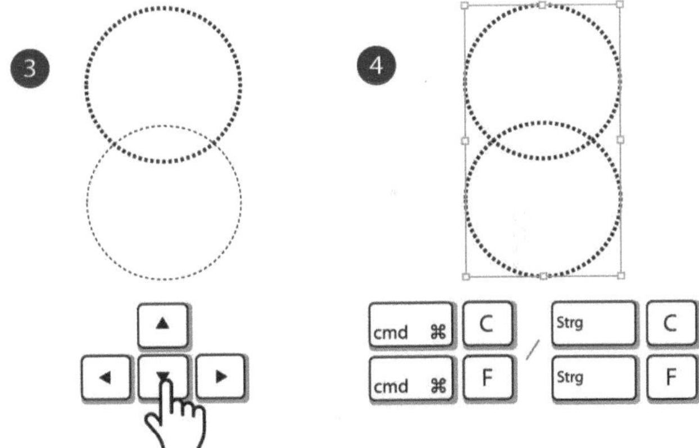

Step 4. Select both objects with the **Selection Tool** (V), copy them with the shortcut Cmd+C/Crtl+C and Cmd+F/Ctrl+F

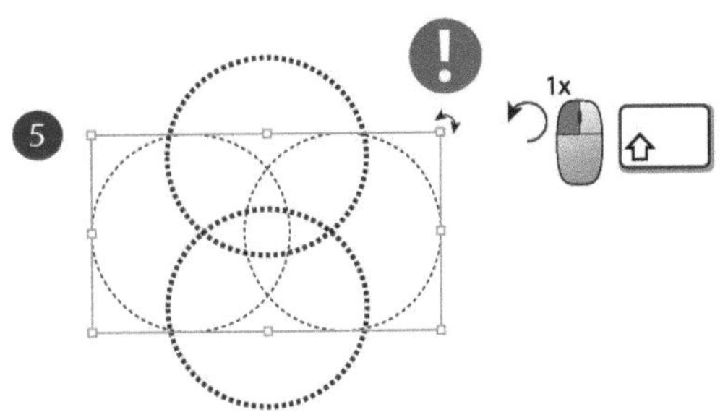

Step 5. Press and hold the left mouse button and drag the copy clockwise or counterclockwise, additionally press the **Shift** key to align the objects at a 90° angle. Then first release the mouse button and then the Shift.

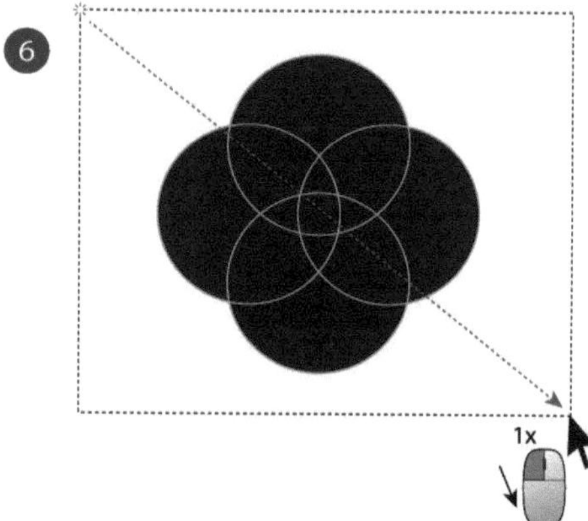

Step 6. Now select all objects with the **Selection Tool** (V).

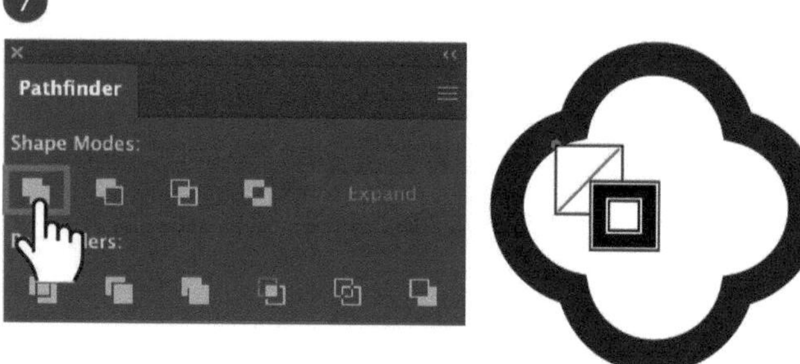

Step 7. Open the "Pathfinder" window **Window > Pathfinder** and click on "Unite" to convert all objects into one object. Switch the "fill" with the "stroke" color, change the "Weight" of the stroke **Window > Stroke** and activate the command **Object > Pattern > Make**.

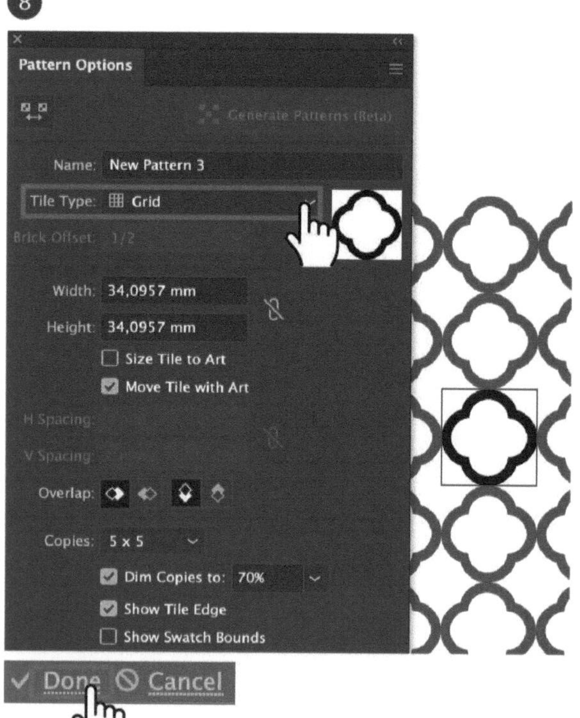

Step 8. In window "Pattern Options" leave the settings as they are, confirm it with "Done" in the control panel (at the top). Now you can find the pattern in the Swatches window **Window > Swatches**.

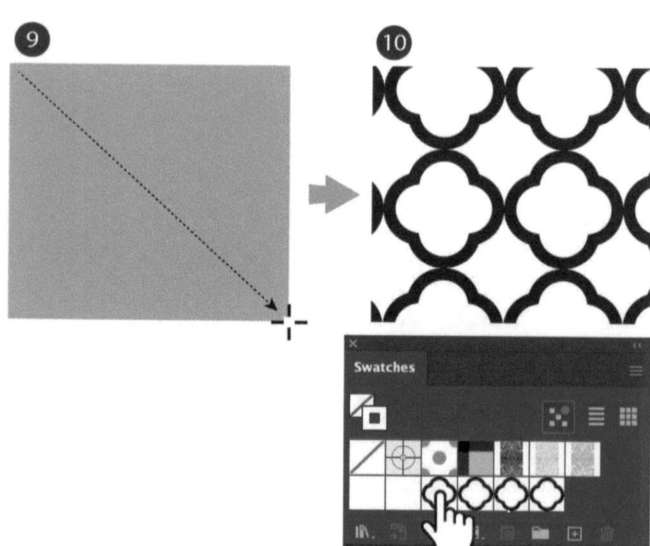

Step 9. Select the **Rectangle Tool** (M) and create a rectangle.

Step 10. Fll in the rectangle with the pattern from the swatches window **Window > Swatches**.

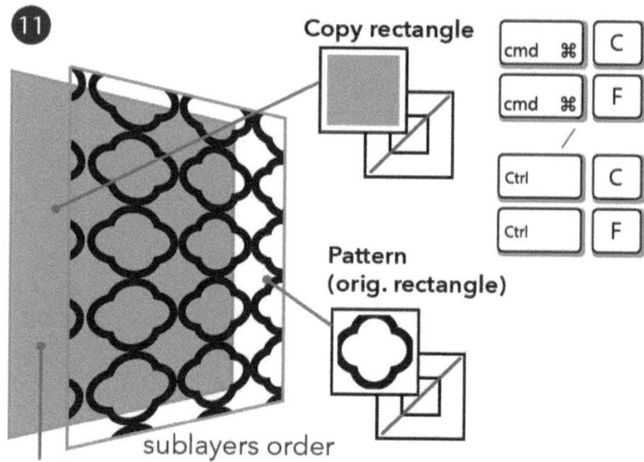

Put the copy in the background **Object > Arrange > Send to Back** and apply a fill color.

Step 11. Create a copy of the pattern rectangle with the shortcut Cmd+C/Crtl+C and Cmd+F/Ctrl+F, then apply a fill color. Place the rectangle in the background **Object > Arrange > Send to Back**. This method is easy to use to add a background to the pattern. Another method to add a background can be found in tutorial 6.23 on page 82.

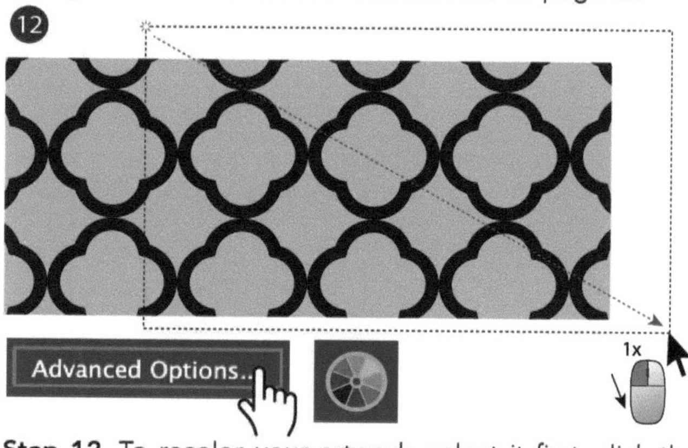

Step 12. To recolor your artwork, select it first, click the **Recolor artwork** button in the control panel or activate the **Edit > Recolor > Artwork** command. In the window that appears, click on the „Advanced Options". Now you can set the colors for multiple objects at the same time.

If you want to resize, rotate or move your pattern, first select it with the **Selection Tool** (V), then right click on the object and go to **Transform > Move..., Rotate..., Scale...**
For a detailed description see step 12 on page 46.

6.10 TUTORIAL: SELECTION TECHNIQUES IN PHOTOSHOP

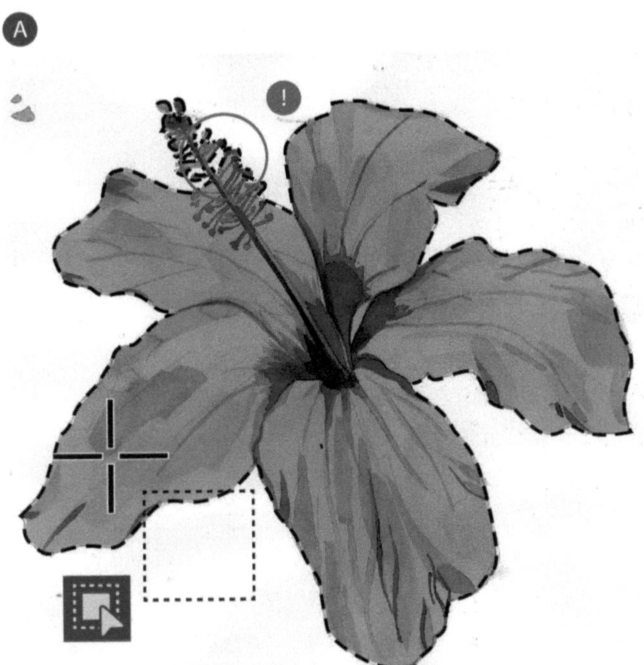

Photoshop offers multiple methods for selection. Here, I outline the most widely used methods. The other techniques are used more on a project-related basis.

A. With the **Object Selection Tool** you can click on an object or drag a selection around an object to select it. The object to be selected is highlighted in blue.

There are other settings for this tool, but since they are too specific they will not be discussed.

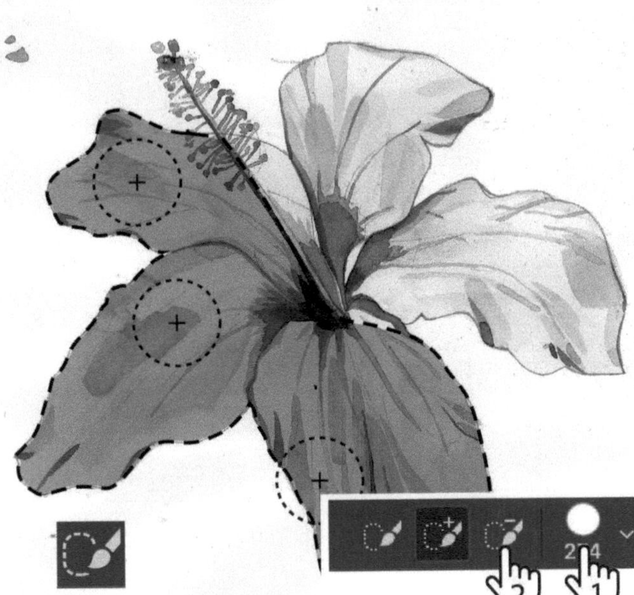

B. With the **Quick Selection Tool** you can click on an object to select it. In the control panel you can select more important setting for this tool e.g. brush size (1) or **add/substract tool** (2).

C. With the **MegicWand Tool** you can click on an object to select it. In the control panel you can select more important setting for this tool e.g. tolerance (1), the higher the value (up to 255), the more similar pixels (colors) are selected, the lower the value, the fewer similar pixels (colors) are selected.

The **shift key** can be used to add or subtract areas from your selection. Activating the **"Contiguous"** option will select pixels only in the closest area instead of all over the document.

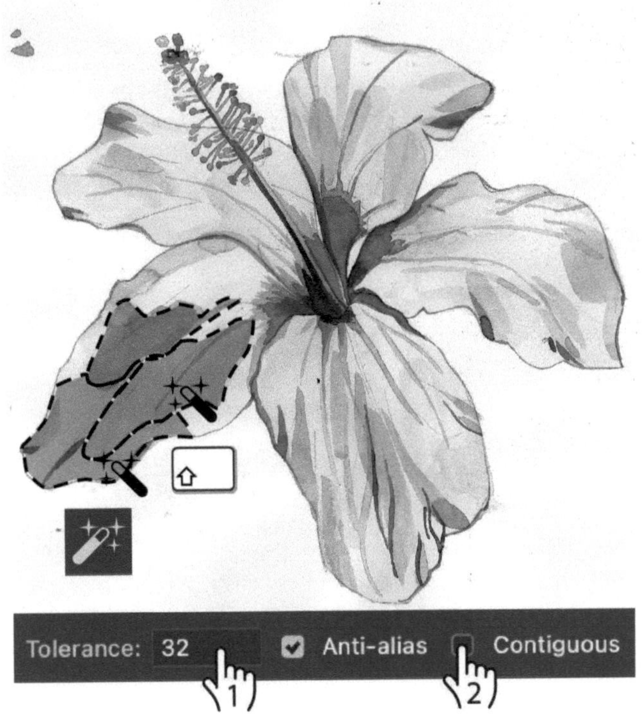

D. With the **Pen Tool** you can draw a line around the object, then the right mouse click on the line or the **"Selection"** button in the control panel (1) opens the window where soft edges (2) can be set so that the selection does not contain too sharp outlines.

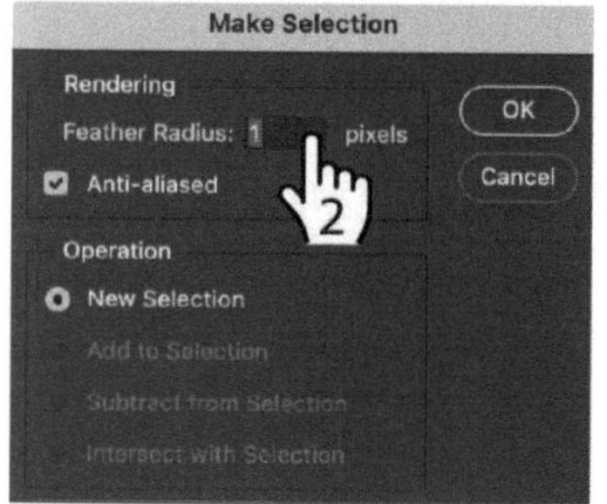

It is also possible to close the shape without any extra curves by holding down the **option key**.

For a path you can add (2) or delete (1) the anchor points with the **Pen Tool** and correct them with the **Direct Selection Tool** (3).

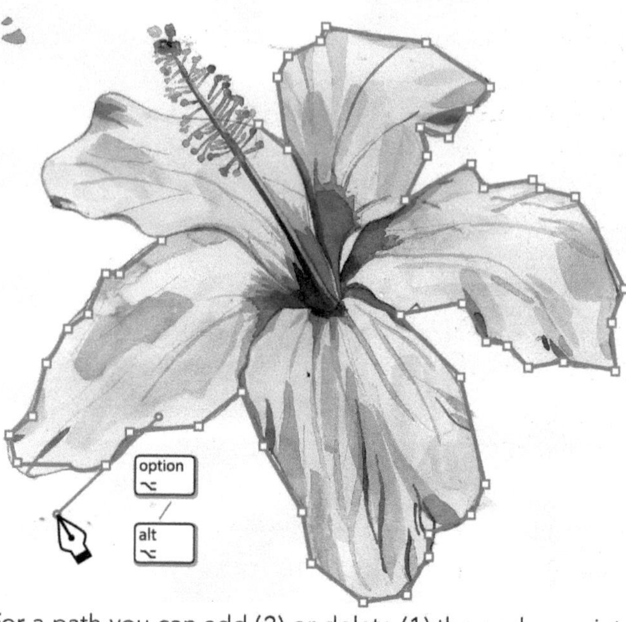

6.11 TUTORIAL: DISSOLVE FILTER

Step 1. Create a new A4 page in Photoshop **File › New › A4**

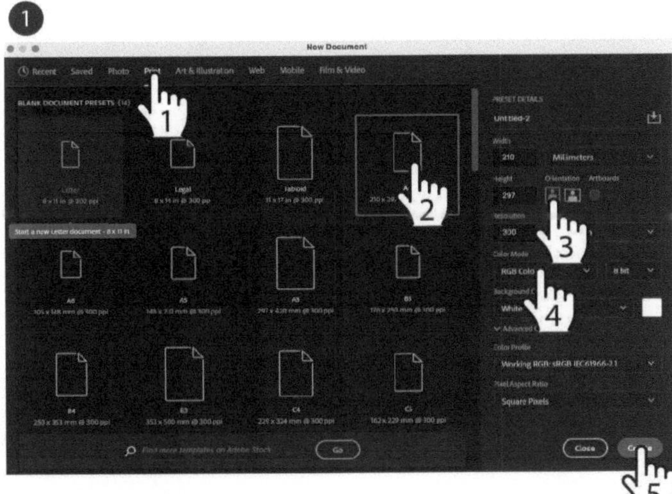

Step 2. Select the **Text Tool** (T), set a new color and font size, click in the empty drawing area with the left mouse button and write a word. Confirm the textbox with **Esc** key or with **Selection Tool.**

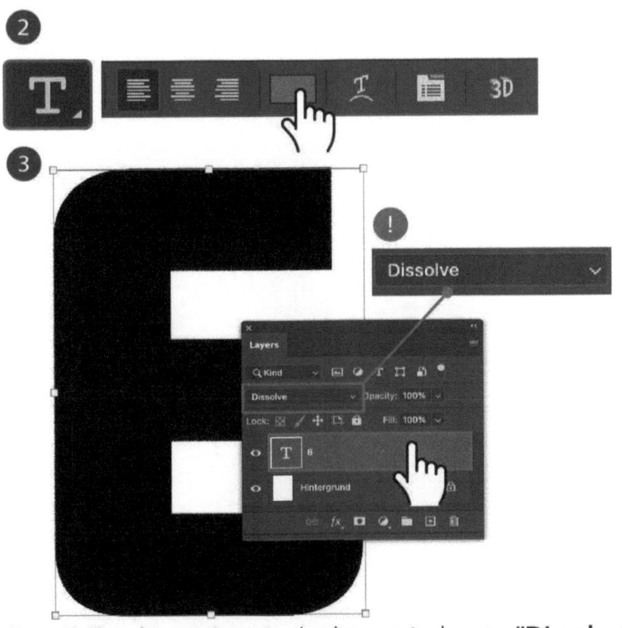

Step 3. Set the settings in the layer window to **"Dissolve"**
Step 4. Turn the text layer into a smart object with the right click.

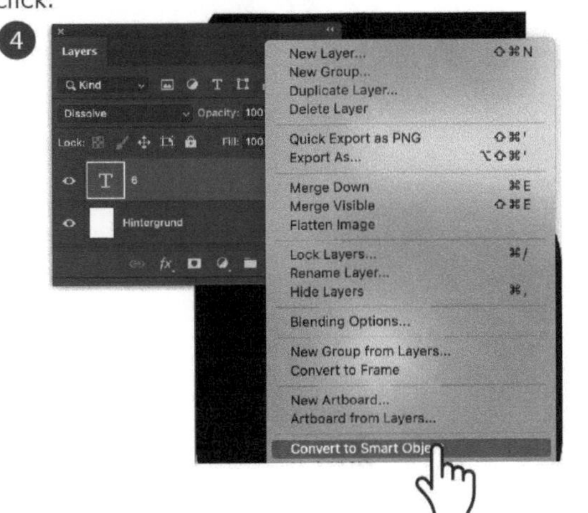

Step 5. Now go to **Filter › Blur Gallery › Path Blur...**

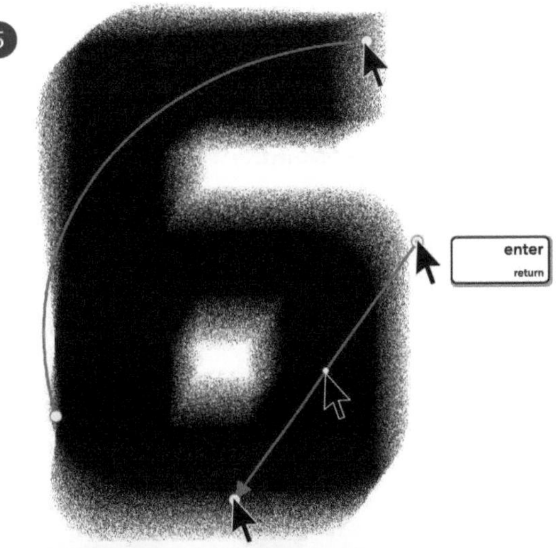

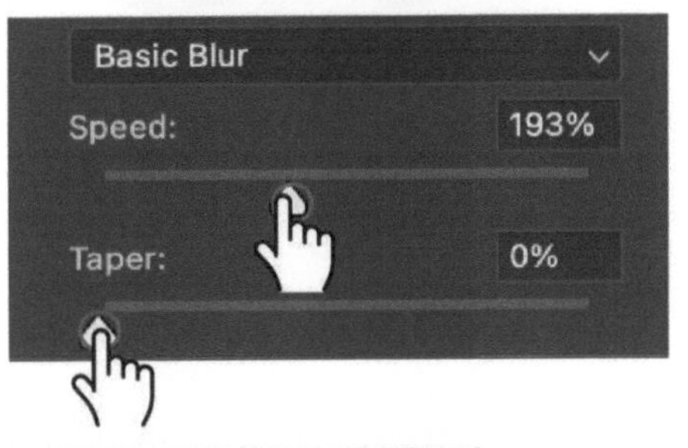

Drag on the blue line to change the direction, click on speed in the right corner to change the settings for the effect. Then click on "OK" or click "enter"key to confirm the settings.

Step 6. To change the settings again, click on the "Blur Gallery" entry in the Layers window.

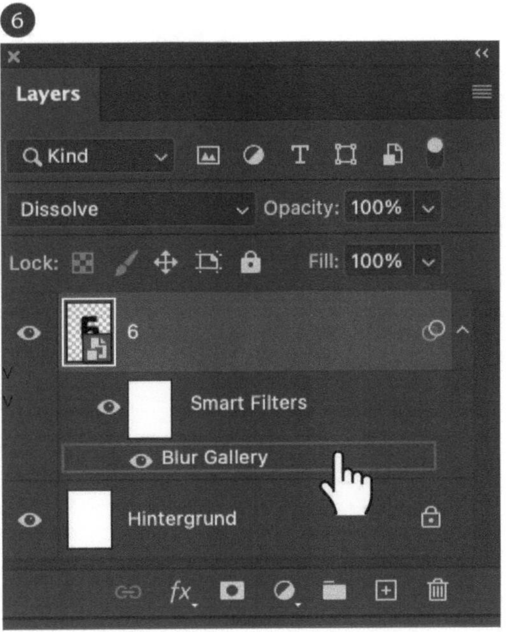

6.12 TUTORIAL: ENVELOPE DISTORT 1

Step 1. Create a new A4 document in Illustrator **File > New >A4**.

Open the font dialog box **Window > Type > Character**. Click with the **Text Tool** (T) in the empty drawing area, set the size of the text to 200pt or bigger, choose font that you like and type for example a series of numbers. Confirm the text rectangle with the „**Esc**" key.

Step 2. Activate the command **Object > Envelope Distort > Make with Mesh...** And enter the value 2 for each row and column, confirm the settings with „OK". You decide how complicated the grid should be. However, simpler grids are easier to handle.

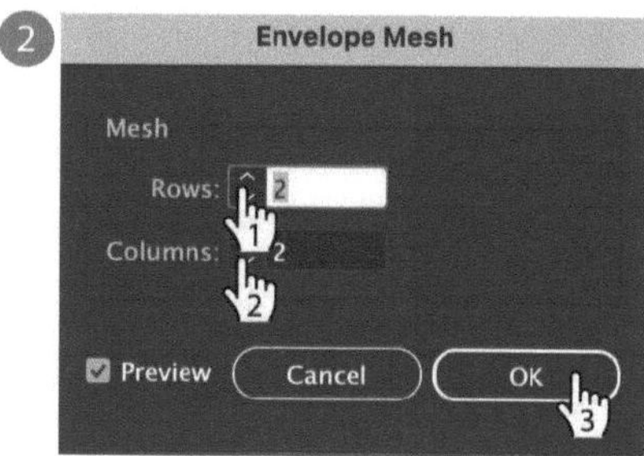

Step 3. Activate the **Direct Selection Tool** (A), press and hold the left mouse button and drag on an anchor point to distort the object.

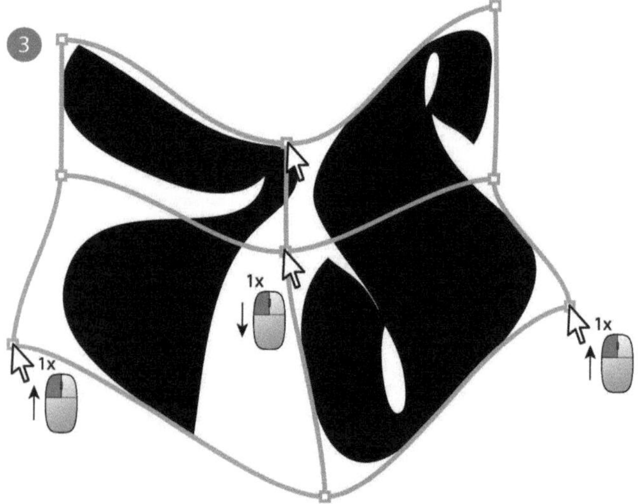

Step 4. If you are satisfied with the result, it is advisable to expand the object to be able to access individual anchor points **Object > Expand...**
But before converting the object, it is better to create a copy of the original so that you can edit anytime the grid.

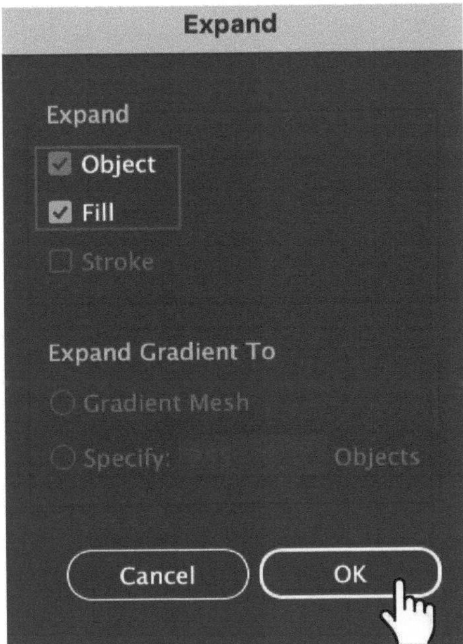

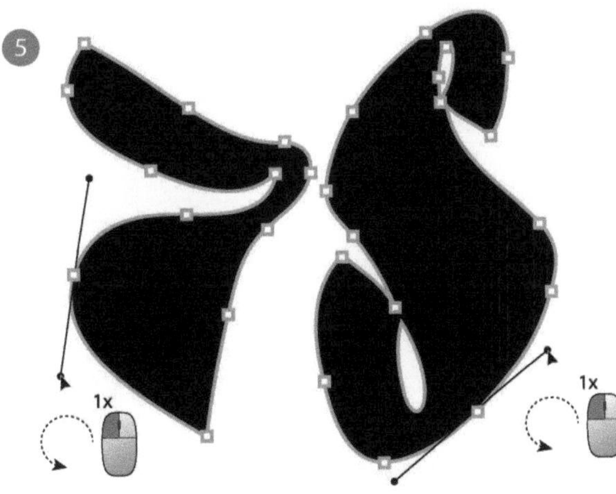

Step 5. Once the object has been expanded, you can begin editing the object's individual anchor points with the **Direct Selection Tool** (A) to refine the shape of the object if necessary.

Step 6. Now you can, for example, create several copies of this object and experiment with strokes and create some patterns **Window > Stroke** & **Window > Swatches**.

6.13 TUTORIAL: ENVELOPE DISTORT 2

Step 1. For the distortion envelope, first create an object with the **Pen Tool** (P) that reflects your ideas. Put this object in the foreground **Object > Arrange > Bring to Front**.

Step 2. Select both objects and activate the command **Object > Envelope Distort > Make with Top Object** or use the shortcut cmd+option+C / Ctrl+alt+C.

Step 3. If the result is distorted too much, you can change the accuracy of the distortion using the distortion options **Object > Envelope Distort > Envelope Options...** (A). Another interesting option is the "Distort Pattern Fill" option. With this setting you can adapt the pattern you created with Illustrator to the shape of the distorting objects (B).

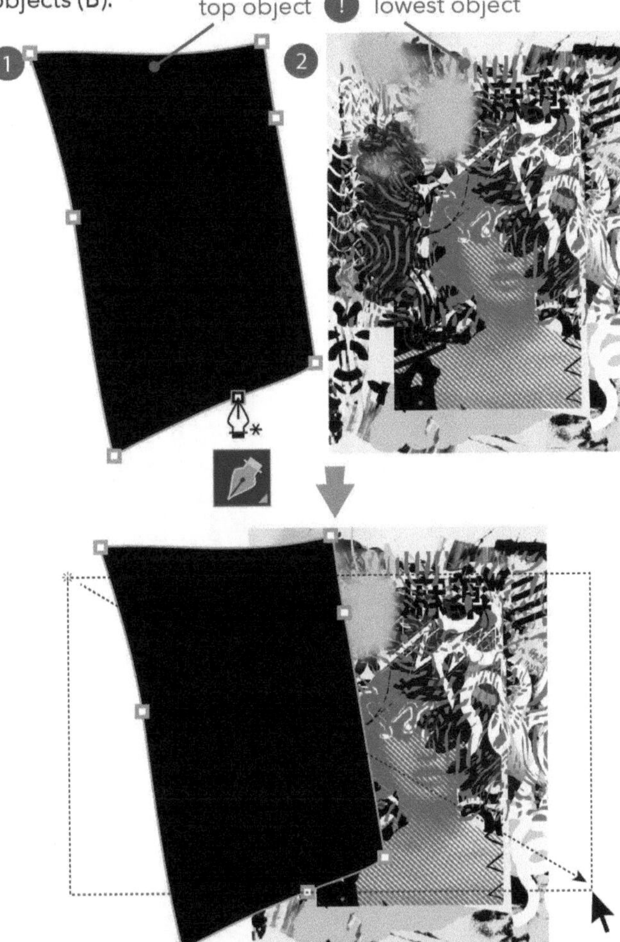

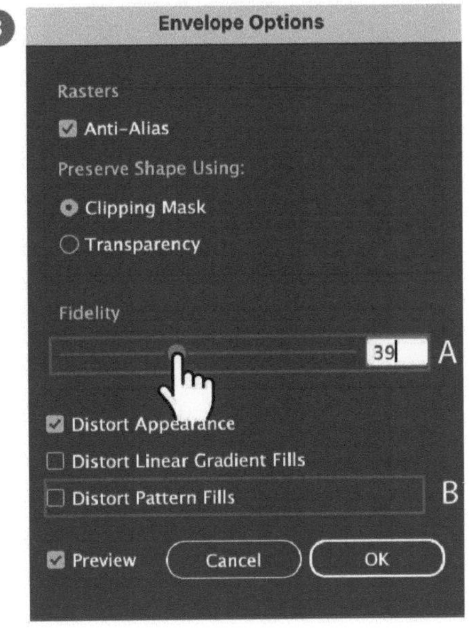

You can also release the envelope distort by activating the following command **Object > Envelope Distort > Release**.

The distortion mesh can be used, among other things, to create mockups, in order to better visualize placement prints on a t-shirt for example.

Distort Pattern Fills is deactivated

Distort Pattern Fills is activated

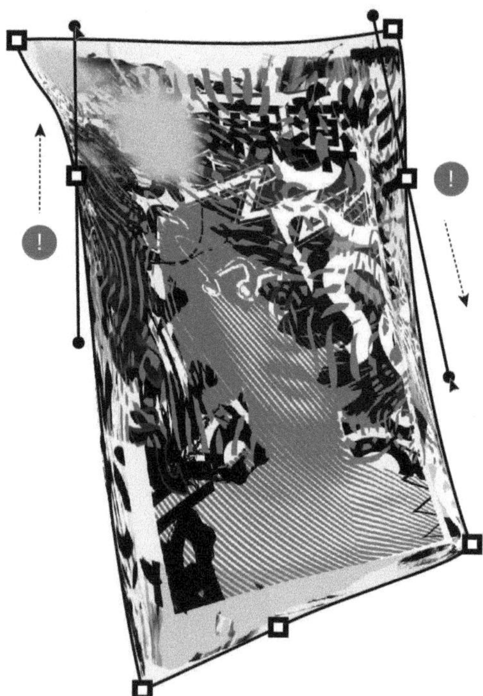

Unexpected outcomes may occur if the „Distort" shape is too complicated or when you start to improve the individual anchor points.

6.14 TUTORIAL: KNIFE TOOL

Step 1. Create a new A4 document in Illustrator **File > New >A4**. Open the font dialog box **Window > Type > Character**. Click with the **Text Tool** (T) in the empty drawing area, set the size of the text to 200pt or bigger, choose font that you like and type a series of numbers. Confirm the text rectangle with the „**Esc**" key.

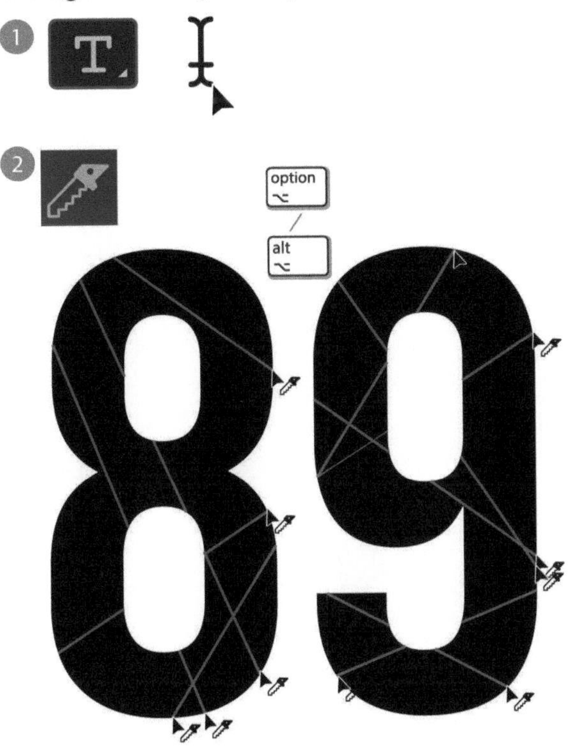

Step 2. To cut through the object, you have to expand the text first. Activate therefor **Object > Expand**. Now activate the **Knife Tool**. You can find this tool in the same group with **Eraser Tool** (right-clicking on the Eraser Tool opens additional tools).
Step 3. To cut through the object with straight lines, hold and press the alt/option key. Then release first the mouse button and then the alt/option key. Then ungroup the object with the command **Object > Ungroup**. Now you can move the objects as you wish.

6.15 TUTORIAL: BLUR FILTER

Step 1. Create a new A4 document in Illustrator **File > New >A4**. Open the font dialog box **Window > Type > Character**. Click with the **Text Tool** (T) in the empty drawing area, set the size of the text in the "Font" window to 200pt or bigger, choose font that you like and type a series of numbers. Confirm the text rectangle with the „**Esc**" key.

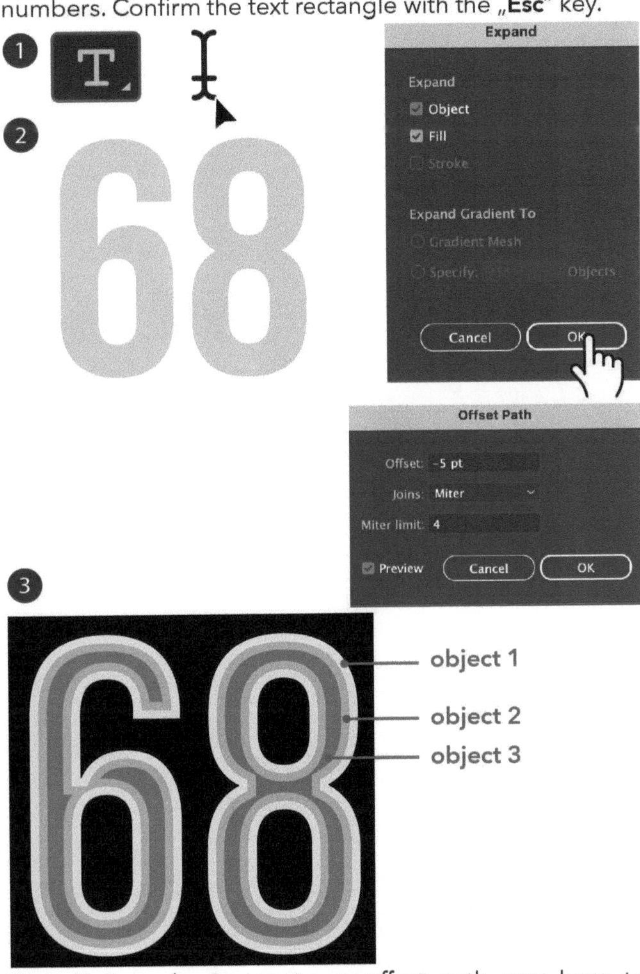

Step 2. In order to create an offset path, you have to expand the text first. Activate therefor **Object > Expand** and then the command **Object > Path > Offset Path**.
Step 3. In the **Offset Path** dialog box change the settings for example to „Offset -5", deactive and activate the preview to see the result and confirm with „OK". The offset size obviously depends on the size of the object. Repeat this step twice.
Step 4. Select all objects with the **Selection Tool** (V) and apply the blur effect **Effect > Blur > Gaussian Blur**.
Step 5. You can change the blur effect settings at any time by opening the **Window > Appearence** window.

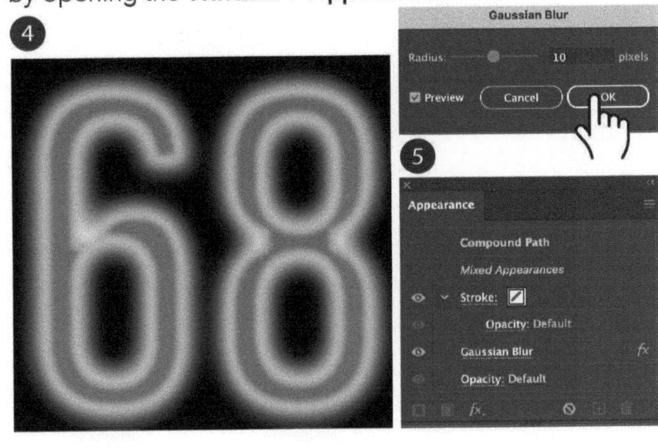

6.16 TUTORIAL:INVERT IMAGES IN ILLUSTRATOR

Step 1. Scan an image or take a photo of it, cut out the background (see tutorial 6.10 on page 61). Create a new A4 document in Illustrator **File > New >A4** and place the artwork there **File > Place...**

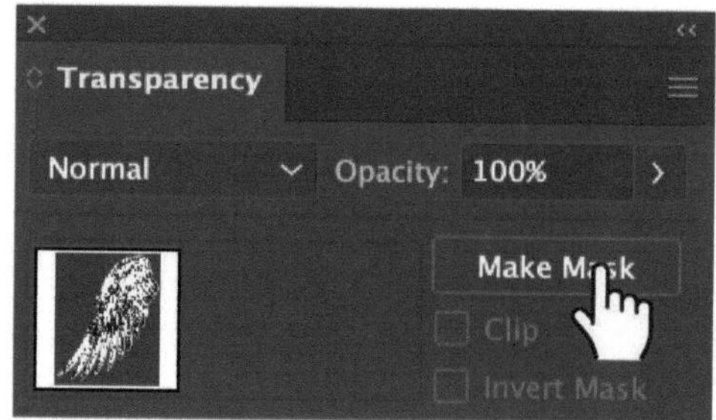

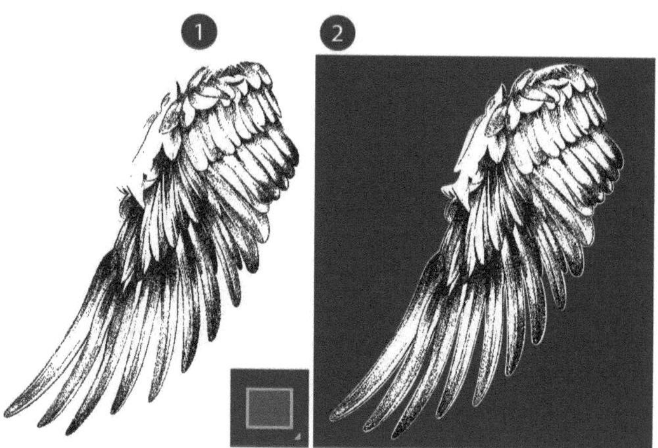

Step 2. Create a rectangle with the **Rectangle Tool** (M) and place it in the background **Object > Arrange > Send to back**.

Step 3. Select both objects with the **Selection Tool** (V).

Step 4. Open the Transparency window **Window > Transparency** and click "Make Mask".

Step 5A. If you click on "Release", you can cancel everything again.

Step 5B. If you click on "Invert Mask", the object will be set in the same color space as the background.

6.17 TUTORIAL: ARTBRUSH

Step 1. Draw a line by hand using ink or other materials. Scan or photograph the drawing and place it in Illustrator **File > Place**.

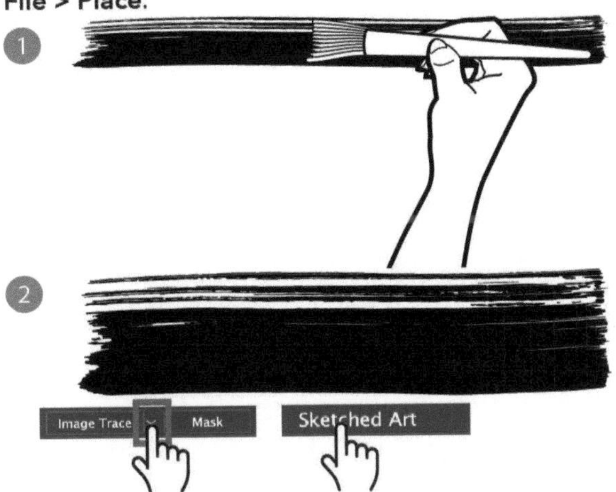

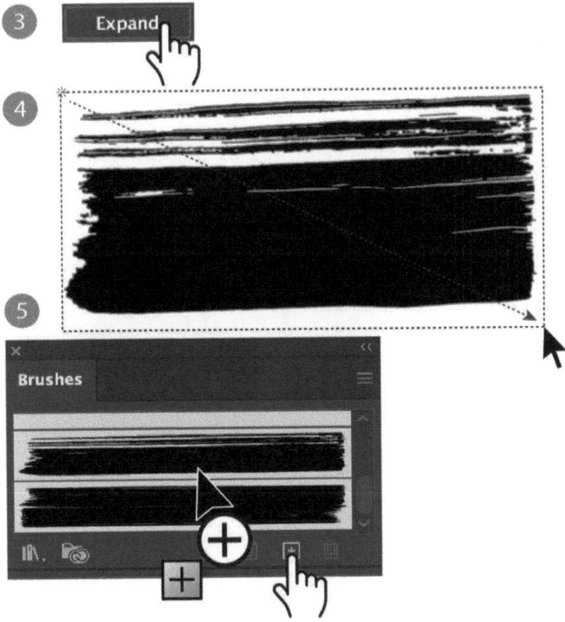

Step 2. Select the object with the **Selection Tool** (V) and click on „Sketched Art" in the control panel.

Step 3. Activate now the command **Object>Expand** and confirm it with „OK".

Step 4. Select the expanded object with the **Selection Tool** (V).

Step 5. Now, open the brushes panel (**Window > Brushes**). Drag the objects to the "Brushes" panel, then drop them using the drag&drop method. Alternatively, click the "New" symbol ⊞ , activate "Art Brush" in the dialog box, and click "OK" to confirm the settings.

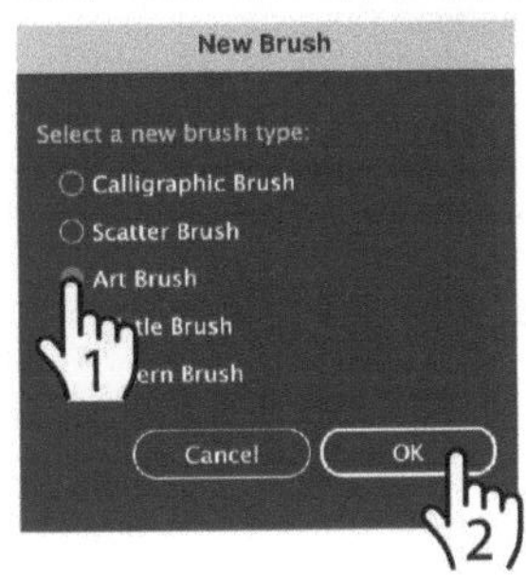

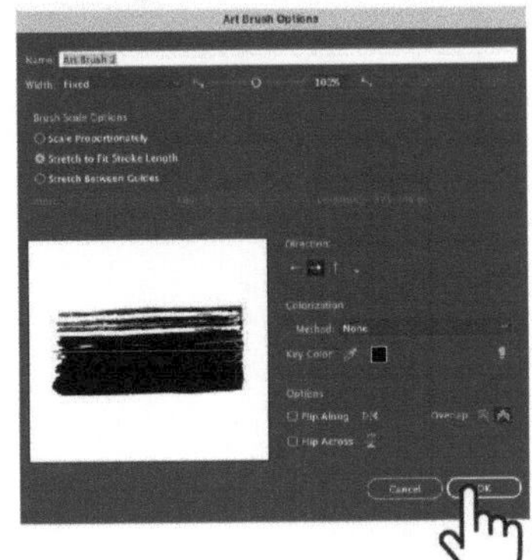

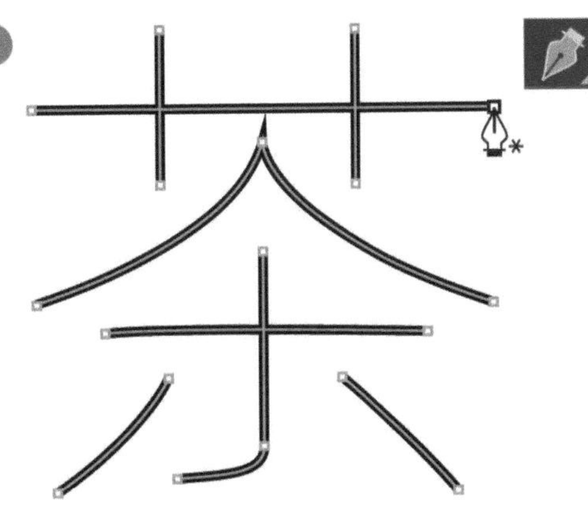

Step 6. Create with the **Pen Tool** (P) for example a drawing made up of several lines.

Step 7. And click on the "Artbrush" you just created in the brushes panel (**Window>Brushes**). In the stroke panel (**Window>Stroke**) you can change the size of the brush ("Weight„ setting).

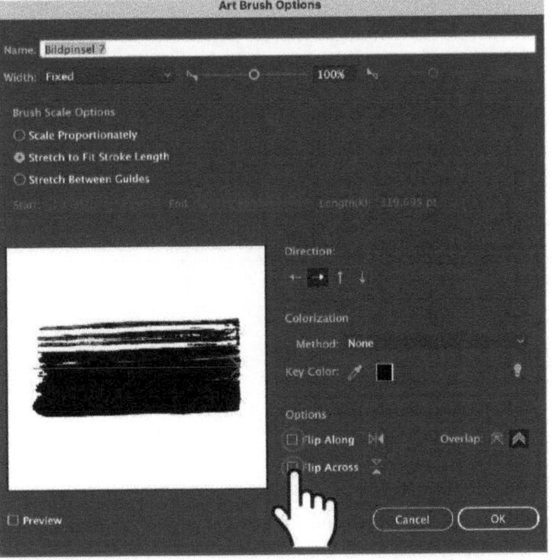

Step 8. To change the brush settings, click "Advanced Options" in the brushes panel (**Window>Brushes**). Here you can apply further settings, for example mirror the direction of the brush.

6.18 TUTORIAL: LINE ART ALLOVER PRINT
LIVE-PAINT BUCKET TECHNIQUE

First, create a new A4 page in Adobe Illustrator **File > New > A4.**
-Choose in the tools panel the stroke color „black" and the fill color „None".

-Set in the stroke panel (**Window > Stroke**) the stroke weight to **1pt** or **2pt**.

Step 1. Place in Illustrator for example a hand drawn sketch first **File > Place**. Trace now the artwork with the **Pen Tool** (P). For complicated drawings like this, you don't need to close shapes, just draw separate lines.
Step 2. For the inner elements you can set the lines thinner.

The only thing you should pay attention to when drawing is that there are no gaps between lines. Otherwise you won't be able to fill the object with „fill" color later.

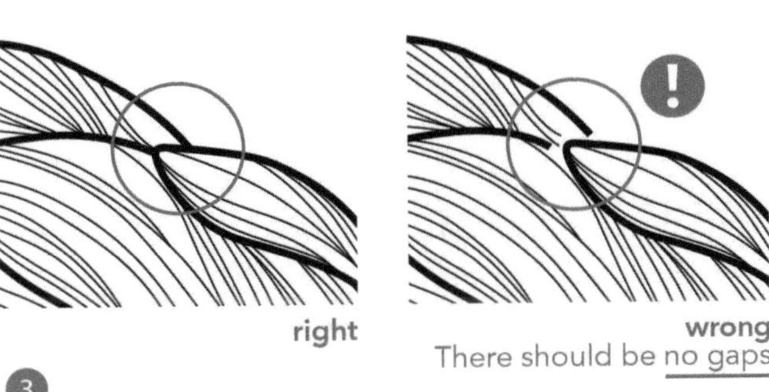

right

wrong
There should be no gaps

Step 3. Now select all objects with the **Selection Tool** (V).
Step 4. Now activate **Live Paint Bucket** (K) and change the fill color in the **tools panel** to grey for example.

Step 5. Click inside the objects with the left mouse button (the stroke is displayed in red). Once all the gaps are filled, it would be better to convert the artwork with the command **Object > Expand** otherwise you can't edit it properly.

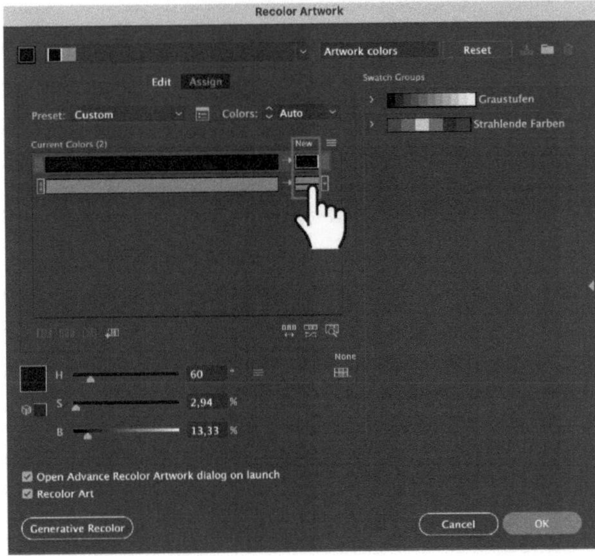

Step 6. To change the colors, click the **Recolor artwork** button in the control panel or activate the **Edit Colors > Recolor > Artwork** command. In the window that appears, click on the „Advanced Options". Now you can set the colors for multiple objects at the same time.

When using the **Live Paint Bucket** (K) tool, pay attention that the tool creates a new object as soon as you fill it. That means there are two objects that overlap at the end.

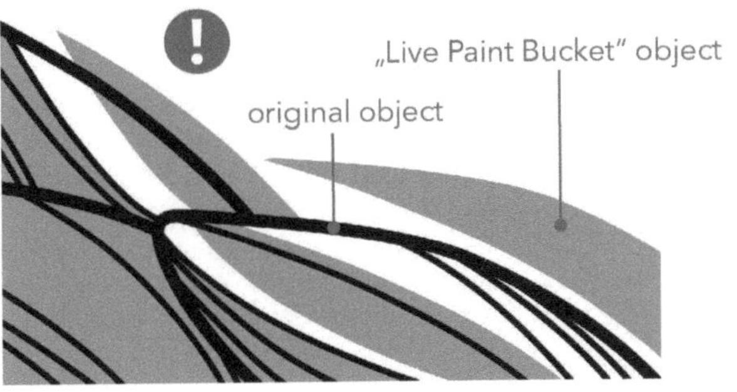

Step 7. Select all objects with the **Selection Tool** (V) and group them with command+G / Ctrl+G.

Create additional object groups (for example flowers) using the same technique.

Step 8. Select all this object groups with the **Selection Tool** (V) and activate the command **Object > Pattern > Make**.
Step 9. In the „Pattern Options" panel that appears set the pattern type to "Hex by Column"(1) and start adjusting the distance between objects using the "Width" and "Height" values (2, 3).
You can also move the objects using the **Selection Tool** (V). With the right click on the object (A) you can for example rotage, scale the objects **Transform > Rotate...**
You can also copy the objects using the drag and drop method (B). Press and hold **alt/option** key, move the object with mouse cursor, then release first the mouse button and then the keyboard keys. A copy of the object is created.
Step 10. When you´re done confirm the settings with "Done" in the control panel (at the top). Now you can find the pattern in the Swatches window **Window > Swatches**.

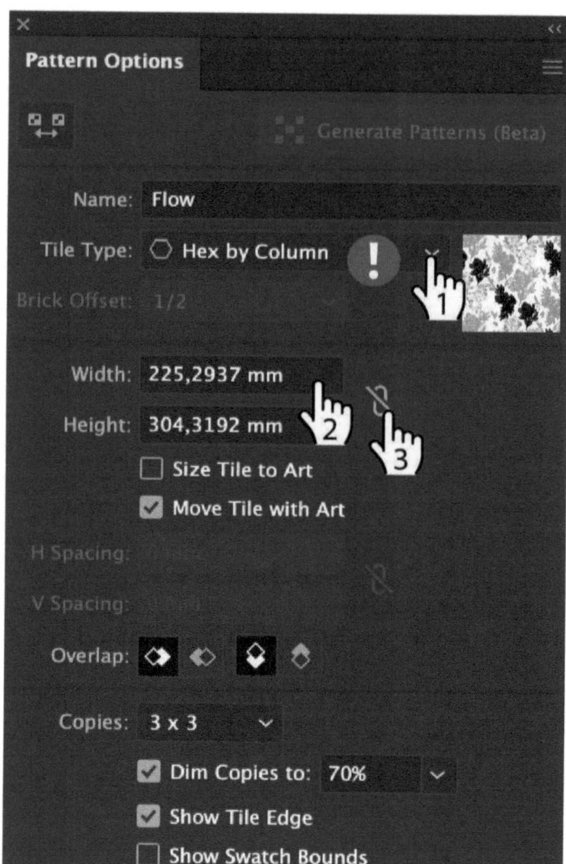

In the hexagon repeat rectangle you can move or copy individual object groups to better adjust the spaces between objects and create a beautiful composition

Remember that a "hexagon" brick is the best way to form a floral pattern because no clear vertical or horizontal transitions will be visible because the transition between objects is harmoniously made invisible by a curved line.

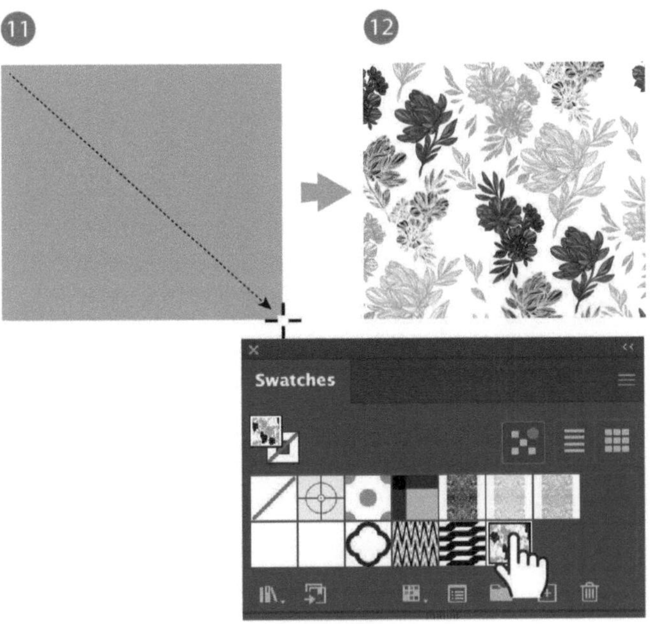

Step 11. Select the **Rectangle Tool** (M) and create a rectangle.

Step 12. And fill in the rectangle with your pattern from the swatches window **Window > Swatches**.

Step 13. Create a black rectangle in the background by simply copy&paste the rectangle with the pattern Cmd+C/Crtl+C and Cmd+F/Ctrl+F, then apply black fill. Place the rectangle in the background **Object > Arrange > Send to Back**.

When designing patterns, the idea of adding an extra rectangle to the background for an all-over print is frequently applied. This method is simple to use. Another method to add a background can be found in tutorial 6.23 on page 82.

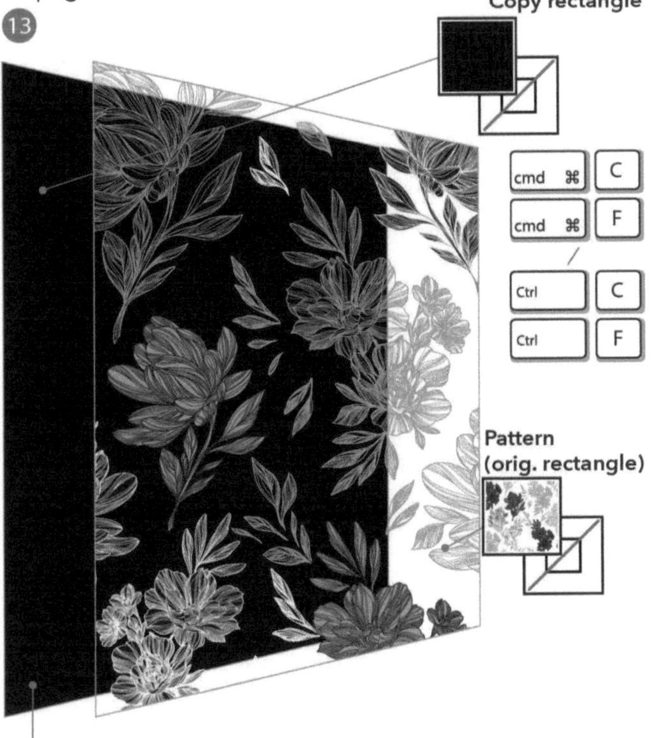

Put the copy in the background **Object > Arrange > Send to Back** and apply black fill color.

6.19 TUTORIAL: CUTOUT TECHNIQUE

Step 1. Select a drawing or photo template and place it on a new A4 document in Illustrator **File > Place**.

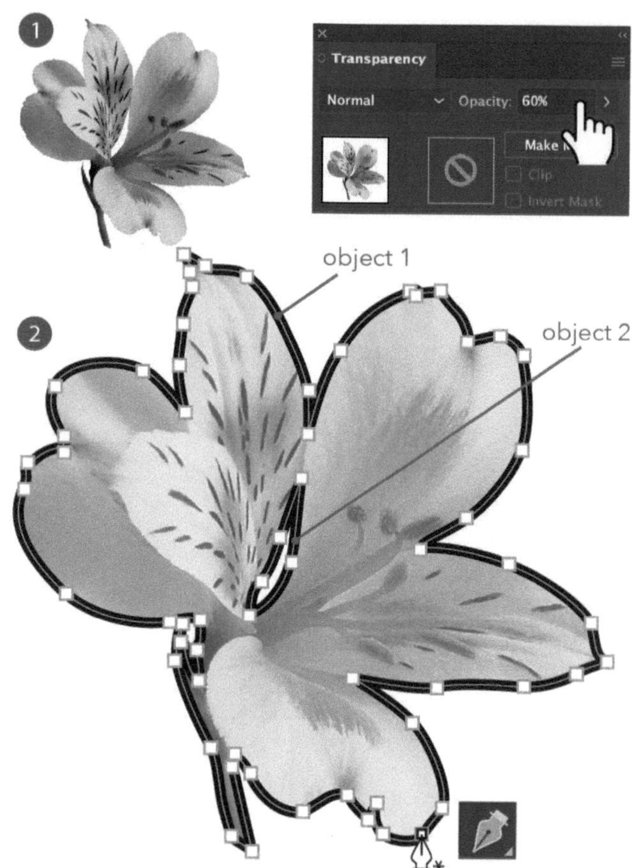

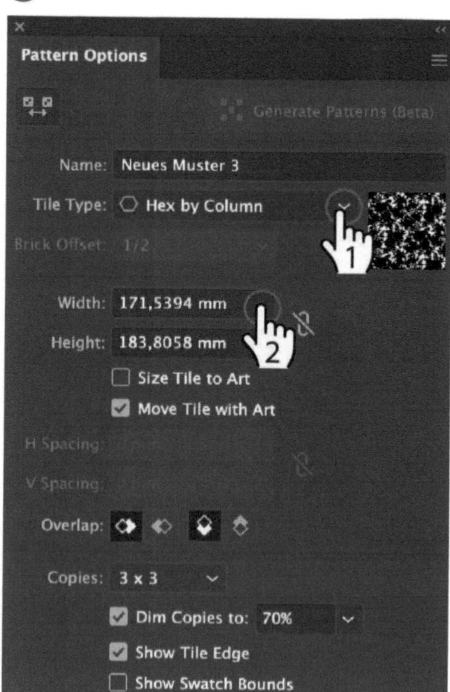

Step 2. Activate the **Pen Tool** (P) and start tracing the outlines.

Step 3. To select every object using the **Selection Tool** (V), click on it while holding down the **Shift** key.

Step 4. You can use **Window > Pathfinder** to merge the objects together. Which setting should be used depends on the complexity of the object. The "Minus Front" setting, which is frequently used when merging objects, was applied in this instance.

Step 5. Create more objects using the same technique. Select the objects with the **Selection Tool** (V) and activate the command **Object > Pattern > Make**.

Step 6. Set the following settings (see figure). Since it depends on the size of the object, the distance (height &width) between each object is set individual for each pattern.

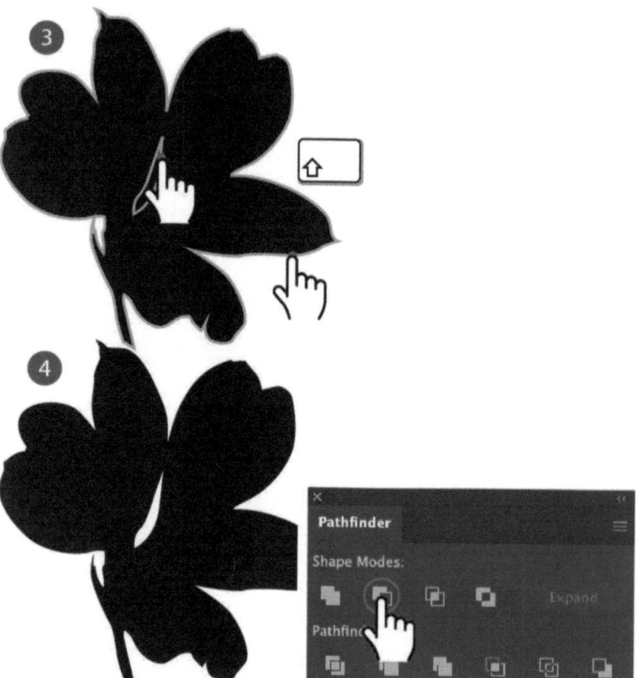

Step 7. The objects can be moved, duplicated, and distorted in the inner area of the repeat rectangle. The outside area's dimmed objects will be automatically adjusted.

Step 8. If you are satisfied with the result, confirm the pattern with "Done" in the option panel.
Step 9. Set the pattern color to white **Edit > Edit Colors > Recolor Artwork** and create a black rectangle in the background using the **Rectangle Tool** (M) or simply copy&paste the rectangle with the pattern Cmd+C/Crtl+C and Cmd+F/Ctrl+F, then apply black fill. Place the rectangle in the background **Object > Arrange > Send to Back**.

When designing patterns, the idea of adding an extra rectangle to the background for an all-over print is frequently applied. This method is simple to use. Another method to add a background can be found in tutorial 6.23 on page 82.

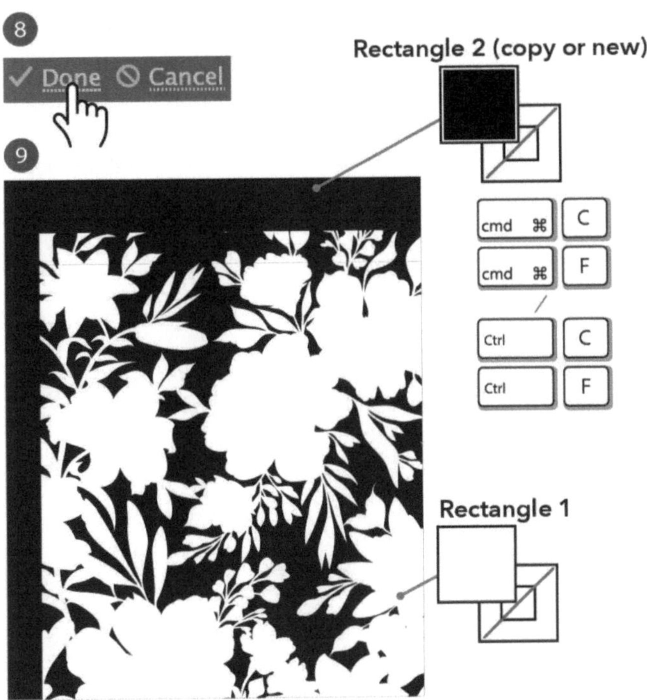

6.20 TUTORIAL: OFFSET PATH TECHNIQUE

Step 1. Create a new A4 document in Illustrator **File > New >A4**.

Step 2. Open the font dialog box **Window > Type > Character**. Click with the **Text Tool** (T) in the empty drawing area, set the size of the text to 200pt or bigger, choose font that you like and type for example a series of numbers. Confirm the text rectangle with the „**Esc**" key.

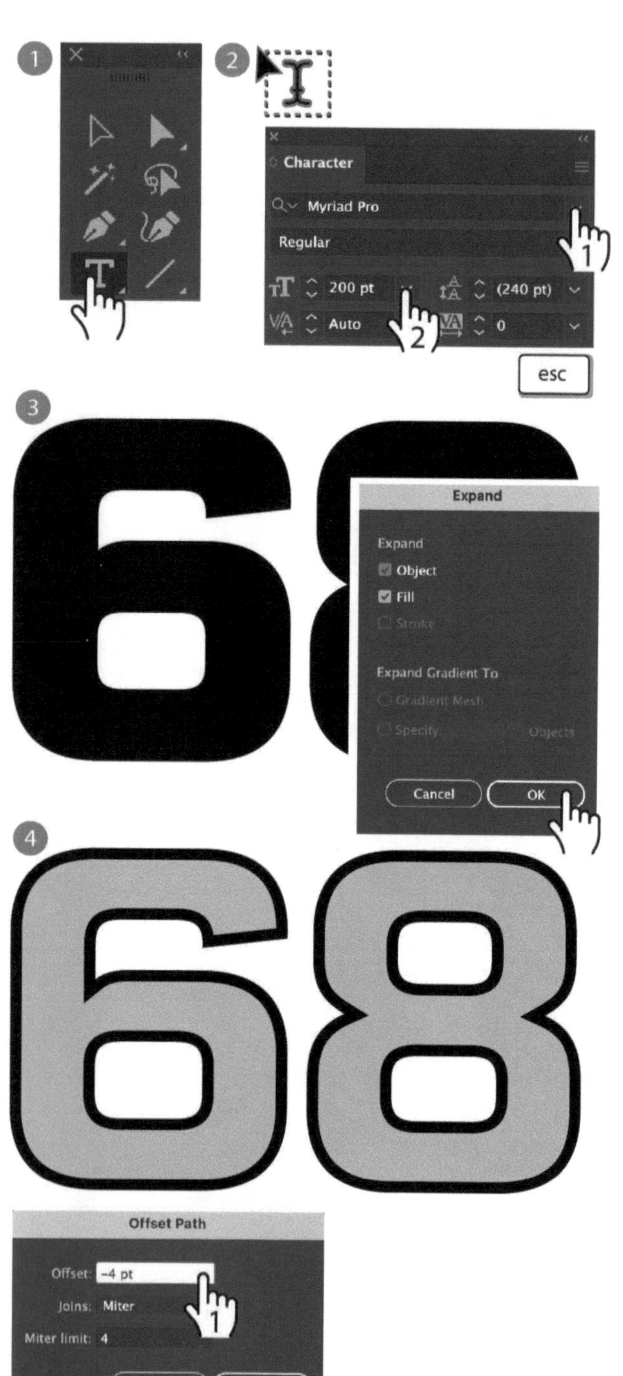

Step 3. In order to create an offset path, you must expand the text first. Activate therefor **Object > Expand** and then the command **Object > Path > Offset Path**.

Step 4. In the **Offset Path** dialog box change the settings to „Offset -4", deactivate and activate the preview to see the result and confirm with „OK". The offset size obviously depends on the size of the object.

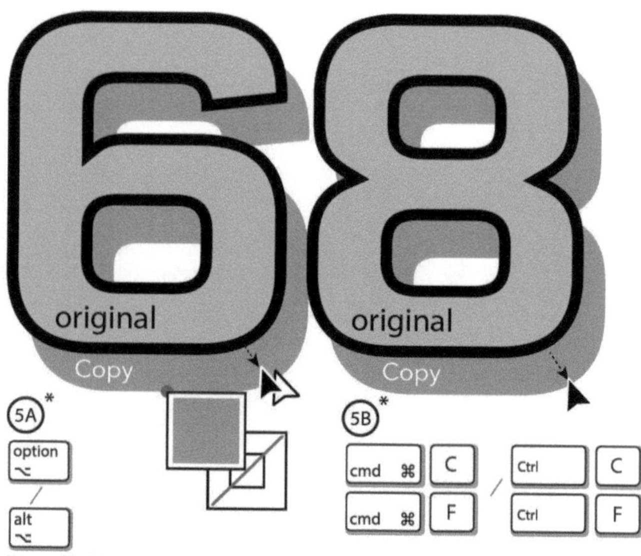

Step 5. Now two copies are created. There are two ways to create copies. (5A) By drag & drop: hold **option/alt** key and drag the object, then release first the mouse button and then the **option/alt** key, (5B) or using the keyboard shortcuts Cmd+C/Crtl+C and Cmd+F/Ctrl+F.

Step 6. Activate the **Blend Tool** (W) and click the both objects (first the „original" and then the „copy" object).
You can use the Blend Tool to create a set of objects to match colors and shapes of multiple objects.

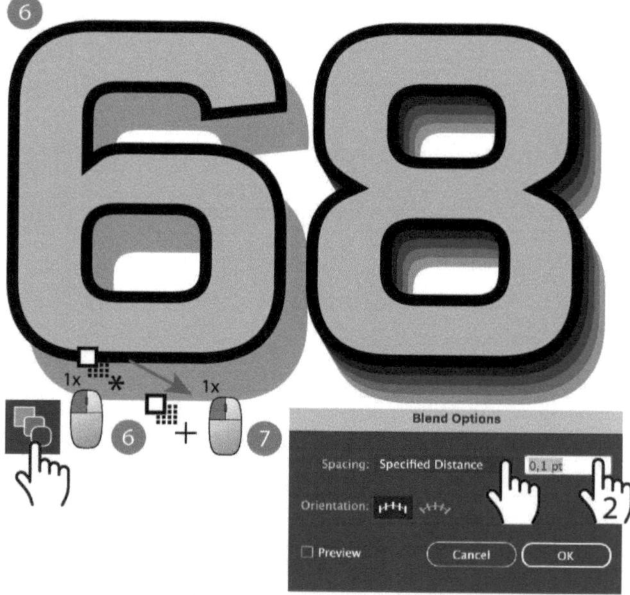

Step 7. Now double-click on the **Blend Tool** (W).
Change the settings in the dialog box (see figure), then confirm with „OK". Activate then the command **Object>Expand Appearance** or **Object>Expand** to access the individual objects.

option 1 (the fill color of the „copy" object is bright).

option 2 (the fill color of the „copy" object is black).

6.21 TUTORIAL: NUMBERS WITH PATTERN

Step 1. Create a new A4 document in Illustrator **File > New >A4**. Open the font dialog box **Window > Type > Character**. Click with the **Text Tool** (T) in the empty drawing area, set the size of the text to 200pt or bigger, choose font that you like and type a series of numbers. Confirm the text rectangle with the „**Esc**" key.

Step 2. Now you have to expand the text, activate therefor the command **Object > Expand**.

Step 3. Create two straight lines with the **Pen Tool** (P). Apply different stroke weight to this two objects **Window > Stroke**.

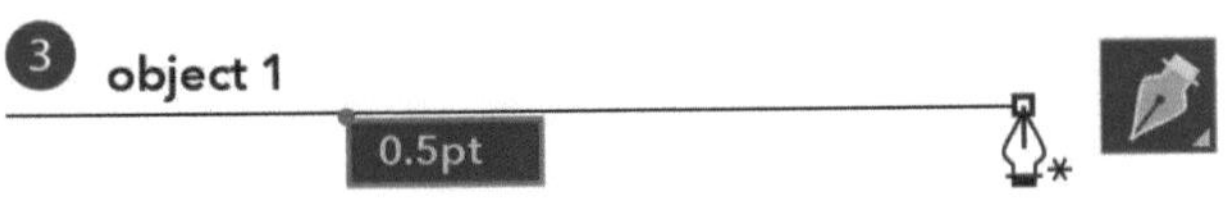

Step 4. Activate the **Blend Tool** (W), click once on the first object (object 1) to define the „initial object" and click once then on the second object (object 2) to create an alignment between this two objects.

Step 5. Double-click on the **Blend Tool** (W) in the tools panel or activate the **Object > Blend > Blend Options** command to set the number of intermediate objects.

Change settings to "Specified Steps" (1), enter the number of intermediate objects (2) and confirm it with „OK"(3).

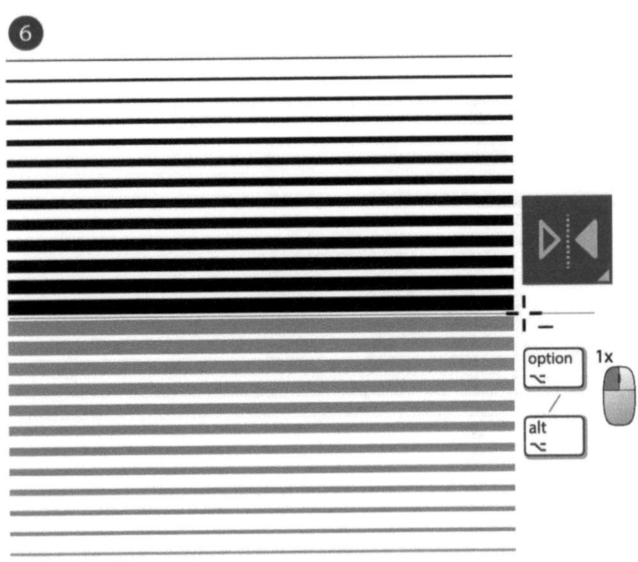

Step 6. Select the **Reflect Tool** (O), position the mouse cursor on the bottom of the object group (horizontal alignment), press and hold the **alt/option** key (do not release the alt/option key) and click the left mouse button. The reflect dialog box appears, then release the **alt** key.

Turn on "Horizontal", "Preview," make sure everything is in order, and then click "Copy." A mirrored duplicate is created.

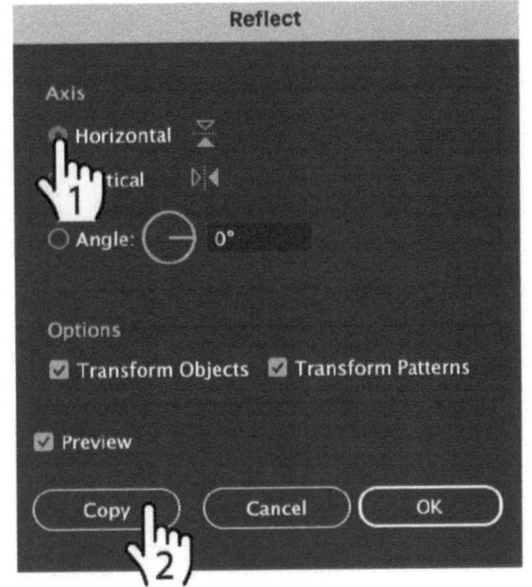

Step 7. Drag with the **Selection Tool** (V) a selection around the objects and move the objects to the swatches panel **Window > Swatches** (drag&drop method) or activate the command **Object > Pattern > Make**.

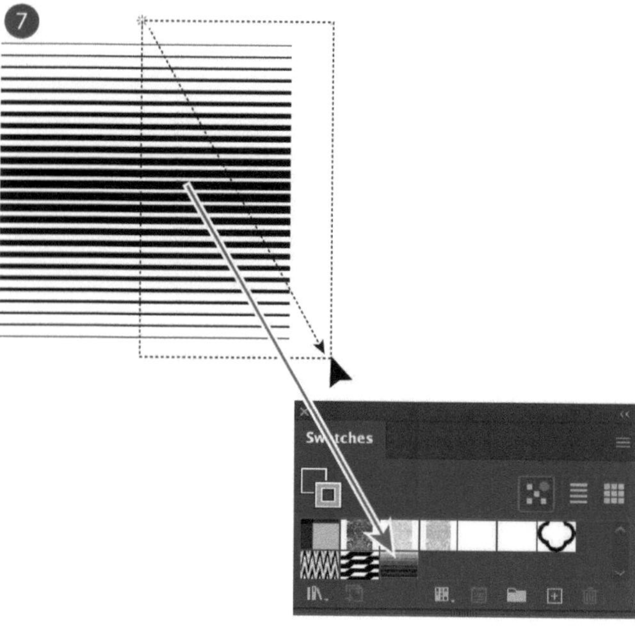

Step 8. Select the numbers with the **Selection Tool** (V) and fill it with the created pattern.

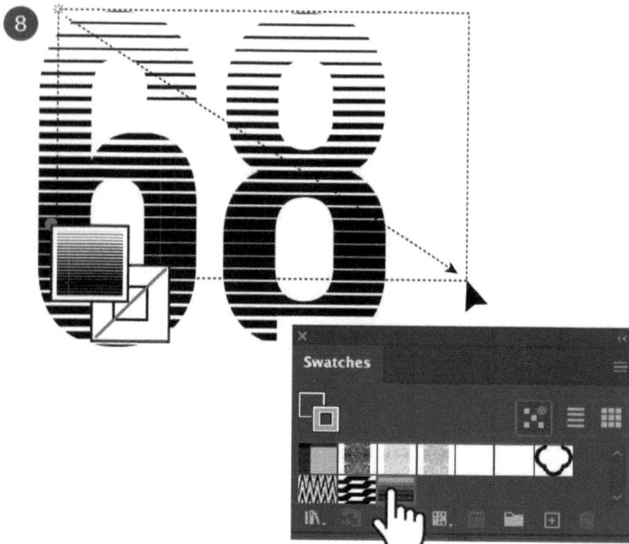

If you need to move the pattern inside the object, right-click on the object and activate the **Transform > Move..** command. In the window that appears, deactivate the "Transform Objects" command to only move the pattern.

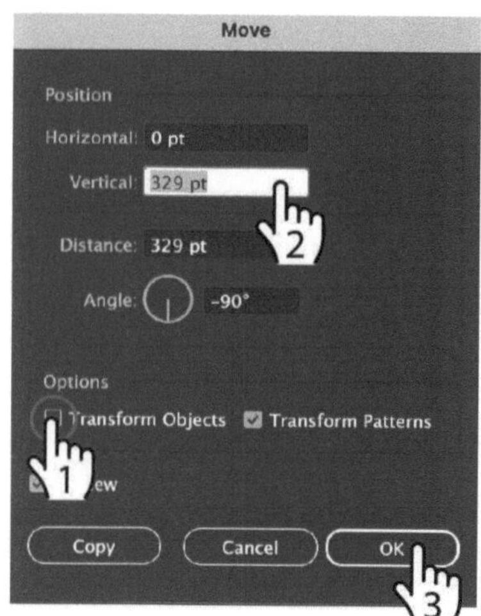

6.22 TUTORIAL: PATCHWORK TUTORIAL

Most elements in Adobe Illustrator are created with the **Pen Tool** (P), **Rectangle Tool** (M) and **Text Tool** (T).

This tutorial shows techniques on how to design a varsity jacket with badges.

TECHNIQUE FOR OBJECTS Ⓐ Ⓕ

Step 1. These shapes are freely drawn with the **Pen Tool** (P). The objects have a stroke and fill color. The stroke thickness can be adjusted in the stroke window **Window > Stroke**.
The inner shapes are cut out with Pathfinder **Window > Pathfinder**.
With the **Direct Selection Tool** (A) you can change individual anchor points and adjust the shape of the object.

Step 2. To cut out the inner object you need to select it first. The object to be cut must be on top **Object > Arrange > Bring to Front**. Then click in the pathfinder window **Window > Pathfinder** "Minus Front". The object is now cut out of the bottom object.
Step 3. Create a copy of the object with command+C / Ctrl+C (Copy) and the shortcut command+F / Ctrl+F (Paste in Front). Add a profile to the object **Window > Stroke**.

TECHNIQUE FOR OBJECTS Ⓑ Ⓙ Ⓚ Ⓒ Ⓖ

Step 1. Open the font dialog box **Window > Type > Character**. Click with the **Text Tool** (T) in the empty drawing area, set the size of the text to 200pt or bigger, choose font that you like and type a letter. Confirm the text rectangle with the „**Esc**" key.

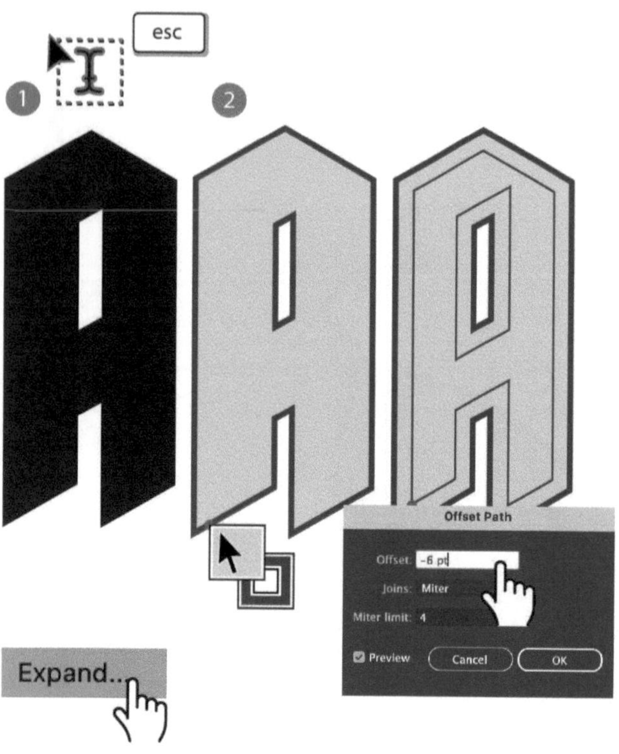

Step 2. In order to create an offset path, you have to expand the text first. Activate therefor **Object > Expand** and then the command **Object > Path > Offset Path**.
In the **Offset Path** dialog box change the settings to for example „Offset -5", deactivate and activate the preview to see the result and confirm with „OK". The offset size obviously depends on the size of the object.

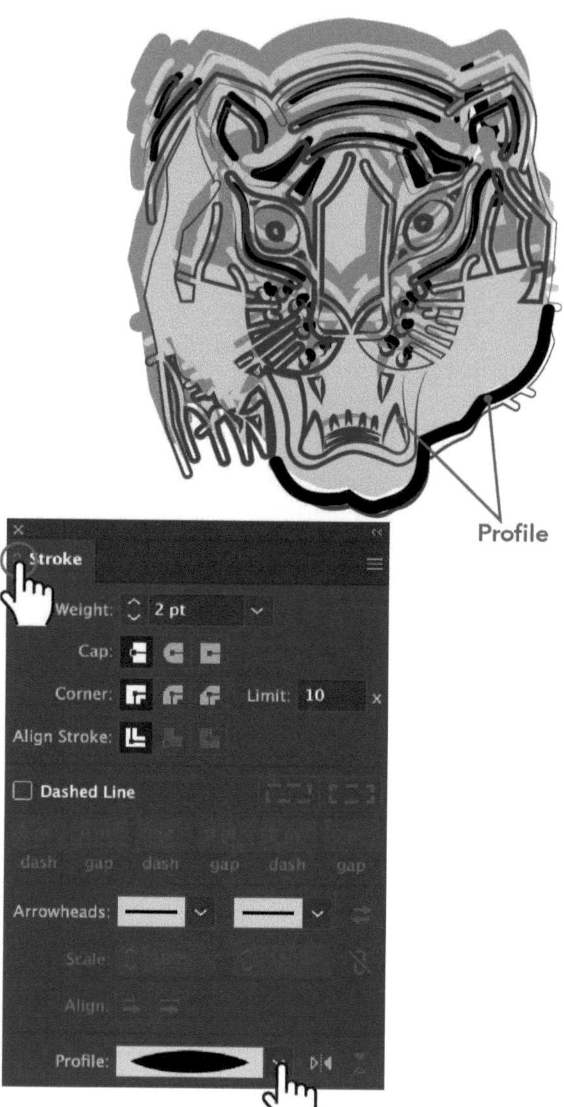

You can also create additional copies and use different profiles from the stroke window **Window > Stroke** to achieve specific graphic aesthetics.

TECHNIQUE FOR OBJECTS Ⓘ Ⓓ

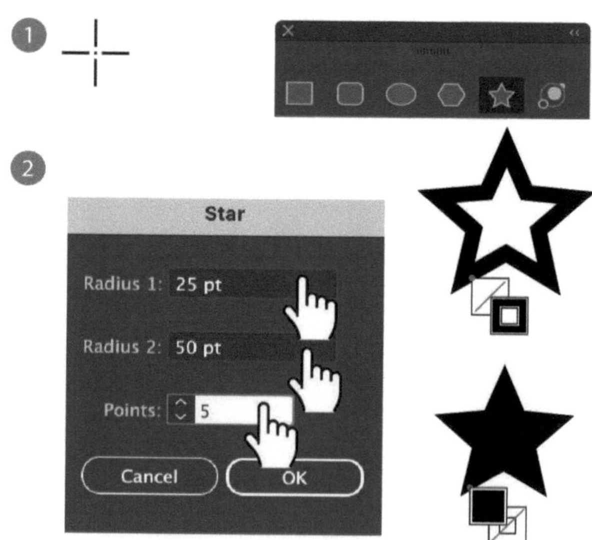

Step 1. Activate the **Star Tool**, you will find it in the same group with the **Rectangle Tool** (M). Click on the workspace with the cursor, a dialog box opens.
Step 2. Enter the following values (see figure) and confirm the window with „OK". In the stroke window **Window > Stroke** you can change the „weight" of the stroke.

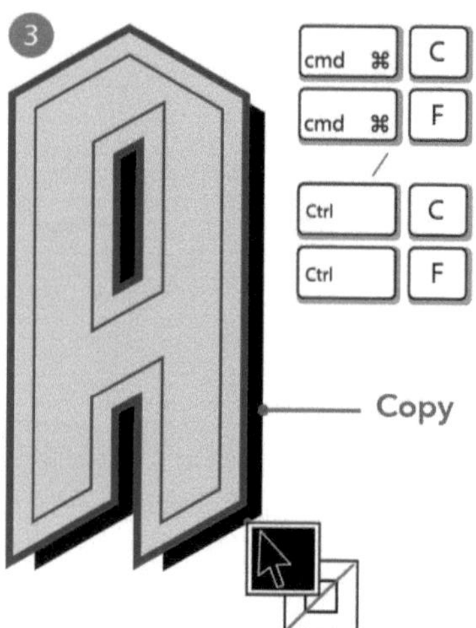

Step 3. Create a copy and place it in the background, color it black and move the copy to the side.

TECHNIQUE FOR OBJECTS Ⓗ

Step 1. Open the font dialog box **Window > Type > Character**. Click with the **Text Tool** (T) in the empty drawing area, set the size of the text to 200pt or bigger, choose font that you like and type a letter. Confirm the text rectangle with the „**Esc**" key.

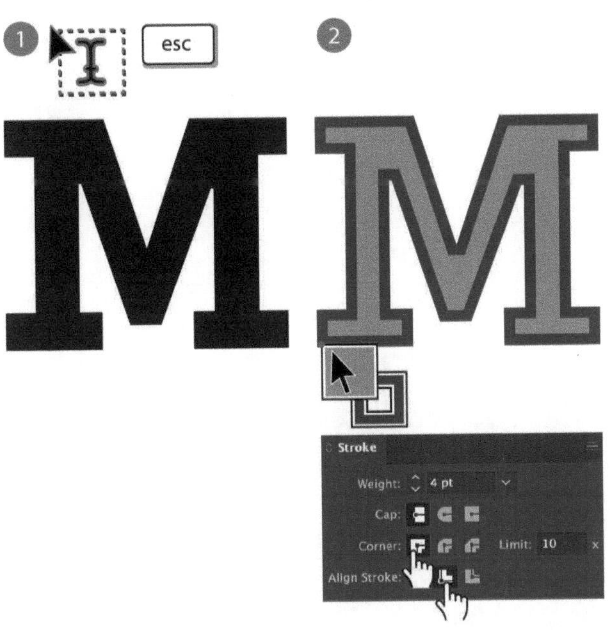

Step 2. In the **Tool panel** change for the object the fill color and apply a stroke. You can change the weight of the stroke in the **Window > Stroke** panel.

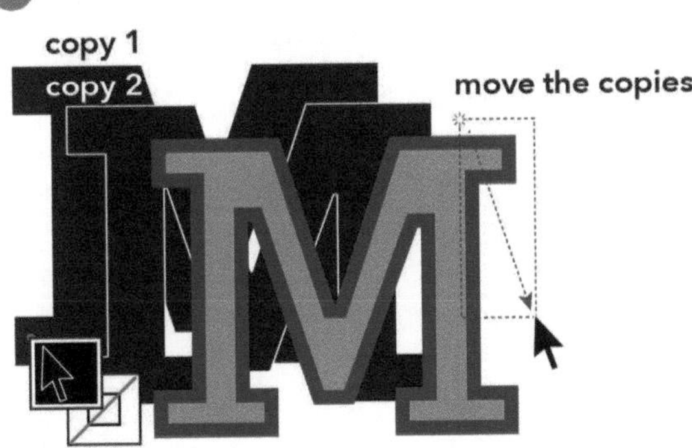

Step 3. Now select the object with the **Selection Tool** (V) and create 2 copies of this object with the shortcut command+C / Ctrl+C (Copy) and the shortcut command+F / Ctrl+F (Paste in Front). Then put the two copies aside.

Step 4. Now use the **Blend Tool** (W) to create a blend. To do this, click on each object once with the left mouse button.

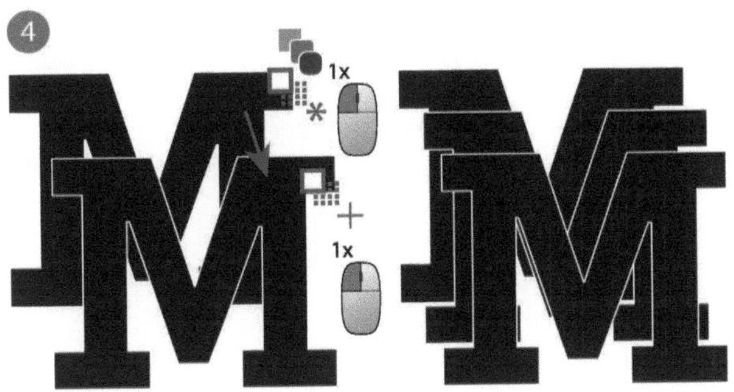

Step 5. To create now more objects in between, double click on the Blend tool to open the Blend tool panel or go to **Object > Blend > Blend Options...**

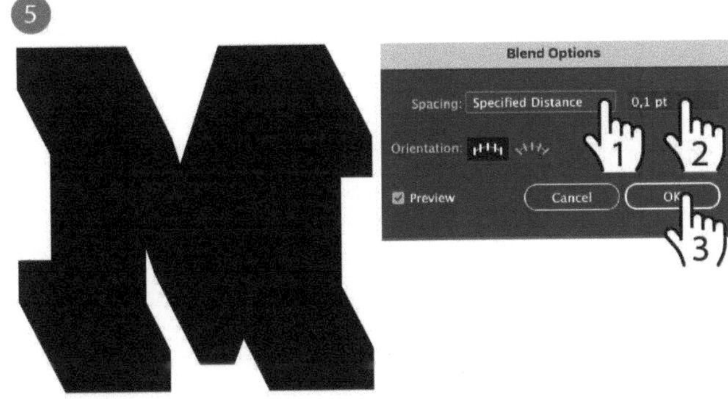

In the tool panel change the „Spacing" to „Specified Distance" and change the value to 0,1pt, then confirm it with „OK".

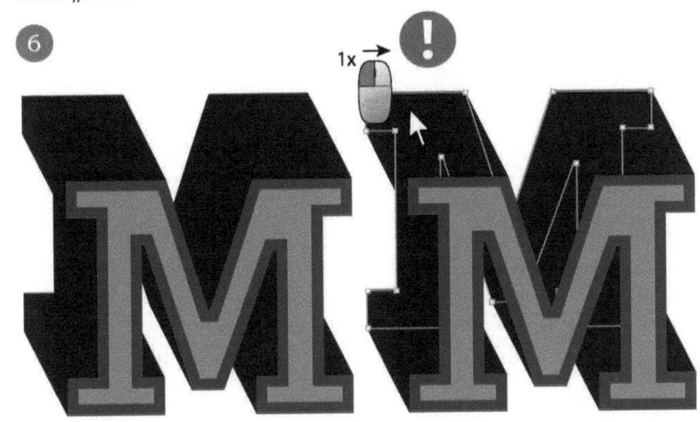

Step 6. You can also move the "blened" objects by clicking and dragging with the **Direct Selection Tool** (A).

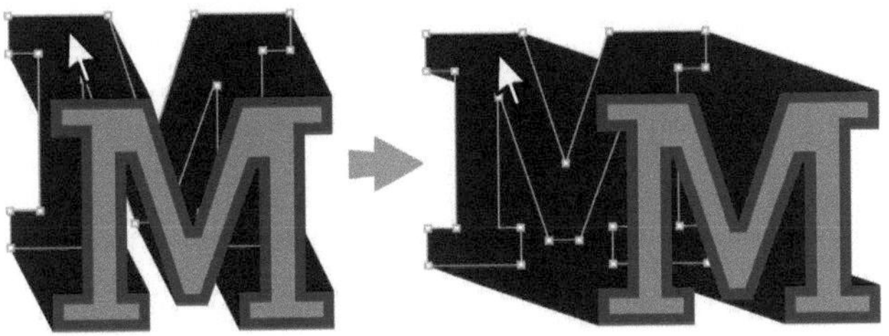

Step 7. You can use the **Pen Tool** (P) to draw additional lines.

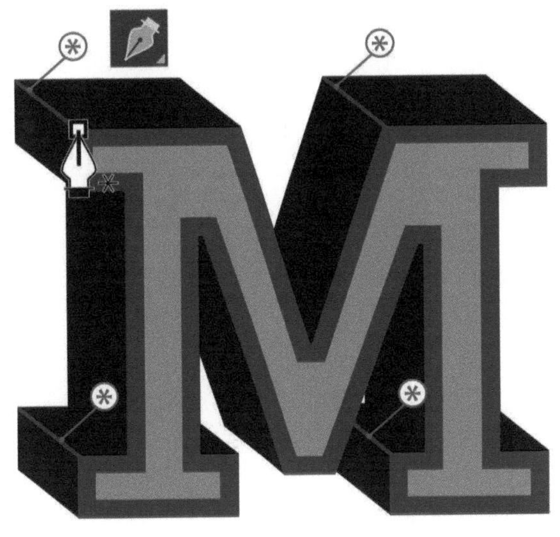

6.23 TUTORIAL: ZIGZAG PRINT

- Choose in the tools panel the stroke color „black" and the fill color „None".

-Choose: **View > Rules >Show Rules, View > Guides > Lock Guides, View > Guides > Show Guides, View > Smart Guides, View > Snap to Point** and place a vertical guide.

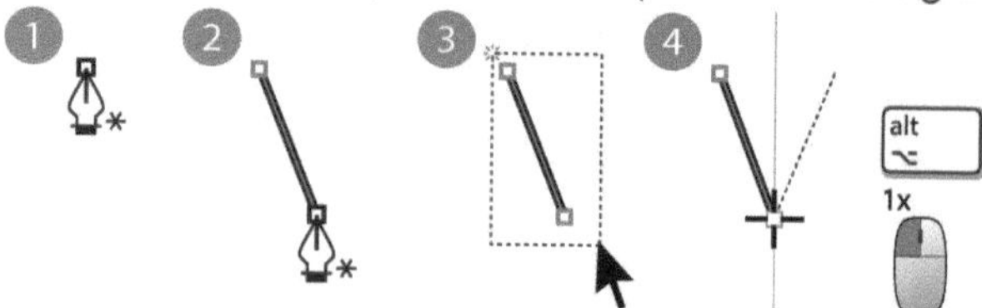

First, create a new A4 page in Adobe Illustrator **File > New > A4.**

Step 1. Activate the **Pen Tool** (P), click in the empty drawing area to create the first anchor point.

Step 2. To create the second anchor point, click on a different location once more.

Step 3. Select the object with the **Selection Tool** (V).

Step 4. Activate the **Reflect Tool** (O), position the mouse cursor on the vertical guide (place the guide first), press the **alt/option** key (do not release the alt key) and click the left mouse button. The reflect dialog box appears ,then release the **alt** key.

Activate the option „Vertical", then „Preview", make sure everything is OK and click „Copy". A mirrored duplicate is created.

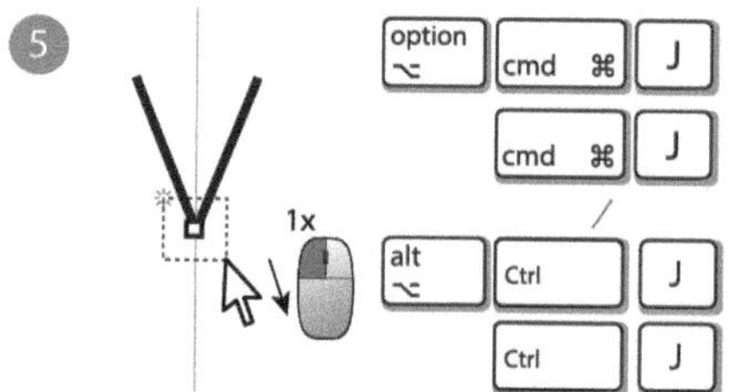

Step 5. Press and hold the left mouse button and drag with **Direct Selection Tool** (A) a selection.

Activate the shortcut option+command+J /alt+Ctrl+J (Average...). In the dialog box activate „Both", then press „OK", then activate the shortcut command+J / Ctrl+J (Join). Two paths have been joined together.

Alternatively you can use the **Join Tool** to connect the two anchor points (see Tutorial 6.26 on page 91).

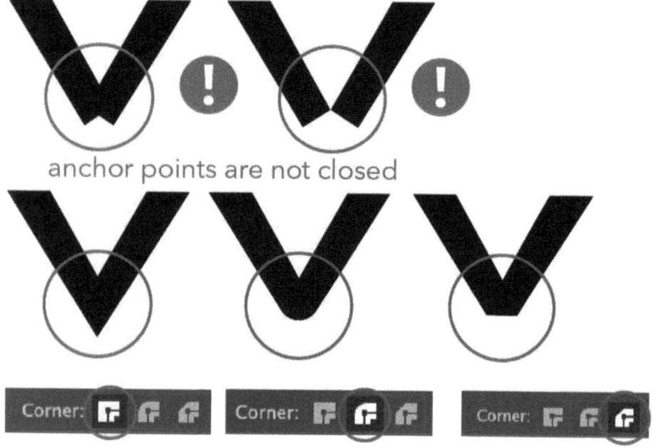

The appearance of the corner can be adjusted in the stroke window **Window >Stroke.**

Step 6. Select the object with the **Selection Tool** (V).
Step 7. Activate the **Reflect Tool** (O), position the mouse cursor on the vertical guide (place the guide first), press the **alt/option** key (do not release the alt key) and click the left mouse button. The reflect dialog box appears ,then release the **alt** key.
Activate the option „Vertical", then „Preview", make sure everything is OK and click „Copy". A mirrored duplicate is created.

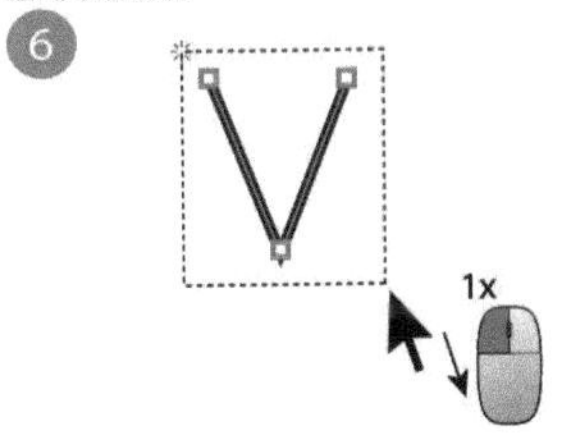

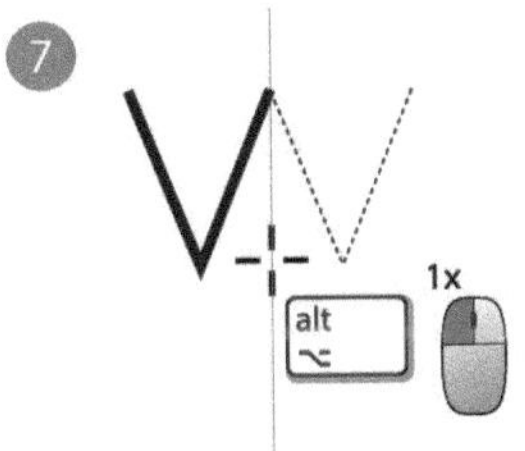

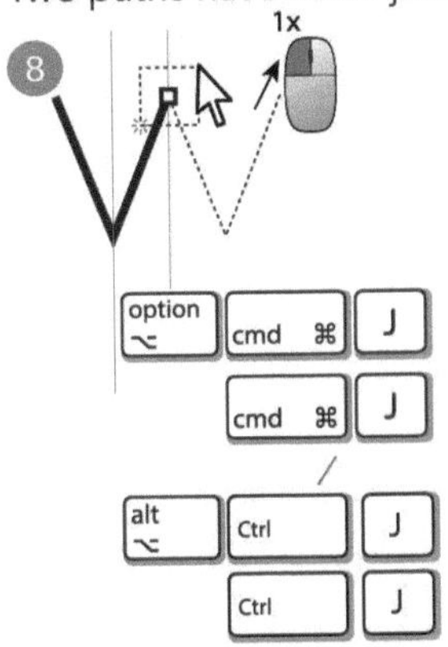

Step 8. Press and hold the left mouse button and drag with **Direct Selection Tool** (A) a selection.
Activate the shortcut option+command+J /alt+Ctrl+J (Average...). In the dialog box activate „Both", then press „OK", then activate the shortcut command+J / Ctrl+J (Join). Two paths have been joined together.

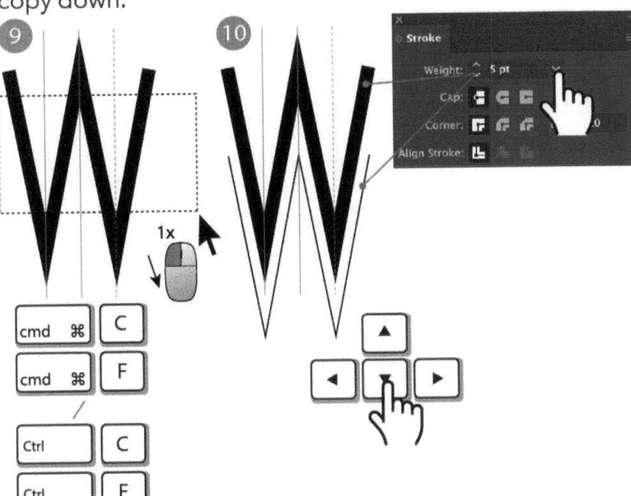

Step 9. Select the object with the **Selection Tool** (V) and activate the shortcut command+C / Ctrl+C (Copy) and the shortcut command+F / Ctrl+F (Paste in Front). Drag the copy down.

Step 10. Set two different stroke thicknesses in the stroke panel **Window >Stroke** for the two objects.
Step 11. Select the both objects with the **Selection Tool** (V).
Step 12. Press and hold **alt/option-** key, move the object with mouse cursor down, additionally press and hold **Shift-**key, then release first the mouse button and then the keyboard keys. A copy of the object is created. Now activate the shortcut command+D / Ctrl+D (Transform again) to create more copies with the same distance.
Step 13. Now place four guides. To ensure a flawless transition, place the guidelines in precisely the same locations.

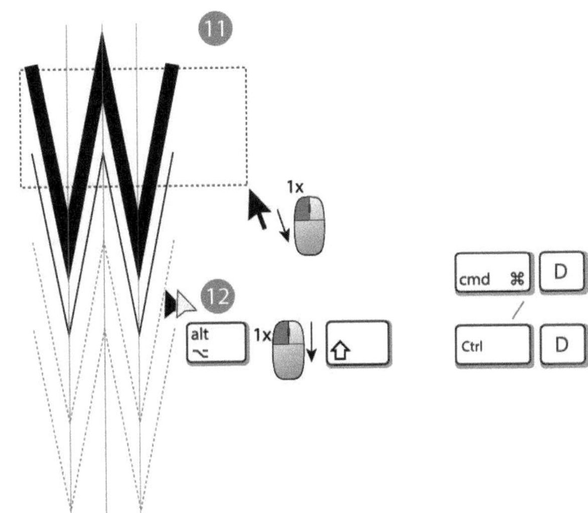

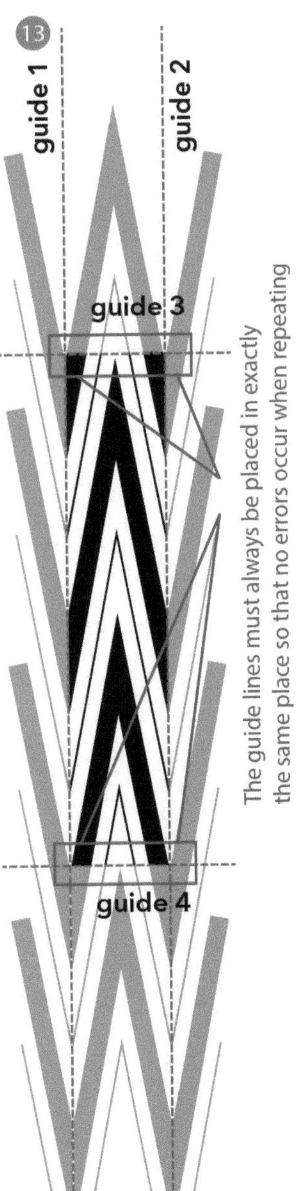

The rapport rectangle is correct

The rapport rectangle is not correct

Step 14. Create a rectangle along the guidelines using the **Rectangle Tool** (M).
Check if the guides are locked **View > Guides > Lock Guides**.

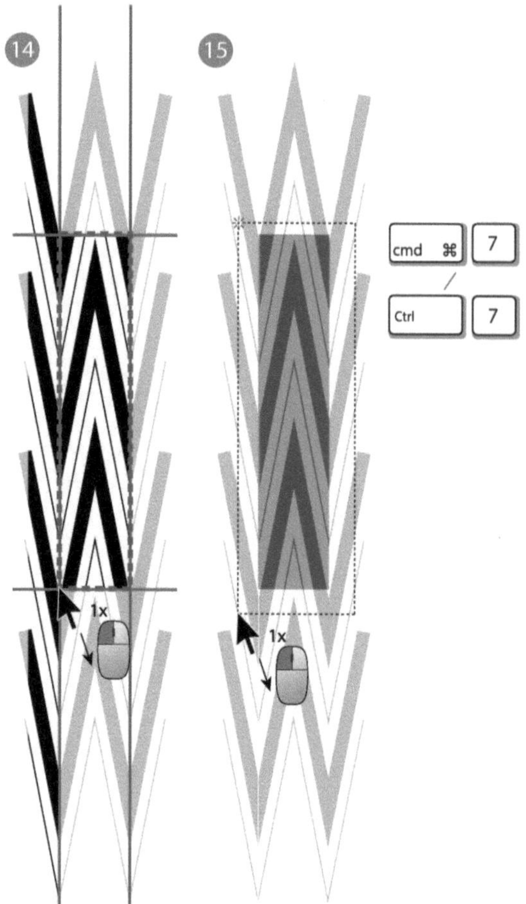

Step 15. Select all objects and create a clipping mask with the shortcut command+7 / Ctrl+7 or **Object › Clipping Mask › Make**.

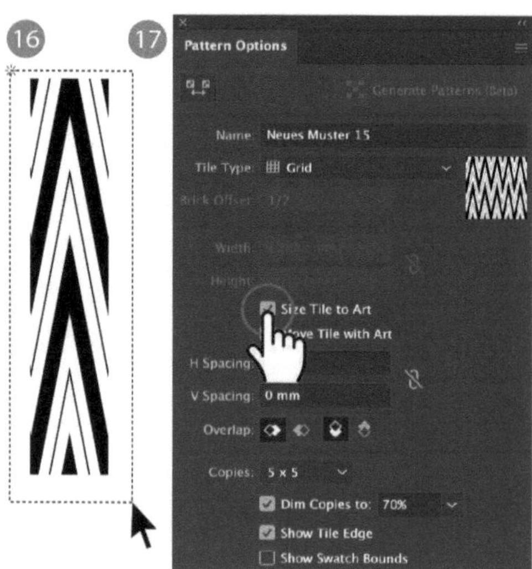

Step 16. Drag with the **Selection Tool** (V) a selection around the object and activate the command **Object > Pattern > Create**.
Step 17. Set the following settings (see figure).
Step 18. Confirm the settings with "Done" in the control panel (at the top). Now you can find the pattern in the Swatches window **Window > Swatches**.

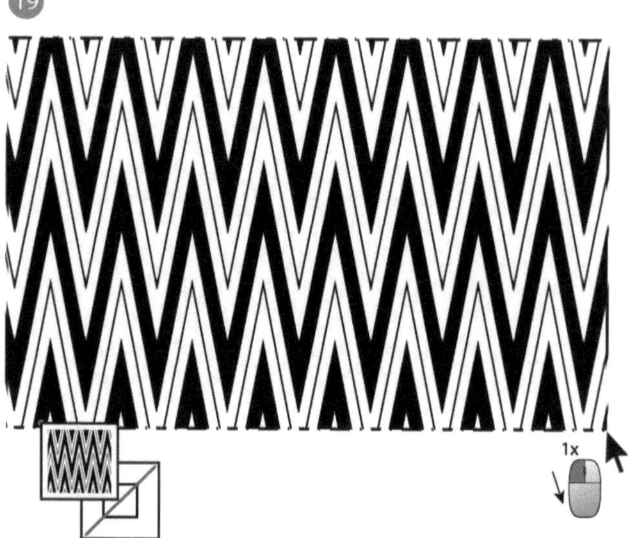

Step 19. Create a new rectangle with the **Rectangle Tool** (M) and fill it with the pattern from the **Window > Swatches** menu.

You can edit the pattern again at any time by clicking **Object > Pattern > Edit Pattern**.

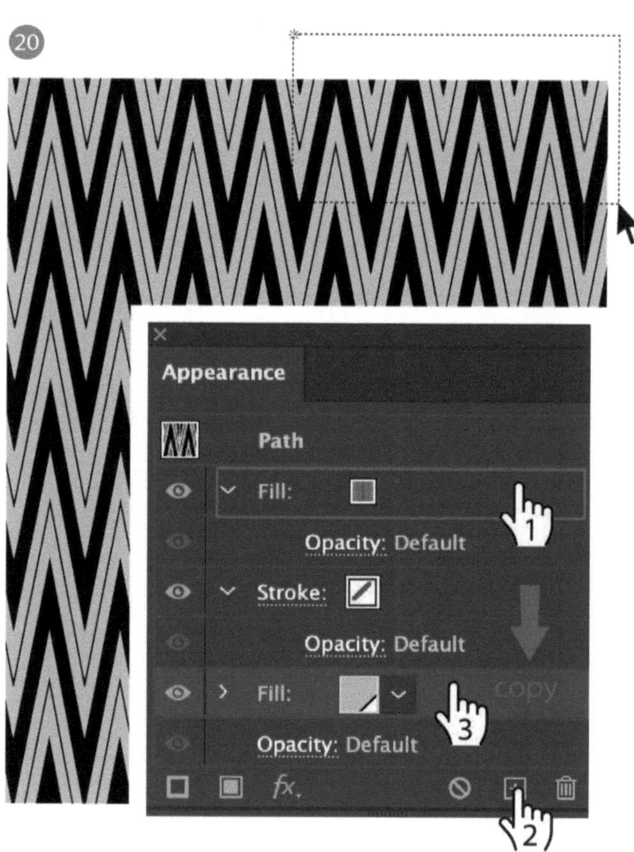

Step 20. One of several ways to add a background for the pattern is via window **Window > Appearance**. First select the object, then open window Appearance, click on the "Fill" to select it (1). Now click on the "Duplicate Selected Item" to create a copy(2). Drag the copy down and set a fill color (3).
However, this method has certain disadvantages if you continue to work with the pattern and for example want to create additional color ways or when you edit the rapport rectangle.

6.24 TUTORIAL: CLIPPING MASK

Step 1. Create a drawing with pencil or other materials. Scan or photograph the drawing and open it in Photoshop **File > Open**. Then open **Image › Adjustments › Exposure...** panel and change the „Exposure" and „Gamma Correcti-on" settings to adjust more contrast and make the image cleaner.

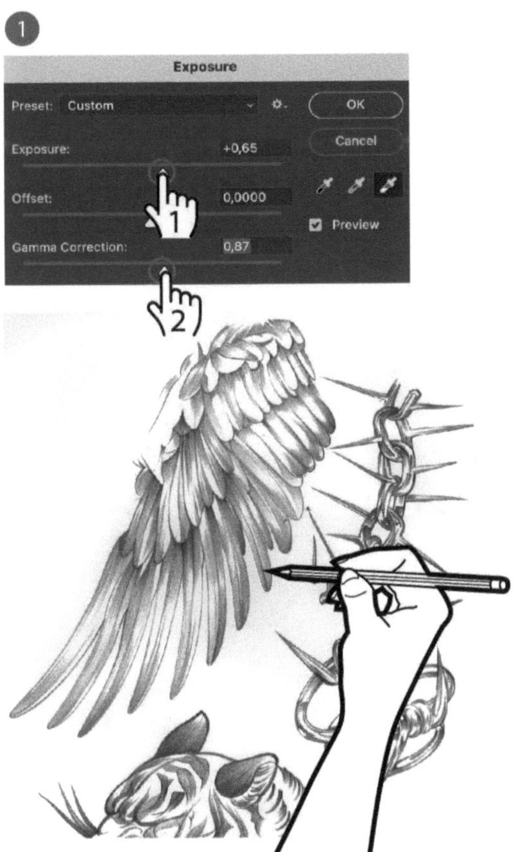

Step 2. Select an object with the **Polygon Lasso Tool** (L). You can find the tool in the Lasso tools group. Now copy the object with the shortcut command Cmd+C/Crtl+C.

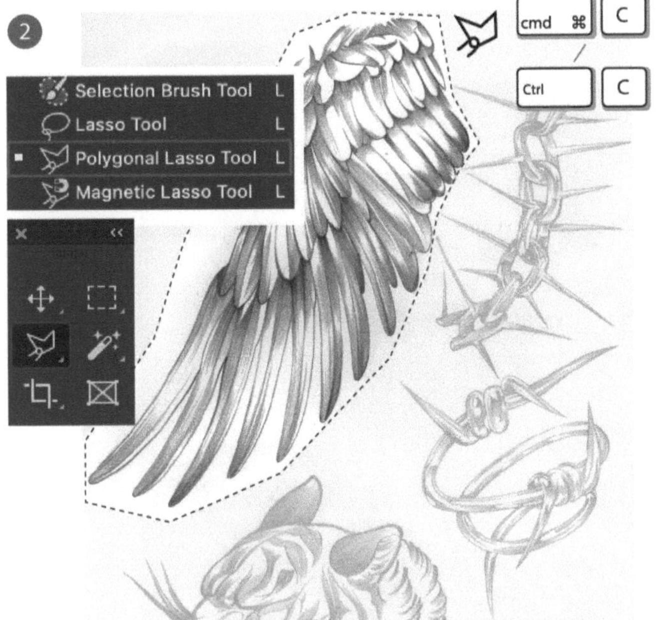

Step 3. Create a new A4 page in Illustrator **File › New › A4** and place the artwork there **File › Place**.

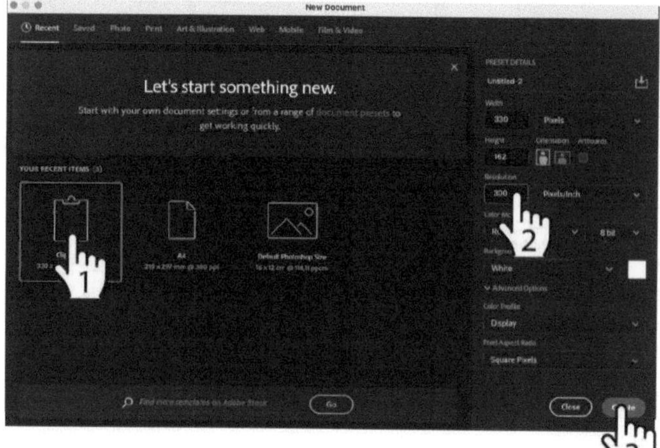

Step 4. Trace the artwork with the Pen Tool (just the outside shape). When you're done, make a copy of the object with the shortcut command+C / Ctrl+C (Copy) and the shortcut command+F / Ctrl+F (Paste in Front). Then place the copy in the background **Object › Arrange › Send to Back**.

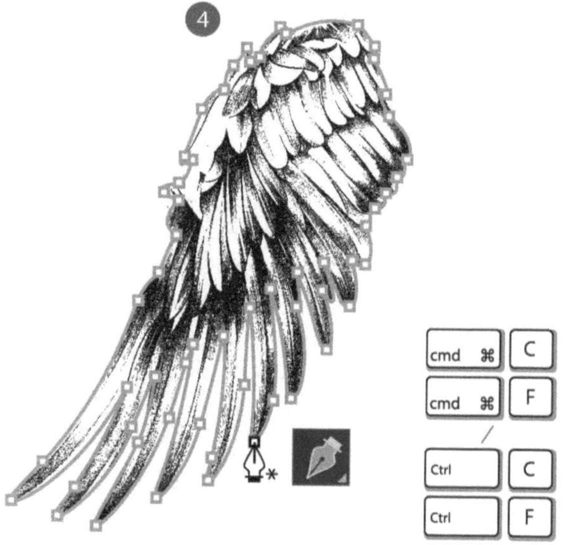

Step 5. Color the copy in white. Change the outline thickness so that the copy appears larger to the outside **Window › Stroke** and lock the „copy" object with the short-cut command+2 / Ctrl+2 to make it easier to select the other two objects later.

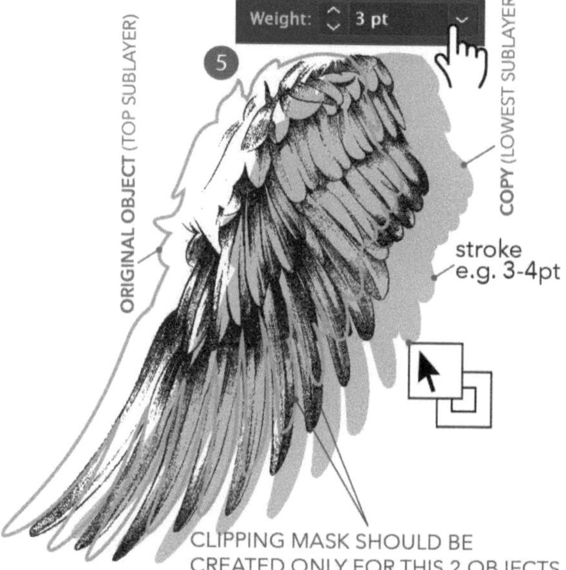

Step 6. Select the two objects and create a clipping mask with the shortcut command+7 / Ctrl+7 or **Object › Clipping Mask › Make**.

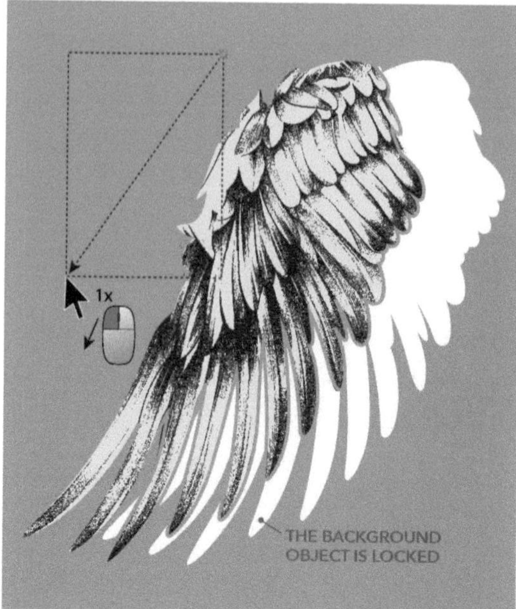

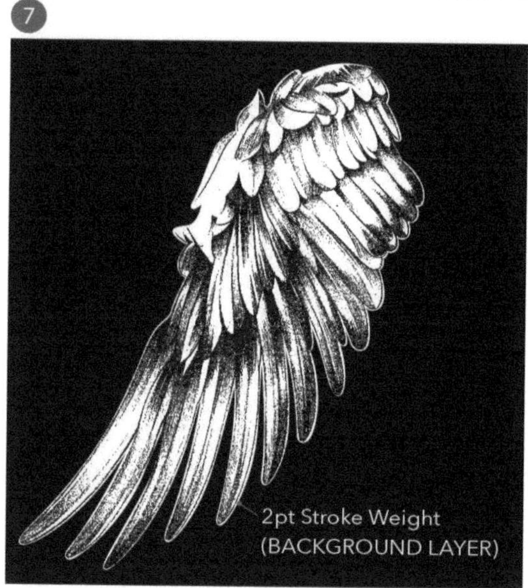

Step 7. Unlock the background object **Object › Unlock All** and see if the contour thickness is sufficient. Otherwise, increase the contour thickness.

The clipping mask in Illustrator is an important tool, among other things, when it comes to masking certain objects in an object composition

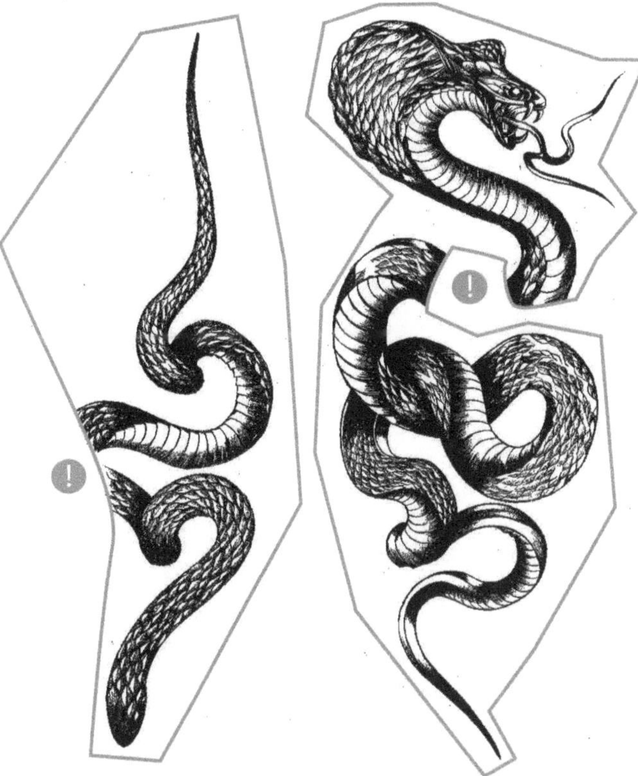

The clipping mask is used to cover particular areas so that the elements meet precisely in order to produce a uniform composition.

Step 8. Once a clipping mask has been created, you can no longer see an outline. Therefore, to determine where the clipping mask is located, activate the outline preview **View › Outline** or the shortcut command+Y / Ctrl+Y.
The outline preview is also good for finding objects that are either behind other objects or have no outline or fill color.

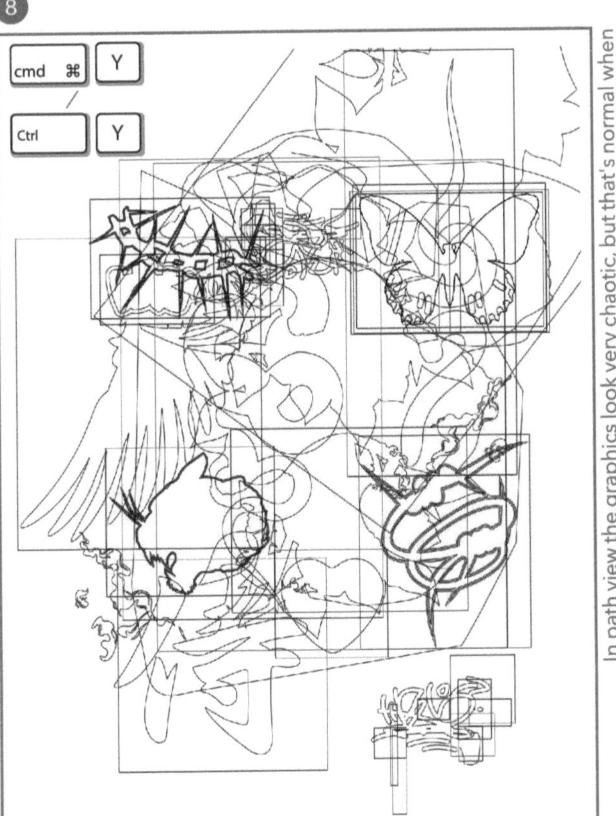

Step 9. If the path has been found in the outline preview, you can edit it directly with the **Direct Selection Tool** (A) (for example move it). You can change the anchor points in both the path preview and the normal preview.

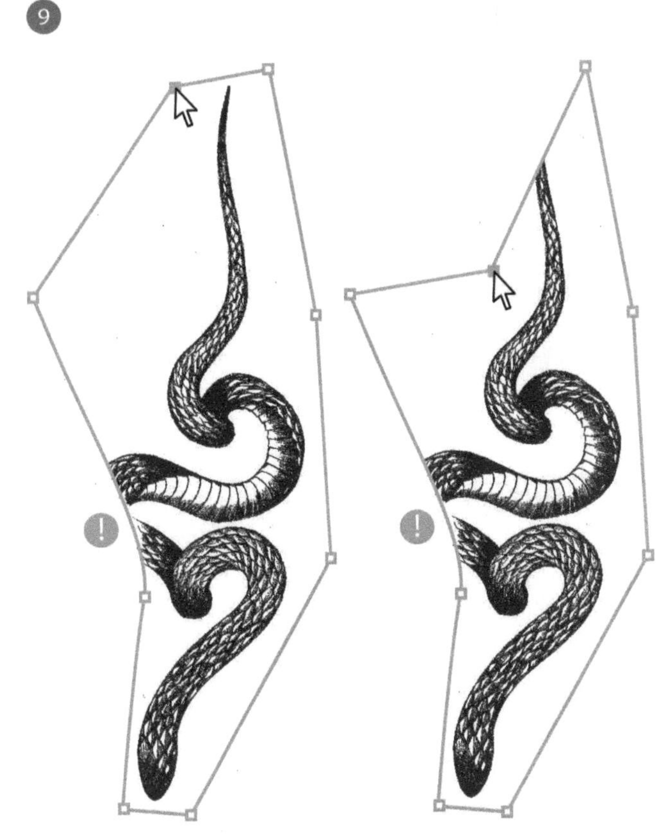

6.25 TUTORIAL: BITMAP TECHNIQUE 1

Step 1. Scan an image or take a photo of an image and open it in Photoshop. Then open **Image › Adjustments › Exposure...** panel and change the „Exposure" and „Gamma Correction" settings to adjust more contrast and make the image cleaner.

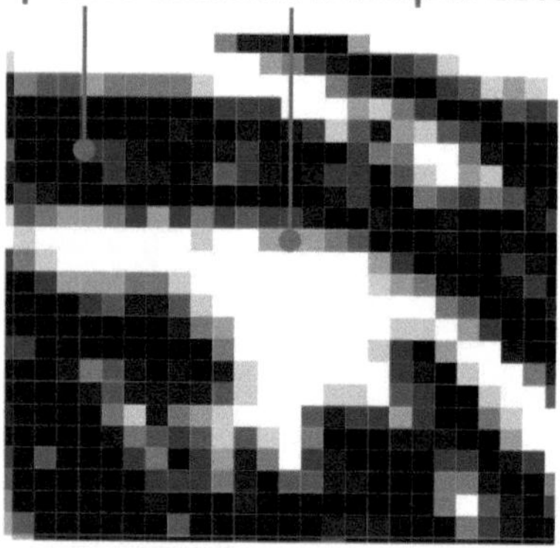

Step 2. Now, open the **Image › Adjustments › Threshold** panel and change the settings so that only black pixels remain after some pixels are removed.

Step 3. Now, activate the settings **Image › Mode › Grayscale**.

Step 4. Now, open the **Image › Mode › Bitmap...** panel.

Step 5. Change the settings (see figure) and confirm it with „OK".

pixels contain multiple colors   original

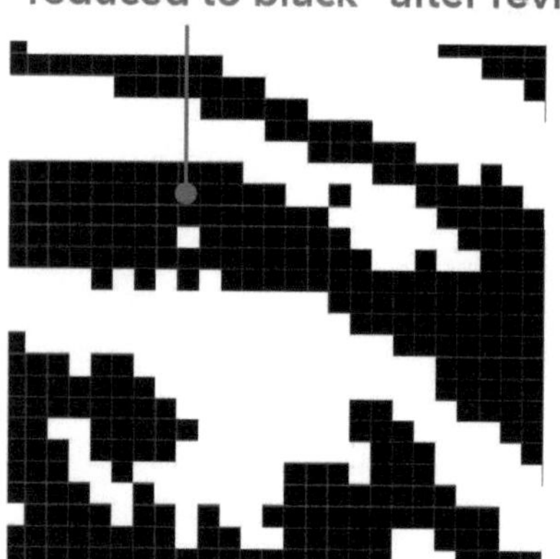

reduced to black   after revision

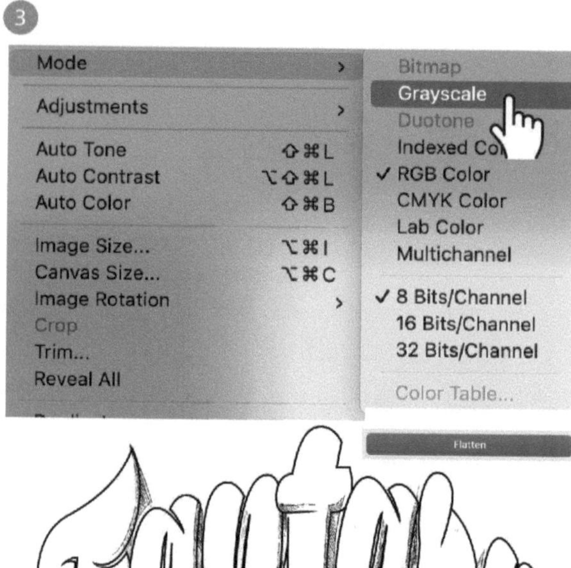

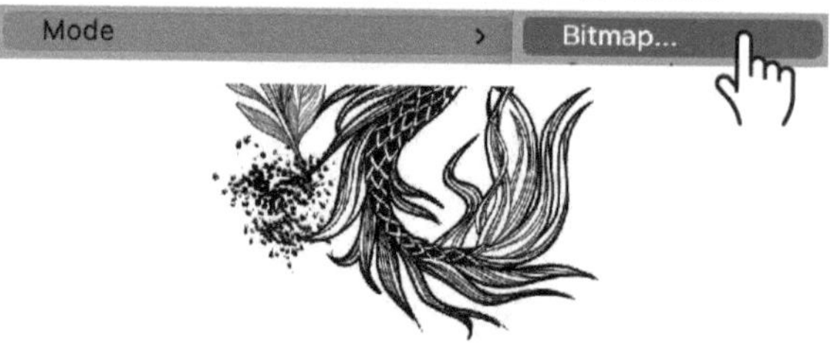

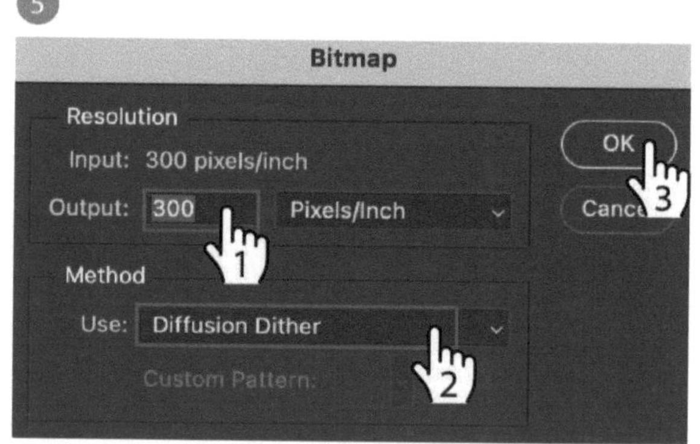

In this example you can see the result with a 300 pixel setting and with a 100 pixel setting

„Output" value is set to „300" (details are finer)

„Output" value is set to „100" (details are less finer)

Step 6. Now you have to save the file as a .tiff file **File › Save As..,** then click on "Save on your Computer". Choose .tiff as format and click on "Save".

⑥

You do not need to set anything in the .tiff options dialog box, confirm the window with "OK".

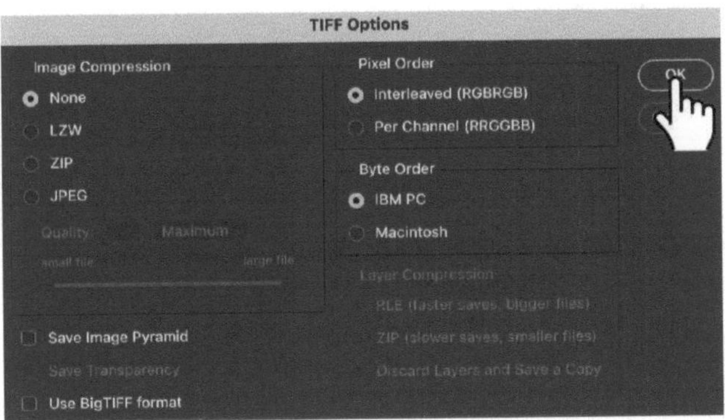

Step 7. Create a new A4 document in Illustrator **File > New >A4** and place the artwork in Illustrator **File > Place.**

Now in the **Tools panel** you can change the "Fill" color of the artwork to black or another color.

⑦

⑧

Step 8. If you need a background for the artwork, create a new object using the **Rectangle Tool** (M) and place it in the background **Object › Arrange › Send to Back.**

Background rectangle color

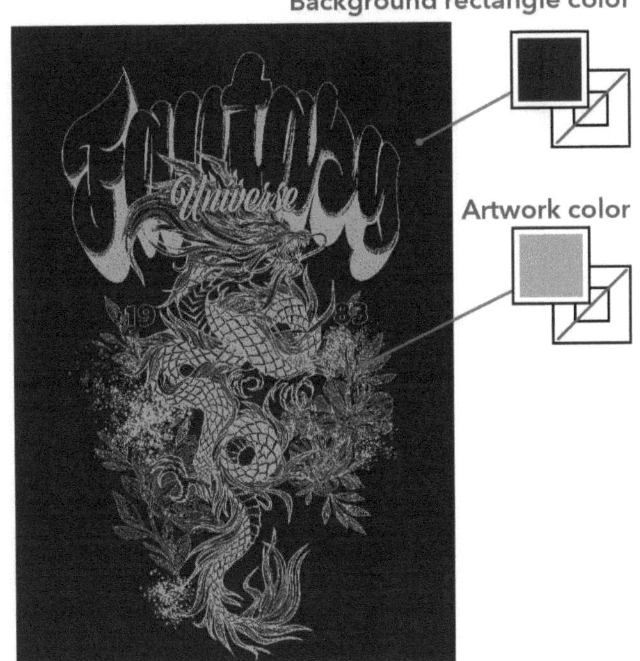

Artwork color

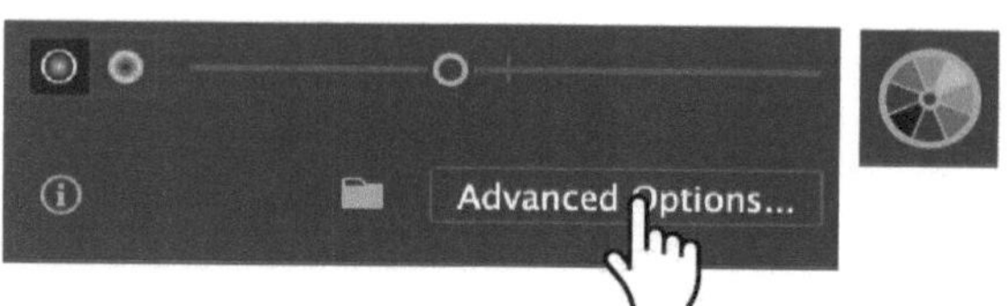

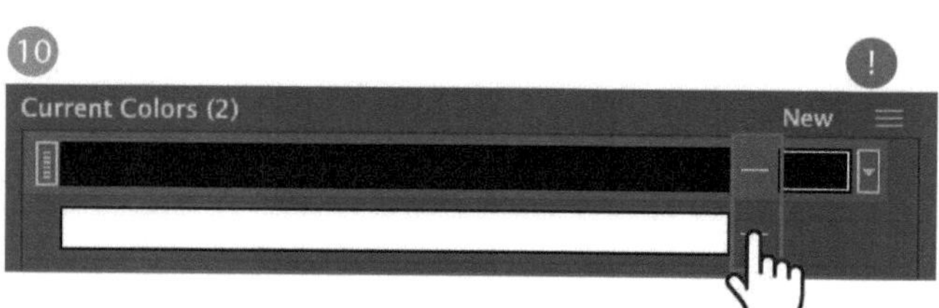

Step 10. When you recolor the artwork for the first time, black and white is always **turned off** by default. To activate black and white, click on the stroke to convert it to an arrow, then confirm the window with „OK" and reopen the recolor window. Now you can also change black and white color.

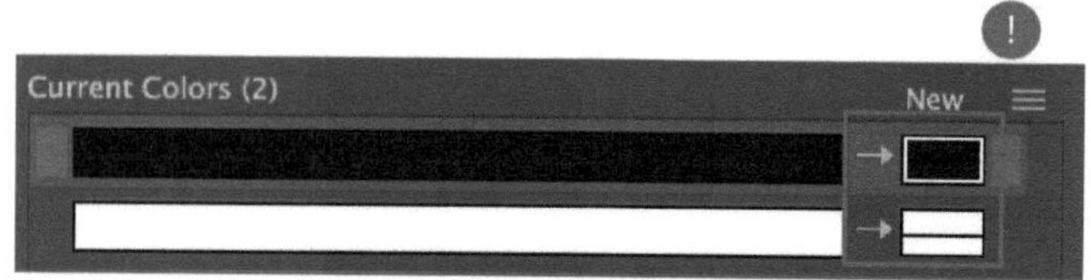

@dimitridesign.org

6.26 TUTORIAL: SWIRLY LETTER DESIGN

First, create a new A4 page in Adobe Illustrator **File > New > A4**.

Step 1. Use the **Pen Tool** (P) to create half of a heart shape.

Step 2. Now select the **Reflect Tool** (O), position the mouse cursor on the vertical guide (placing guides see page 24), press and hold the **alt/option** key (do not release the alt/option key) and click the left mouse button. The Reflect dialog box appears, then release the **alt** key.

Turn on "Vertical," "Preview," make sure everything is in order, and then click "Copy." A mirrored duplicate is created.

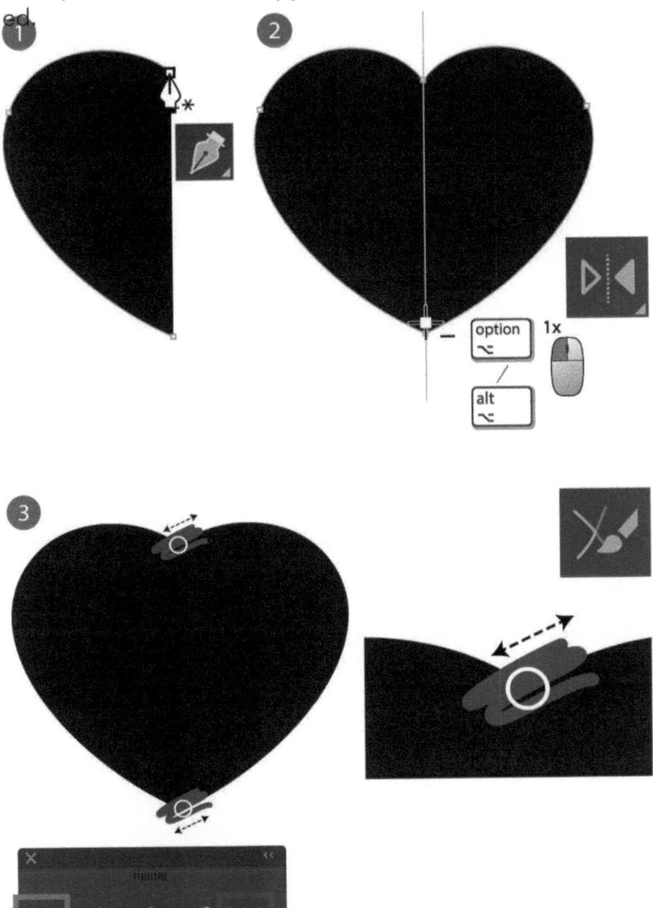

Shaper Tool   Join Tool

Step 3. Now you have to join two halves. You can use the **Join Tool** for this purpose. You can find this tool in the same group as the **Shaper Tool**.

First select the objects with the **Selection Tool** (V), then with the **Join Tool** drag over the anchor points of the two halves several times. This will connect the anchor points, do this at both connection areas.

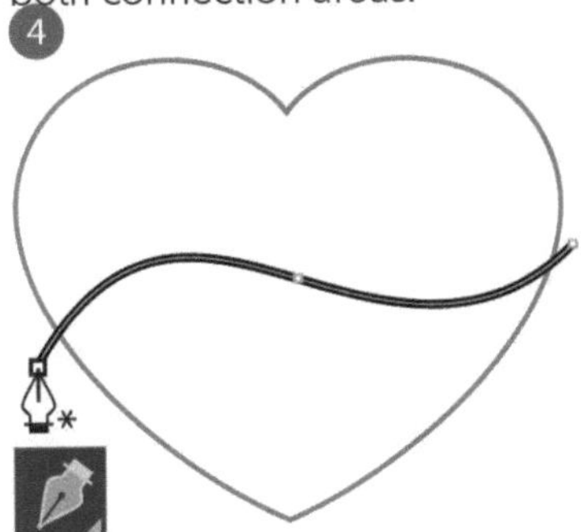

Step 4. Create with the **Pen Tool** (P) another line.

Step 5. Create a copy of this object with the shortcut command+C / Ctrl+C (Copy) and the shortcut command+F / Ctrl+F (Paste in Front). Drag the copy up or down.

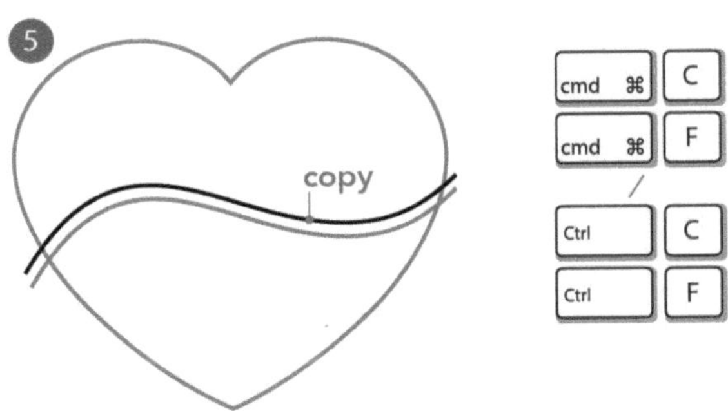

Step 6. Select the objects with the **Selection Tool** (V).

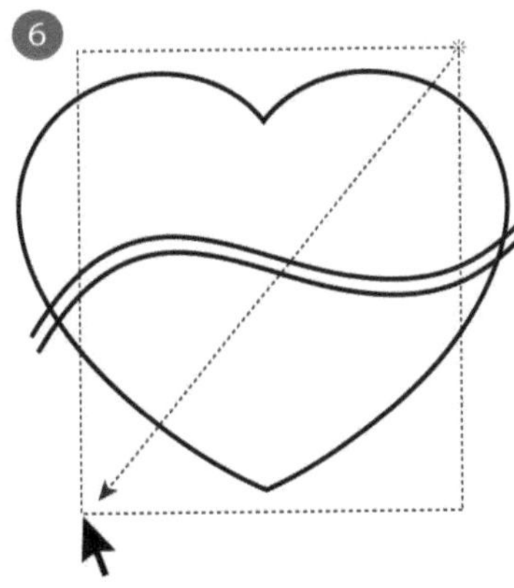

Step 7. Activate the **Live Paint Bucket** (K). Change the fill colour for example to grey. Then click inside the objects with the left mouse button (the stroke will be displayed in red).

Step 8. Then activate the command **Expand** in the control panel or the command **Object>Expand..** After that command the objects are grouped together.

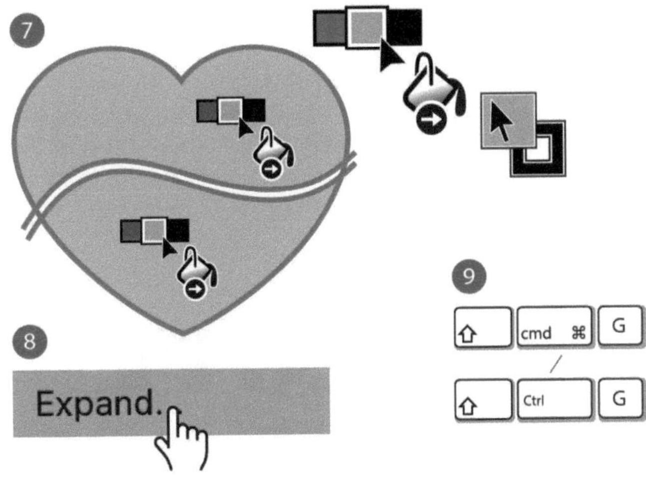

Step 9. Activate **several times** the shortcut Shift+cmd+G / Shift+Ctrl+G (or choose **Object>Ungroup**, also several times) to ungroup the objects.

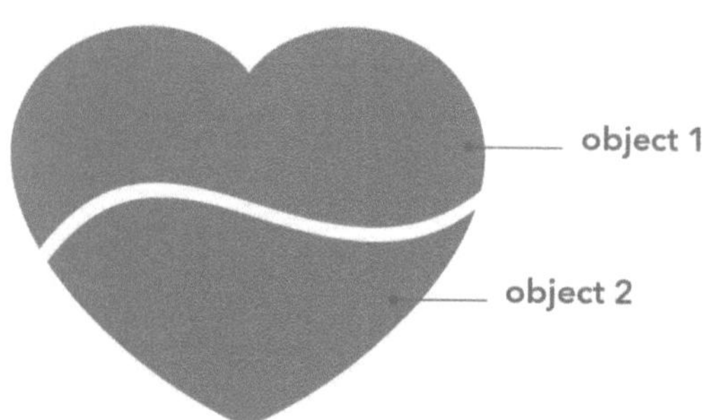

The two objects are now ungrouped and you can access them individually.

Step 13. First select the first two objects (group1) and activate the shortcut option+cmd+C / alt+Ctrl+C (or choose **Object> Envelope Distort > Make with Top Object**.

LOVE
PEACE

Step 14. Repeat step 13 for the „group 2" objects.

Step 10. Open the font dialog box **Window > Type > Character**. Click with the **Text Tool** (T) in the empty drawing area, set the size of the text to 200pt or bigger, choose font that you like and type a word. Confirm the text rectangle with the „**Esc**" key. Repeat this step for the second word.

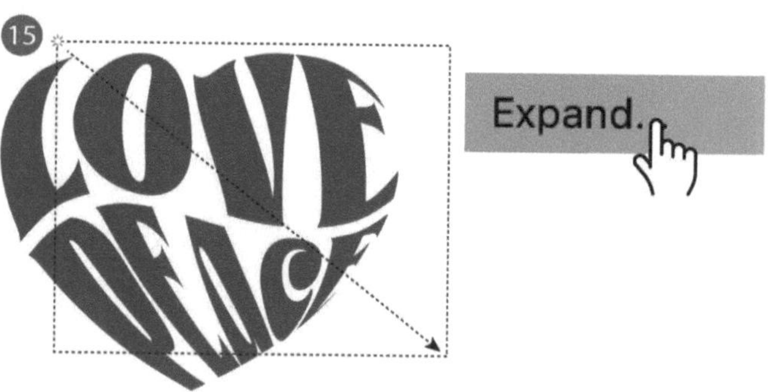

Step 15. Select all objects with the **Selection Tool** (V) and activate the command **Expand** in the control panel or the command **Object>Expand..** Now you can access the individual anchor points to further refine the artwork.

Step 11. Select both objects with the **Selection Tool** (V) and activate the command **Expand** in the control panel or the command **Object>Expand..**

Step 12. Place the two objects in the foreground **Object >Arrange>Bring to Front**

Step 16. Use the **Direct Selection Tool** (A) to finally adjust the shape.

Now you can set for the object different strokes, fill colors and various effects.

pattern fill

artistic outline

You can find many interesting outlines (artistic brushes) under this menu **Window > Brush Libraries > Artistic**.

Under **Effects** you can find many interesting filters such as the blur filter **Effect > Blur > Gaussian Blur...** which is often used in the artwork development.

6.27 TUTORIAL: TRACE PIXEL IMAGES

Step 1. Scan an image or take a photo of it and open it in Photoshop **File > Open**.

Step 2. Then open **Image › Adjustments › Exposure...** panel and change the „Exposure" and „Gamma Correction" settings to adjust more contrast and make the image cleaner.

Step 3. Create a new A4 document in Illustrator **File > New > A4** and place the artwork there **File > Place...**
Select the object with the **Selection Tool** (V) and click on „Sketched Art" in the control panel or open **Object › Image Trace › Make**.

Step 4. Now open „Image trace panel" in the control panel.

You can now change the outcome by modifying different settings.

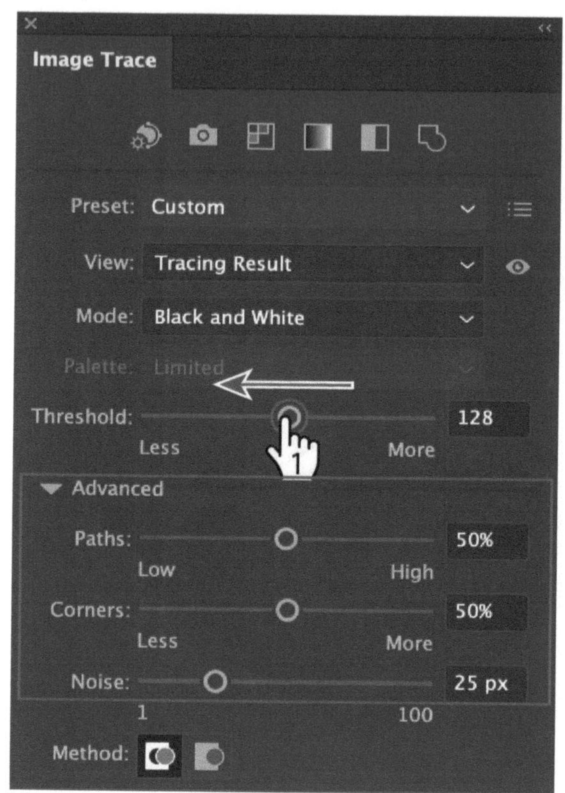

Threshold (1)

Another option is the "Advanced" control panel, but the outcome is dependent on the artwork. Some images will show no results at all, while the results for the other artworks become more visible.

Step 5. Now click on „Expand" button (option panel) to finally convert the artwork into paths (vector graphic).

(5)

(6)

Step 6. Activate the command **Object › Path › Simplify…**

original

simplified

In this dialog box you can determine the number of anchor points and thereby simplify the appearance of the object.

(7)

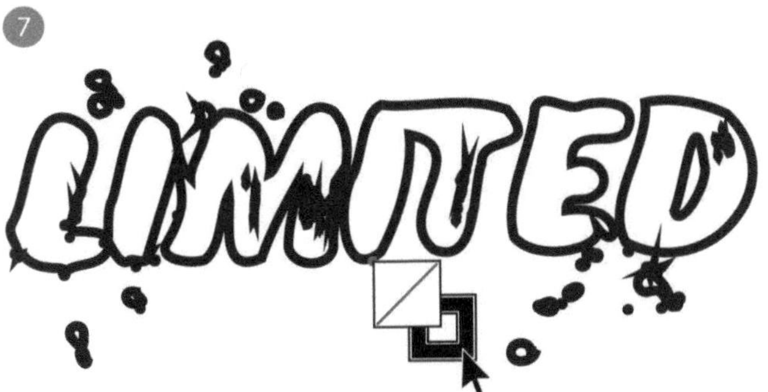

Step 7. Another interesting way to achieve effects is to add an outline to the object **Window › Stroke**.

Here you can for example change the stroke weight (1) and add a profile (2).

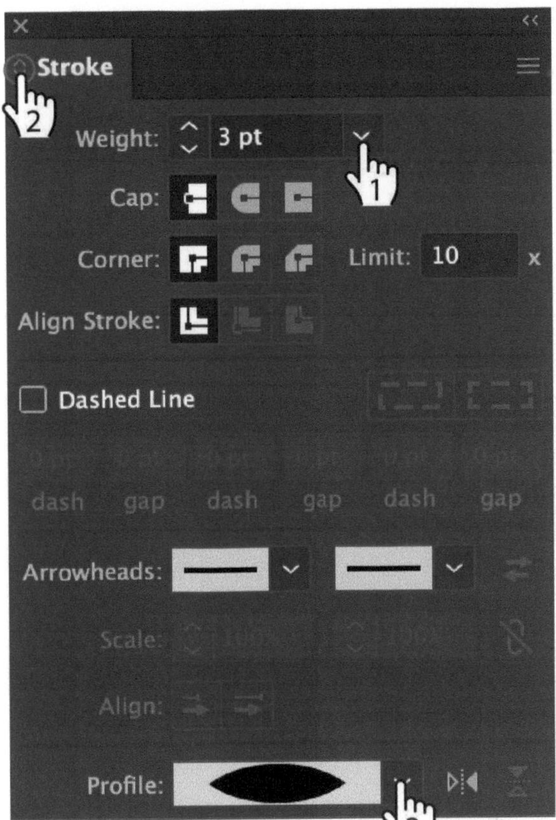

(8)

Step 8. Another interesting option is to work with "artistic brushes". **Window › Brush Libraries › Artistic › Artistic ScrollPen**. There are of course many more options and effects but the result always depends on your ingenuity.

6.28 TUTORIAL: INFRARED CAMERA EFFECT

Step 1. Open an image in Photoshop. A high-resolution image is necessary for this technique, so make sure the quality is appropriate.

To check this go to **Image › Image Size...** Next, make sure the dimensions result in roughly one Din4 page and that the resolution is set to at least 300 ppi.

Then open the layers window and deactivate the lock to access all settings **Window › Layers**.

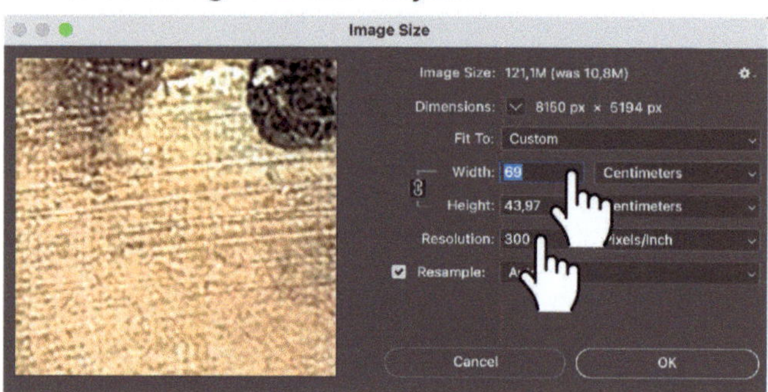

Step 2. To achieve the infrared effect, open the **Image › Adjustment › Curves...** window.

Now you can start forming new anchor points and bending the curve into a zigzag line in this window.

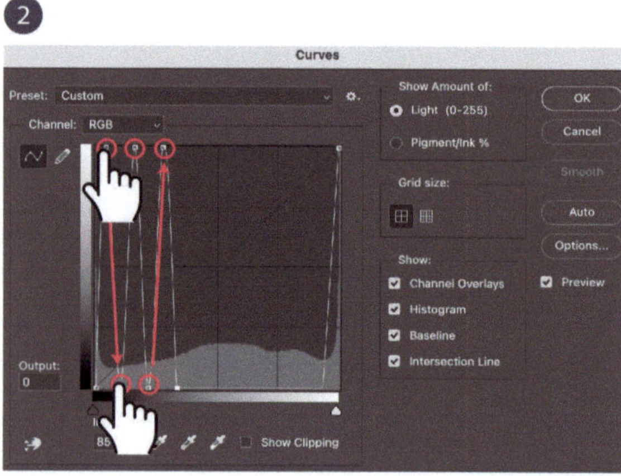

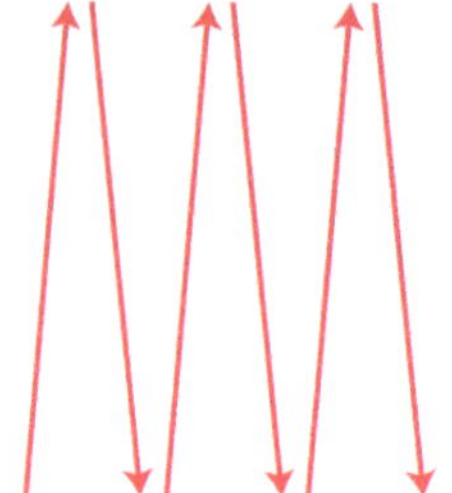

Create as many points until you are satisfied with the result. Then confirm the window with OK.

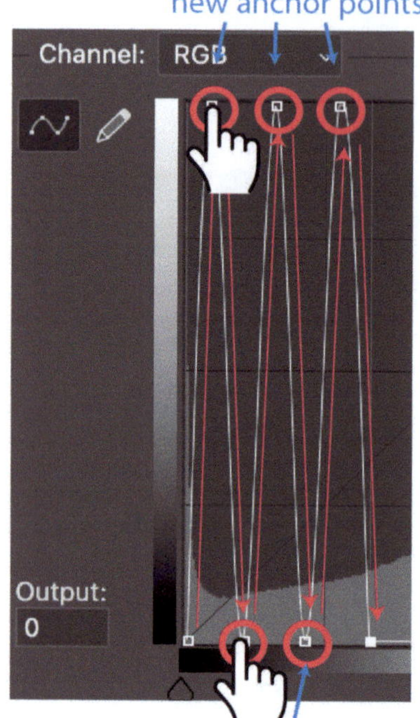

The number of anchor points and the density of the zigzag curve determines the final result (A,B,C).

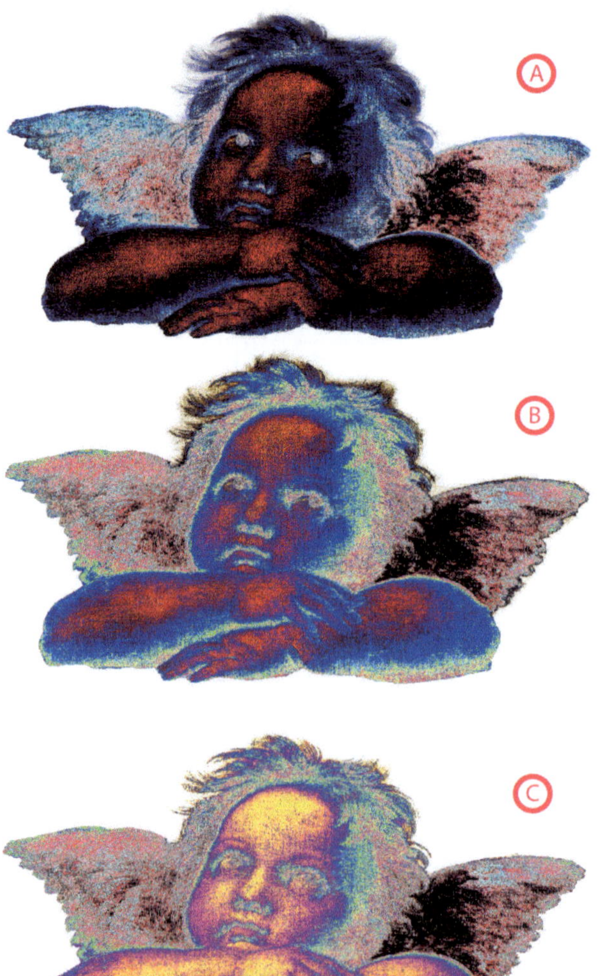

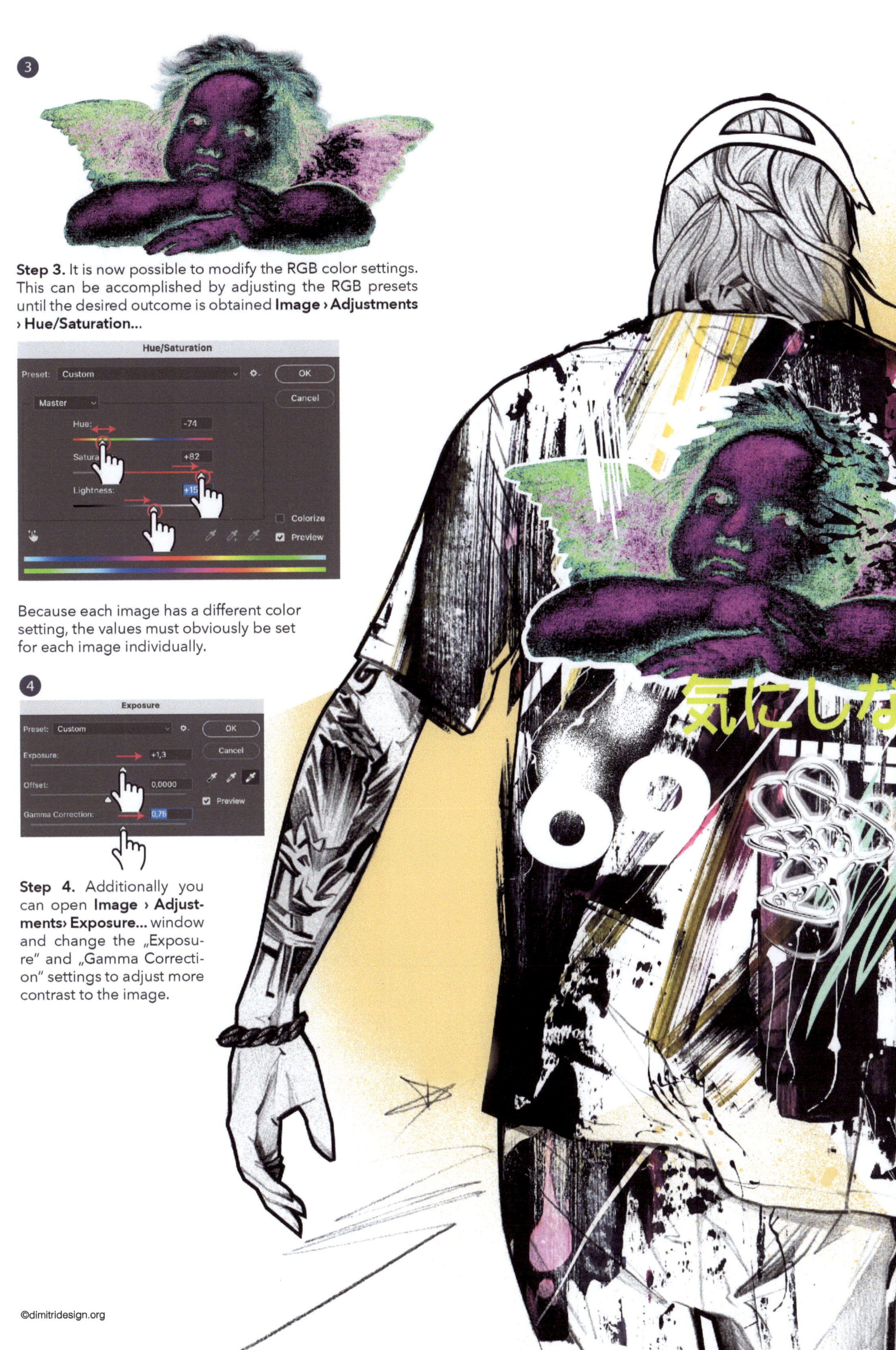

③

Step 3. It is now possible to modify the RGB color settings. This can be accomplished by adjusting the RGB presets until the desired outcome is obtained **Image › Adjustments › Hue/Saturation...**

Because each image has a different color setting, the values must obviously be set for each image individually.

④

Step 4. Additionally you can open **Image › Adjustments› Exposure...** window and change the „Exposure" and „Gamma Correction" settings to adjust more contrast to the image.

6.29 TUTORIAL: DISTORTION TECHNIQUE

Step 1. Open a new A4 document in Photoshop **File>-New...** Select the **Text Tool** (T), set a new color and font size, click in the empty drawing area with the left mouse button and write a word. Confirm the textbox with **Esc** key or with **Selection Tool.**

Step 2. Convert the object into a smart object **Layer>Smart**

Objects > Convert to Smart Object.
Step 3. Now open the panel **Liquify (Filter>Liquify...)** and distort the object as you wish. Using these four tools (see figure) is the best approach to accomplish this. To operate more accurately, adjust the tool's size as well (see figure). Then confirm the settings with „OK".
Save the file in .psd (Photoshop) format **File>Save as..**

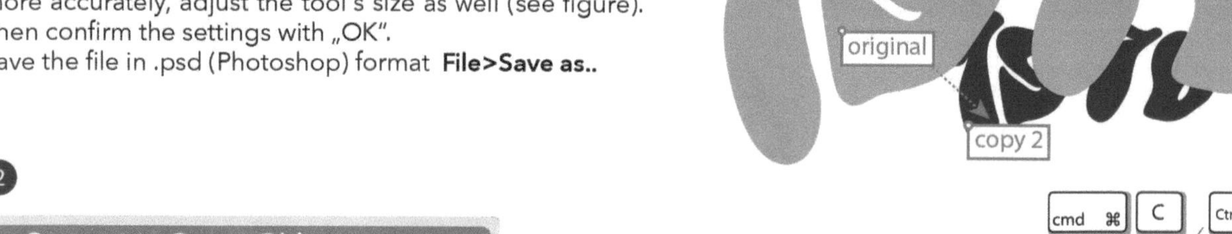

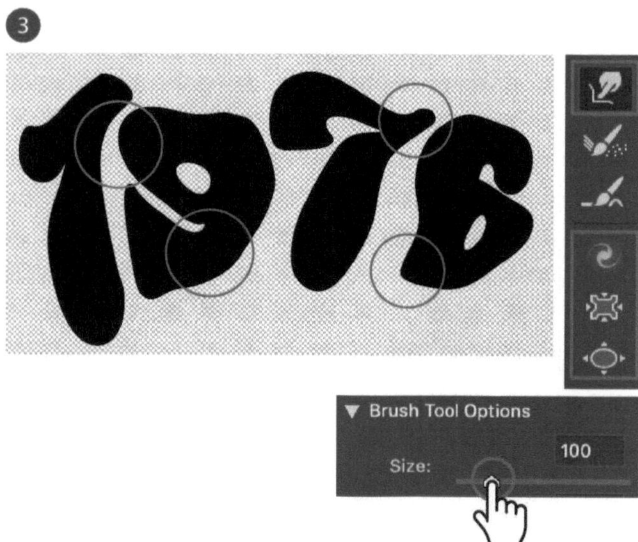

Step 4. Then create a new A4 page in Illustrator **File > New > A4.** Place the artwork in Illustrator **File>Place...**
Select the object with the **Selection Tool** (V) and click on the **"Sketched Art"** button in the option panel.

Now click on the "Expand" button to expand the artwork so you can apply further steps.

Step 5. Now select the object with the **Selection Tool** (V) and create 1 copy of this object with the shortcut command+C / Ctrl+C (Copy) and the shortcut command+F / Ctrl+F (Paste in Front).

Then move the copy and make it smaller with the **Selection Tool** (V).
Step 6. Now use the **Blend Tool** (W) to create a blend. To do this, click on each object once with the left mouse button.

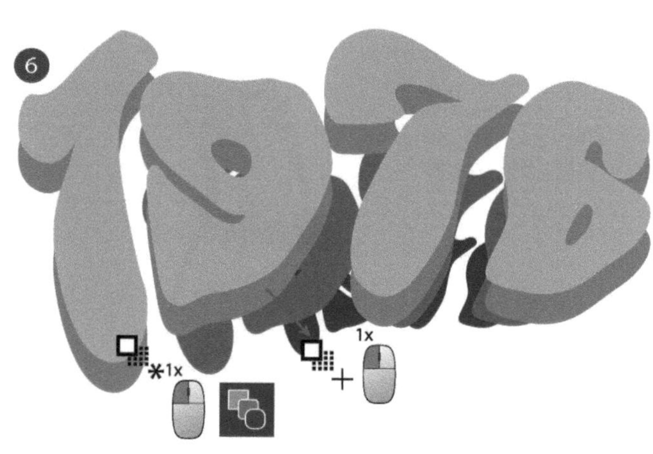

To create now more objects in between, double click on the mix tool to open the mix tool panel or go to **Object > Blend > Blend Options.**

Step 7. In the tool panel change the „Spacing" to „Specified Distance" and change the value to 0,1pt, then confirm it with „OK".

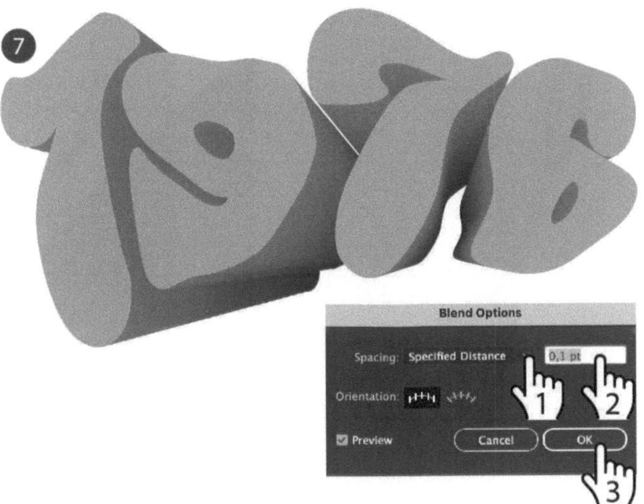

Step 8. To change the color space of the graphic go to **Edit > Edit Colors > Recolor Artwork** or click on the circle icon in the control panel.

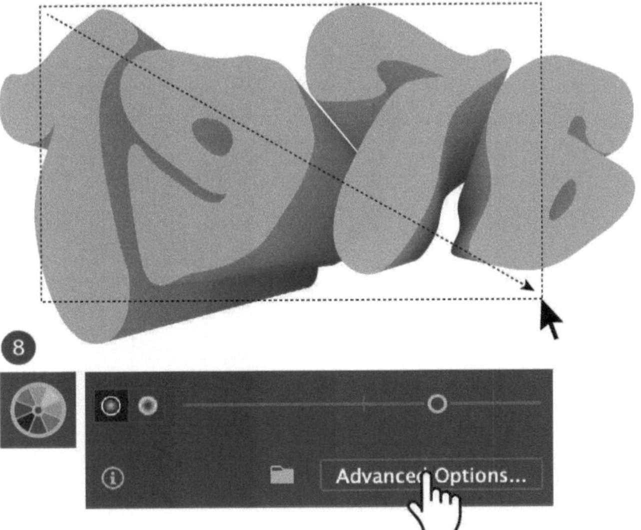

In the window that appears, activate the „Advanced options" button. Now you can change each color individually by double clicking on "New" (see figure).

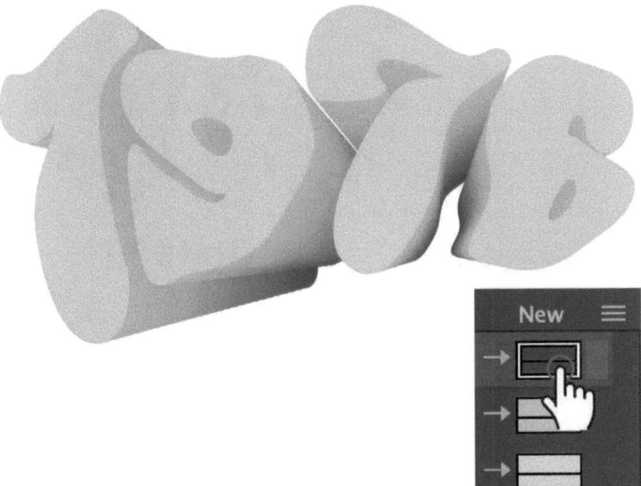

©dimitridesign.org

6.30 TUTORIAL: BITMAP TECHNIQUE 2

In this tutorial, various bitmap images are combined and prepared so that they can be recolored with Illustrator.

Step 1. Scan an image or take a photo of an image and open it in Photoshop. Then open **Image › Adjustments › Exposure...** panel and change the „Exposure" and „Gamma Correction" settings to adjust more contrast and make the image cleaner.

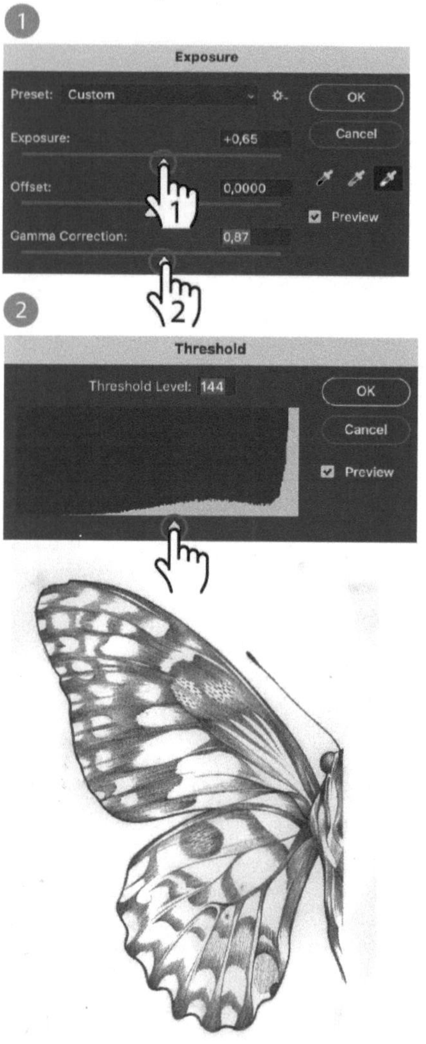

Step 2. Now, open the **Image › Adjustments › Threshold** panel and change the settings so that only black pixels remain after some pixels are removed.

Step 3. Set the image to grayscale **Image › Mode › Grayscale**.

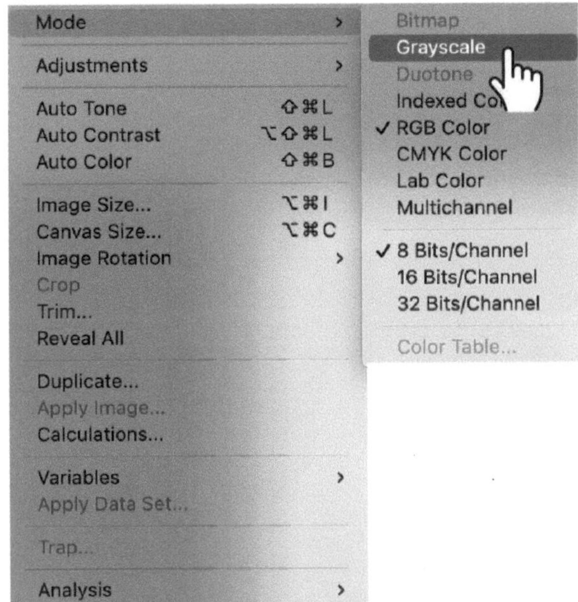

Step 4. Activate the command **Image › Mode › Bitmap**.

Step 5. Now change the following settings:
Set the „Output" to „300". The higher the value, the finer the details. But this setting also increases the file size. A good setting is between 100-300.
Set the „Method" to „Diffusion Dither" and confirm the settings with „OK". The first object is created.

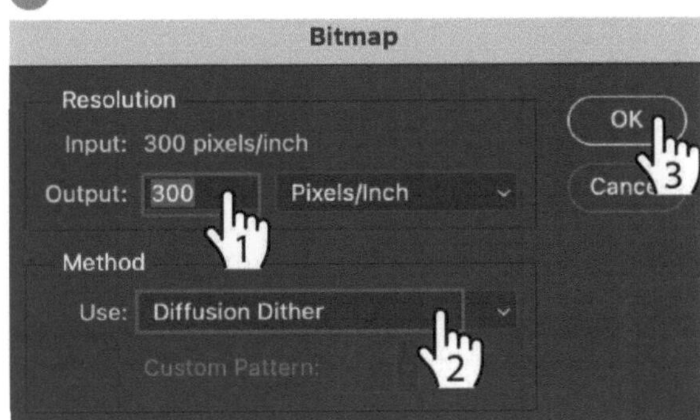

Step 6. Now it's about creating different surface structures using the bitmap technique.
Choose an image with an uneven structure, e.g. old paper, denim fabric, images with surface structure. Then repeat the steps 1-4.

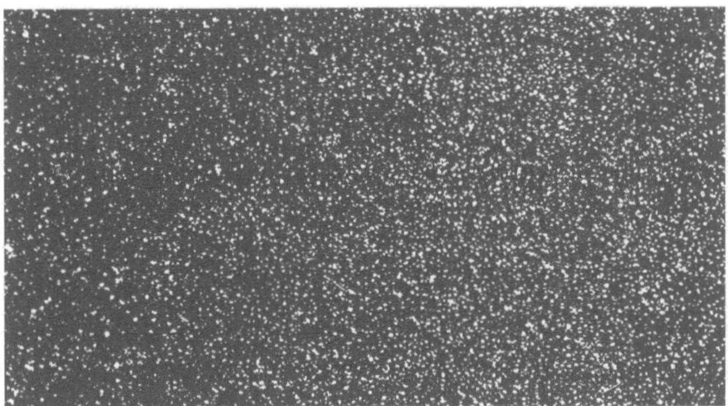

Step 7. Now change the following settings:
Set the „Output" to „150".
Set the „Method" this time to „Halfton Screen.." and confirm the settings with „OK".

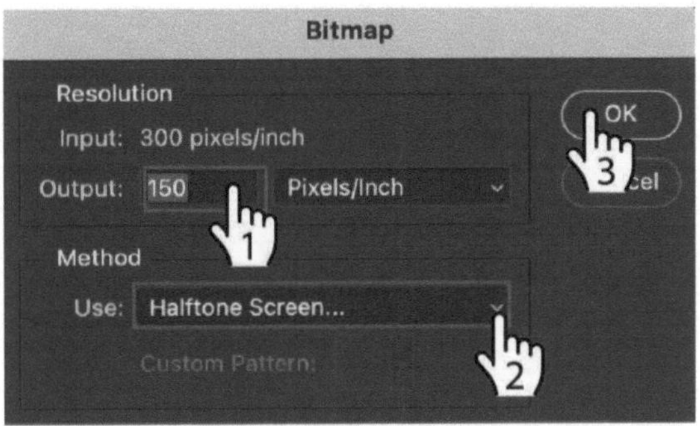

Shape „Line" with „Frequency" 15

Shape „Line" with „Frequency" 25

Step 8. Now set the shape to "Line" with the following settings (see figure). Try out other shape settings (you have to undo first this step to try out other options).

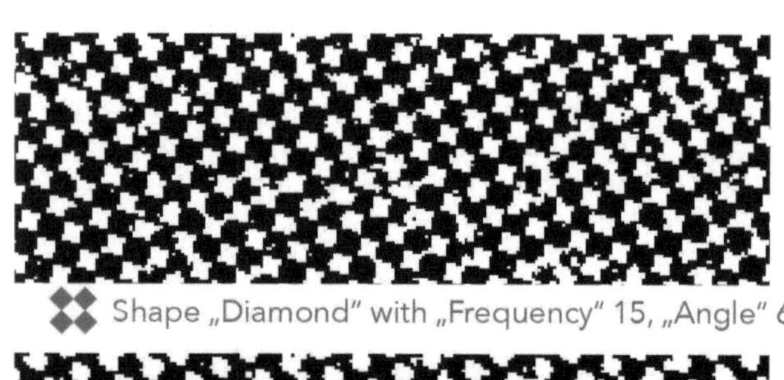

Shape „Diamond" with „Frequency" 15, „Angle" 60

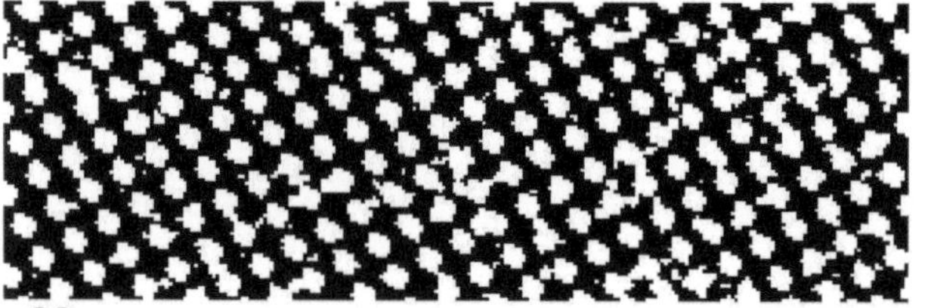

Shape „Ellipse" with „Frequency" 15, „Angle" 60

Shape „Square" with „Frequency" 15, „Angle" 60

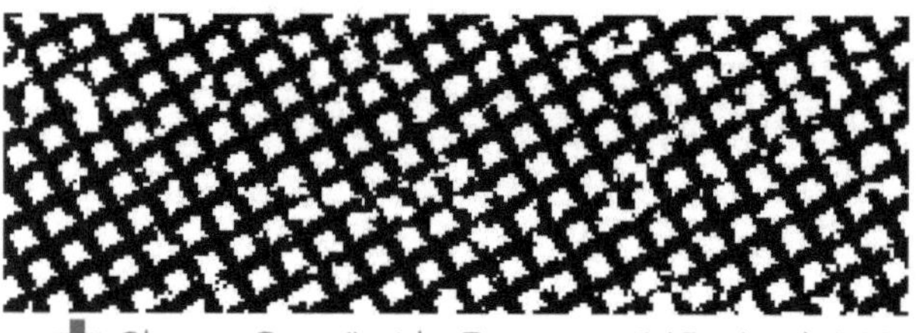

Shape „Cross" with „Frequency" 15, „Angle" 60

Step 9. Now save the file in .tiff format **File>Save As...** choose a destination, choose .tiff as format and confirm with „Save".

Format: TIFF

Step 10. From now on you will continue to work with Illustrator.
Create a new A4 page in Illustrator **File > New > A4.** Place the structure you've created first in Illustrator **File > Place.** While placing, deactivate "Link"

Link

Create a pattern with this object **Object > Pattern > Make** (you have to select the object first).

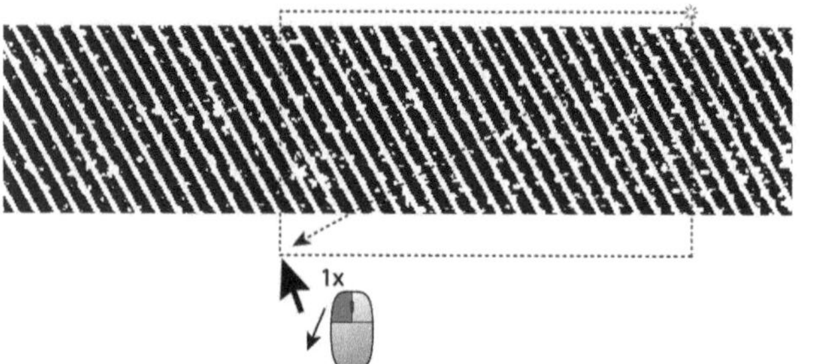

Confirm the settings with "Done".

Step 12. Place your first artwork from this tutorial in Illustrator **File > Place** (While placing, deactivate "Link").

Now trace the outside shape with the **Pen Tool** (P).

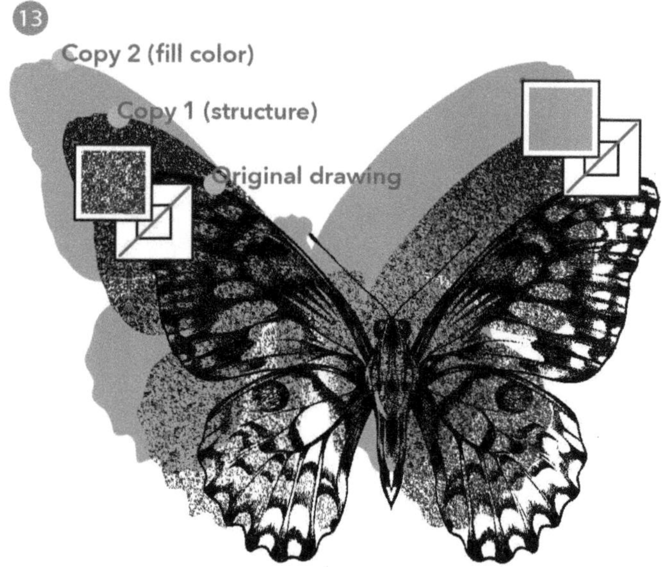

Step 13. Create 1 copy of the traced object with the short-cut command+C / Ctrl+C (Copy) and the shortcut command+F / Ctrl+F (Paste in Front).

Now for better understanding, you have 3 objects that are on top of each other. Fill the 2 drawn objects one with a color and the other object with the structure created before from the swatches library **Window > Swatches.**

How complicated the artwork is designed depends on the task and your desire. But this is the classic approach to designing multi-layered artwork in Illustrator.

To get a better overview, either move the individual objects to the side or access the layer order **Window > Layers.**

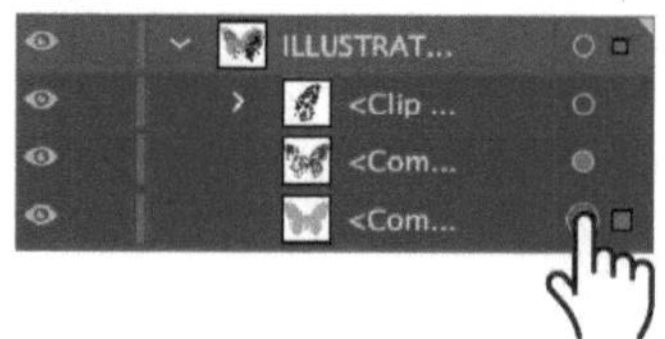

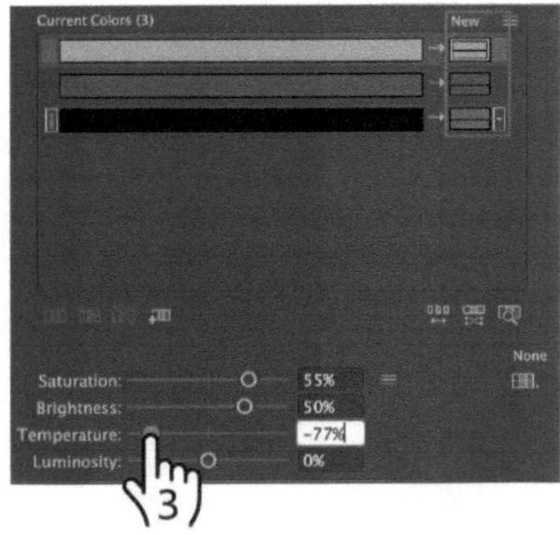

Step 14. When you place a bitmap image in Illustrator, the program shows a question mark in the toolbar. Double click on the "fill" in the tool panel to set a color, then the question mark disappears.

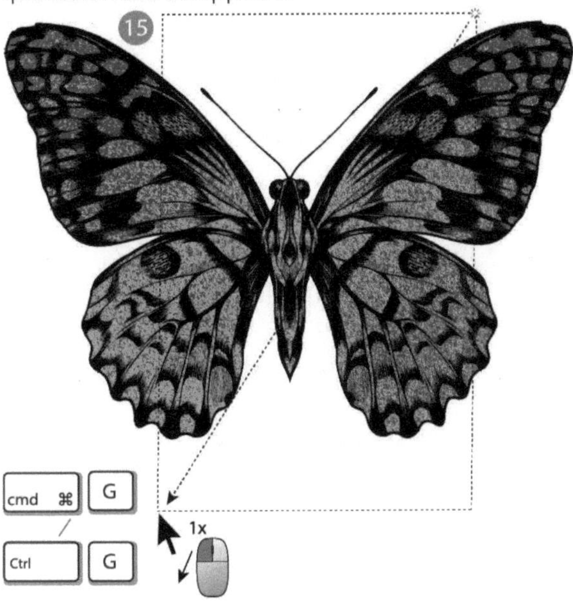

Step 15. Now select all objects with the **Selection Tool** (V) and group the objects with the shortcut cmd+G / Ctrl+G or **Object > Group**.

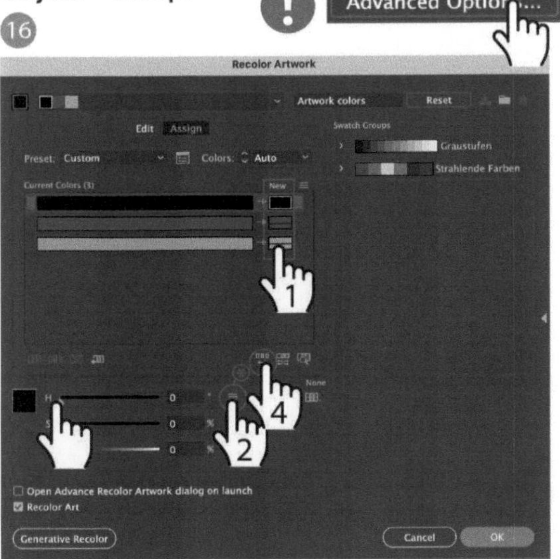

Step 16. To recolor the artwork, open the command **Edit › Edit Colors › Recolor Artwork**. When the window appears, click on the „Advanced Options..." and then the required window will open. Here you have the opportunity to set specific colors (1). If you click on this button (2) and set „Global Adjust" then you have further options to manipulate the colors (3).

colorway 1

Step 17. If you click on the "Randomly change color order" (4) button you have the opportunity to change the colors among each other as you wish. This keeps the set colors exactly the same while producing other interesting colorways.

colorway 2

6.31 TUTORIAL: REDYE WITH LAYERS 1

Step 1. Scan an image or take a photo of an image and open it in Photoshop. Then open **Image › Adjustments › Exposure...** panel and change the „Exposure" and „Gamma Correction" settings to adjust more contrast and make the image cleaner.

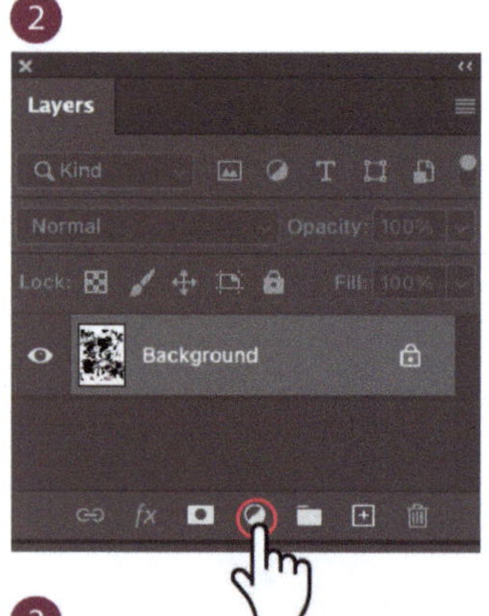

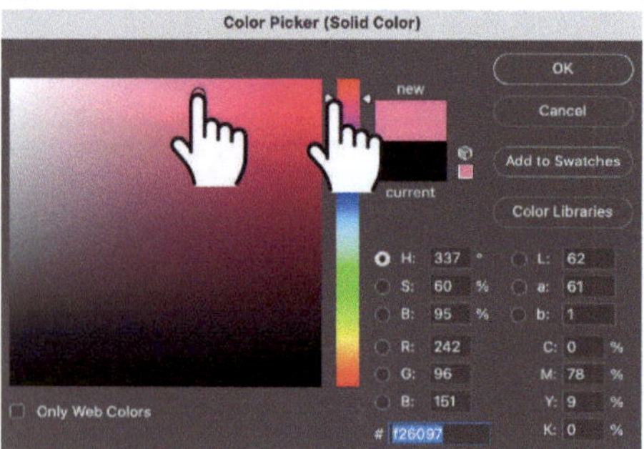

Step 2. Open the menu "Create new fill or adjustment layer" and click on "Solid Color".
Step 3. In the menu choose the color you prefer and confirm it with "OK".

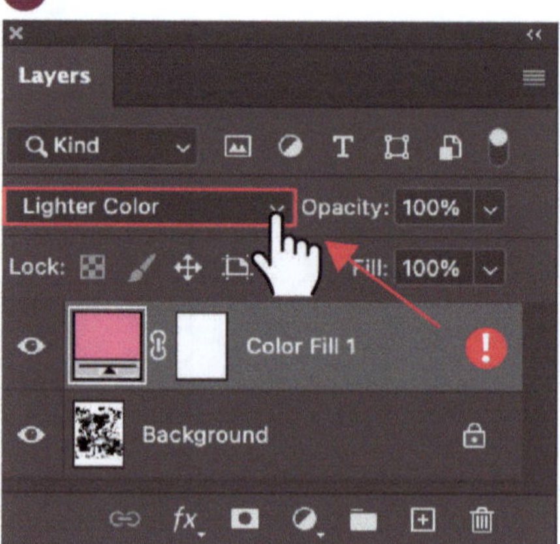

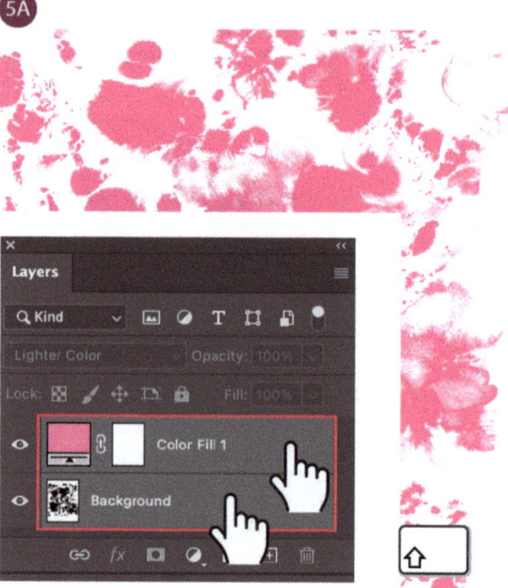

Step 4. In the layer window change the value to "Lighter Color" (see figure).
Step 5A. Press and hold the Shift key, then go to the layer panel and click on **Layer › Merge Down** or use the shortcut command+E / Ctrl+E to merge the layers.

Step 5B. Instead of a fill color, you can also set a gradient. To do this open the menu "Create new fill or adjustment layer" and click on "Gradient..". Remember that before you create a new "fill or adjustment layer", you should deactivate the existing color layers.

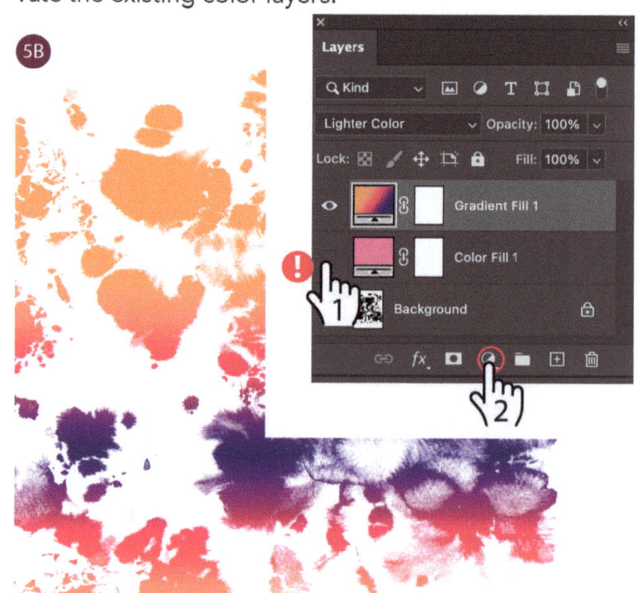

Step 6. In the window that appears, click on the „Gradient" entry. Additionally, you can change some more settings like gradient's scale and angle.

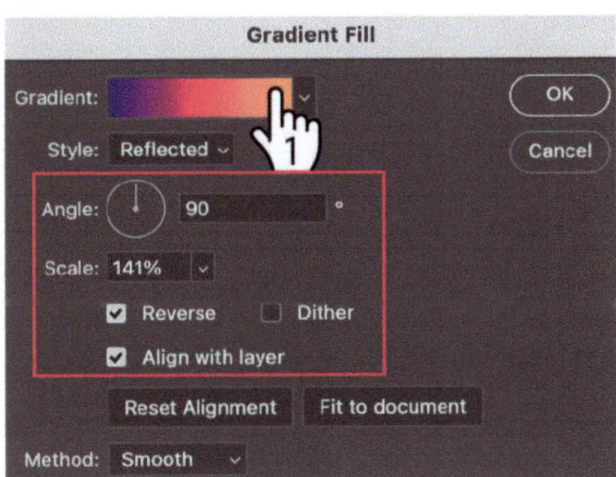

Step 7. In the "Gradient" drop-down menu select first a standard gradient (1). Next, you can double-click the slider to adjust the colors (2), add new colors, or remove existing ones (3).

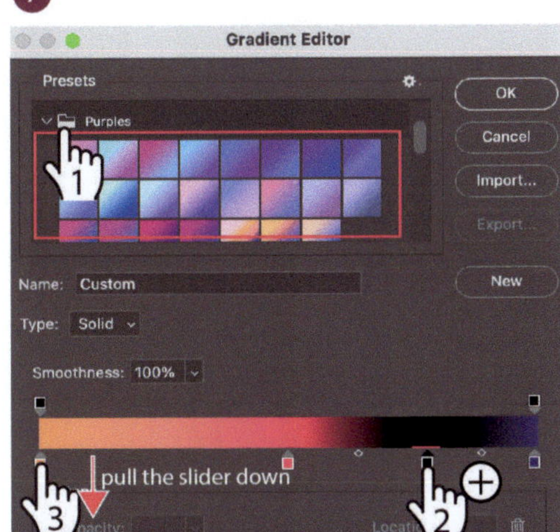

To change the colors, double click on the slider, set the colors and confirm with "OK"

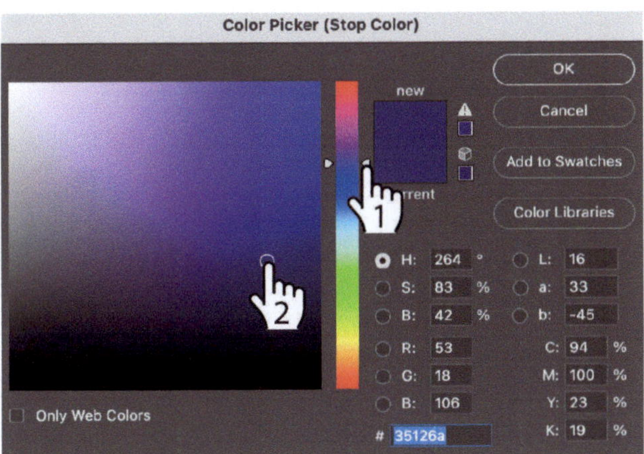

6.32 TUTORIAL: REDYE WITH LAYERS 2

There are numerous options in Photoshop for image corrections. Due to the variety of techniques in this area, only some interesting possibility will be discussed in this book. You can find the most important settings for image corrections under the menu **Image › Adjustments.** In this tutorial we will work with the **Channel Mixer** and **Hue/Saturation**

Of course, all of these tools offer much more possibilities, but here the author presents some techniques that he uses every day in graphic design field for fashion.
Try these techniques with different images to better memorize the knowledge.

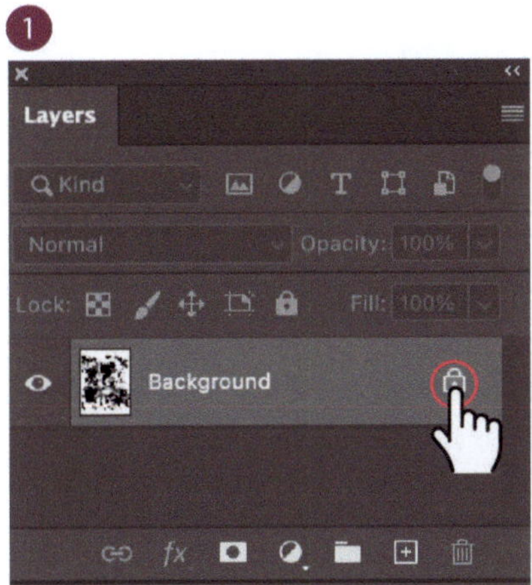

Step 1. Open an image and disable the lock button in the layers window.

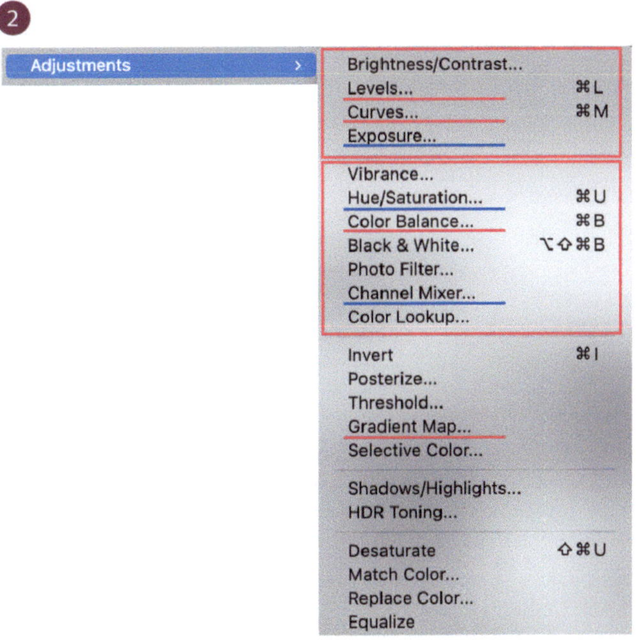

Step 2. Create first an additional „solid color" layer (see previous tutorial). Go now to **Image › Adjustments › Chanel Mixer...** in the menu panel.

Step 3. Now you have the possibilitie to change the RGB color settings. To achieve this, go through the RGB presets and change the values until the desired result is achieved.

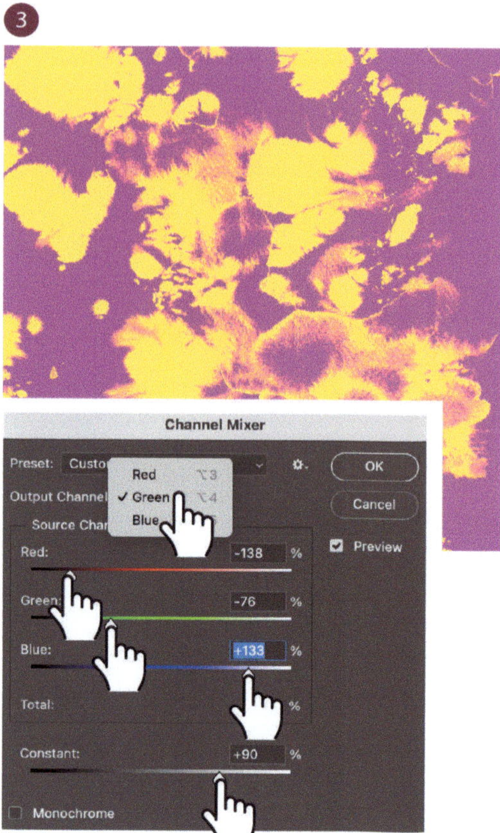

The values must of course be set individually for each image because every image has its own color settings.

Step 4. After you've selected some interesting color values, select **Image › Adjustments › Hue/Saturation..** You can adjust the image's color range globally using this dialog box.

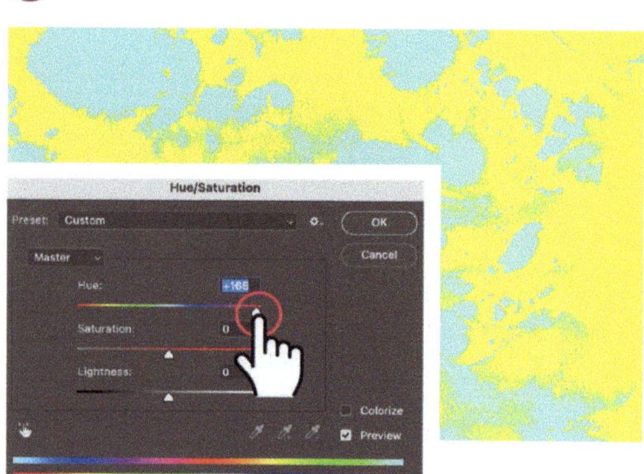

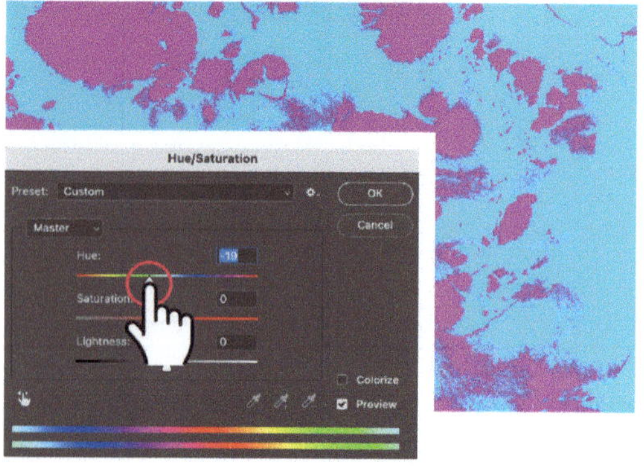

6.33 TUTORIAL: RGB DISTORTION EFFECT

Step 1. Open an image in Photoshop. You can open an image in color as well as in grayscale. If you want to convert the image to grayscale, open **Image › Adjustments › Hue/-Saturation** and take the saturation out.

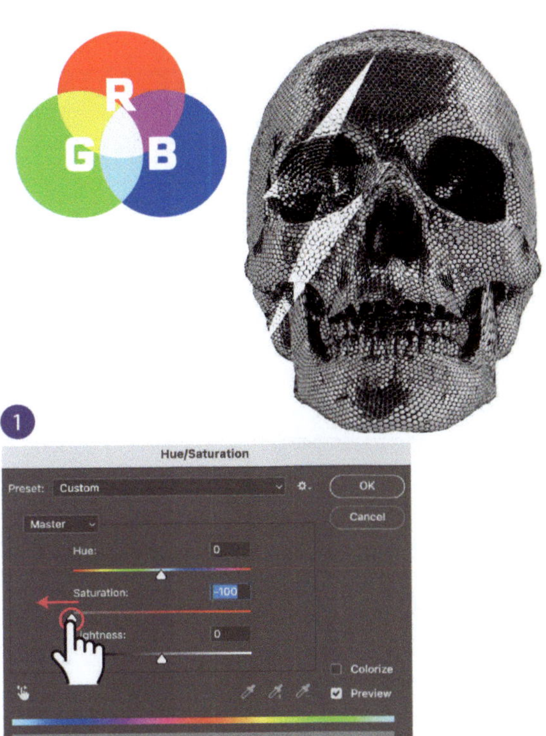

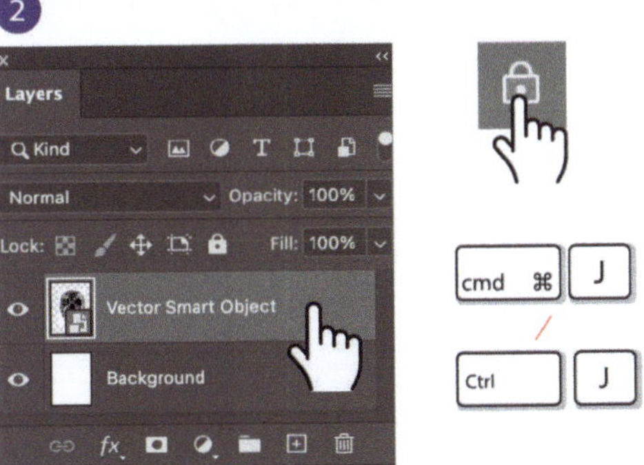

Step 2. Now create two copies of the layer with the shortcut command+J / Ctrl+J. If the layer is „locked", „unlock" it first.

Step 3. Double-click **copy 2** and uncheck **R** and **G** channels in the dialog box (see figure).

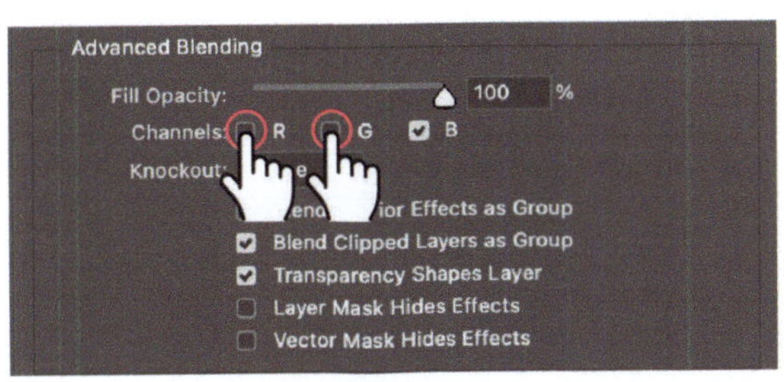

Step 4. Now move the object in the layer window using the right arrow key (copy 2).

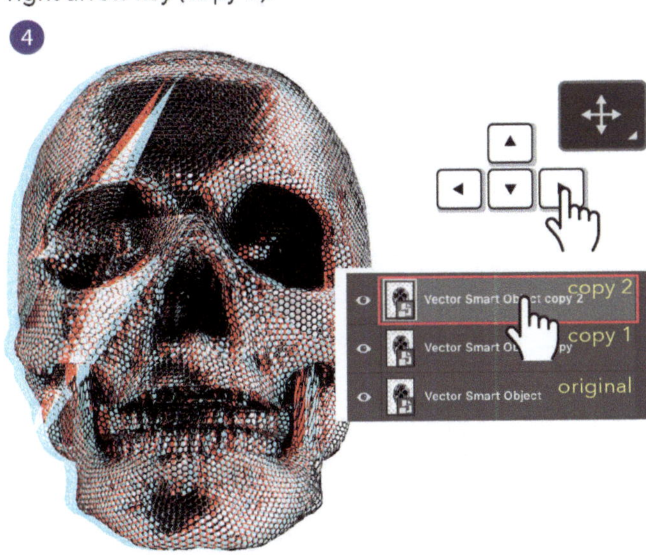

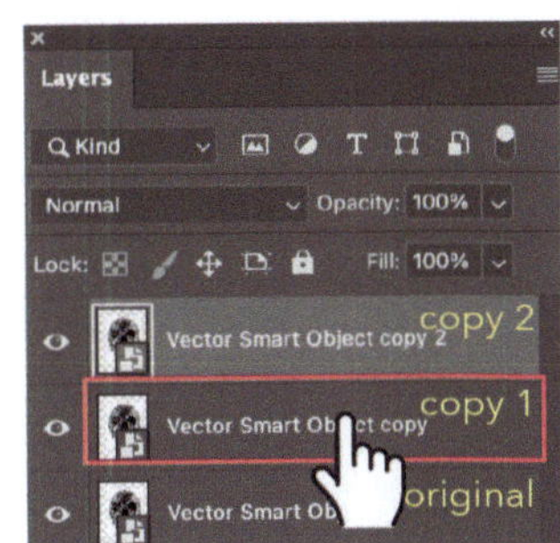

Step 5. Double-click **copy 1** and uncheck this time **R** and **B** channels in the dialog box (see figure).

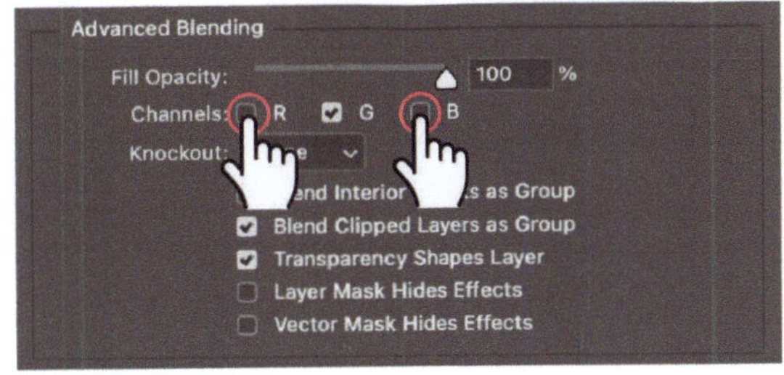

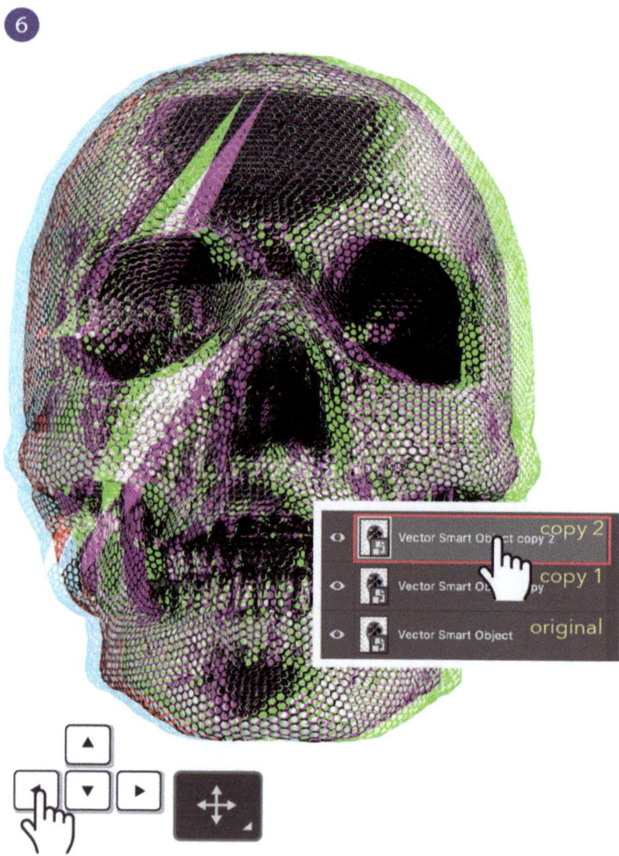

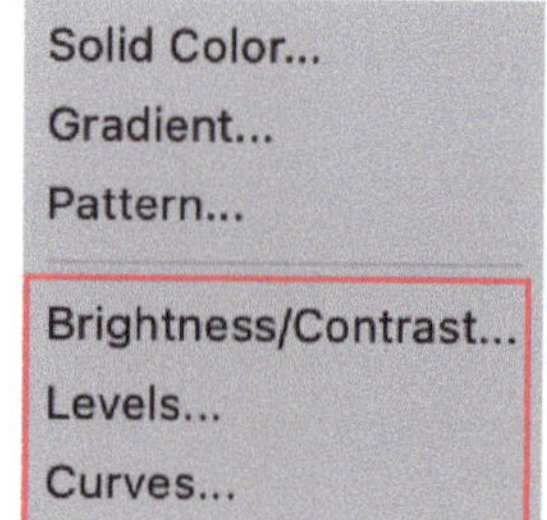

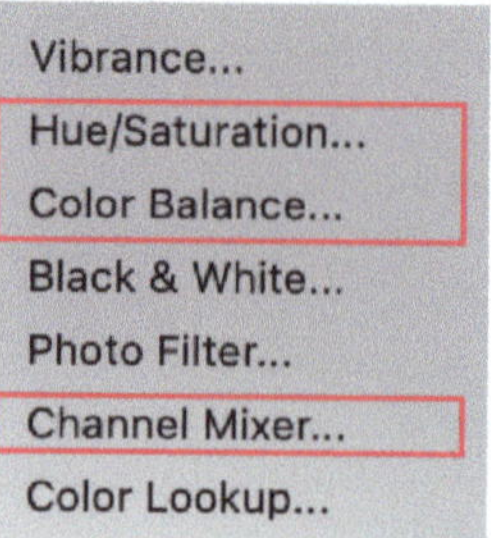

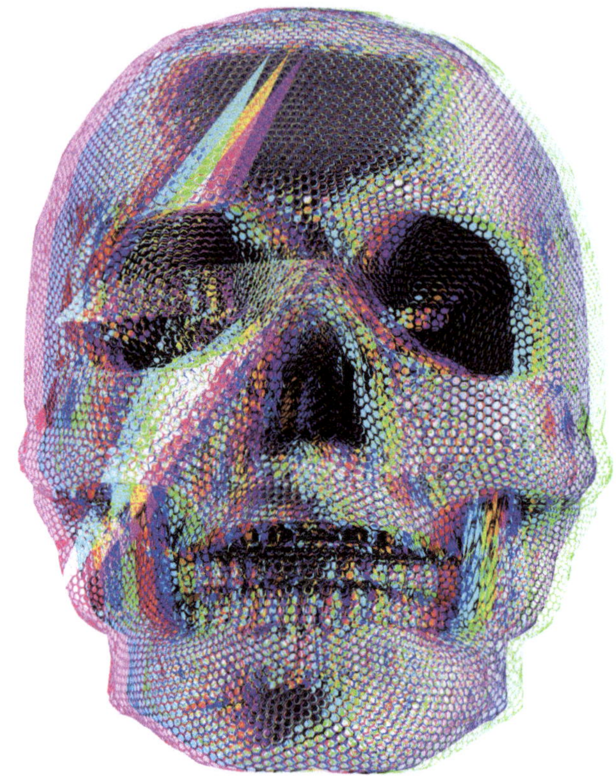

Step 6. Now move the object in the layer window using the left arrow key (copy 1). Move the layers until a color shift becomes visible.

The end result depends on your skill and willingness to experiment with this settings.

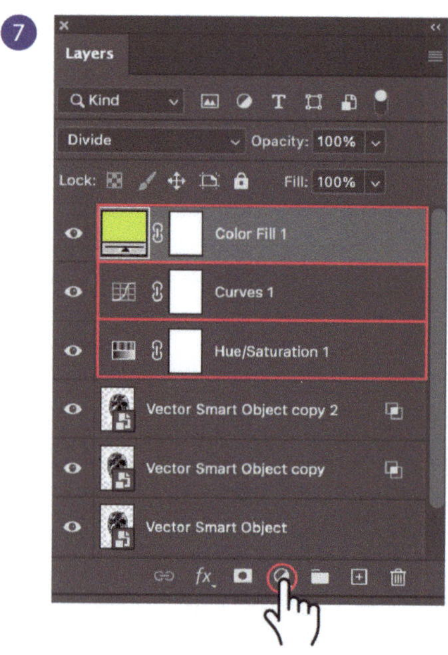

Step 7. To further experiment with colors and contrast, you can activate **Create new fill or adjustment layer**. You can use e.g. "Curves", "Brightness/Contrast", "Hue/Saturation" and other settings.

©dimitridesign.org

6.34 TUTORIAL: 3D LETTERING DESIGN

First, create a new A4 page in Adobe Illustrator **File > New > A4.**

Step 1. Open the font dialog box **Window > Type > Character.** Click with the **Text Tool** (T) in the empty drawing area, set the size of the text for example to 200pt or bigger, choose font that you like and type a number or a letter. Confirm the text rectangle with the „**Esc**" esc key.

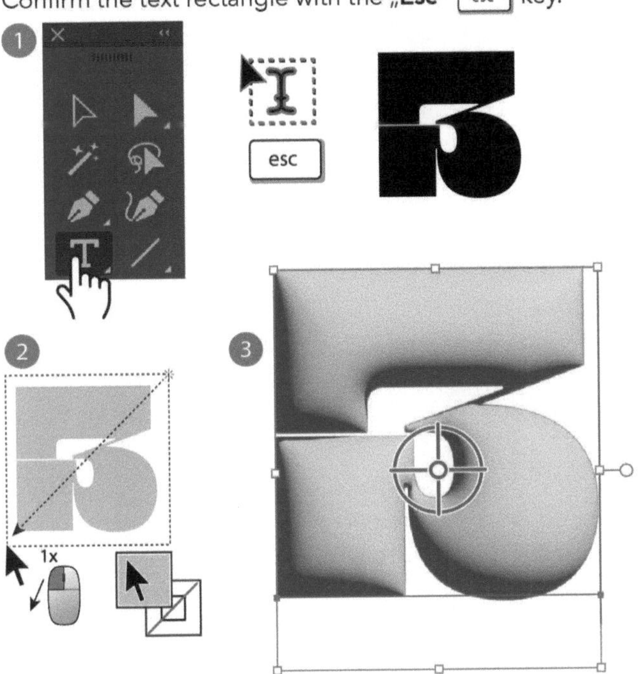

Step 2. Change the "fill" color to yellow, for example.
Step 3. While the object is still selected, activate the effect **Effect > 3D and Materials > Inflate...**

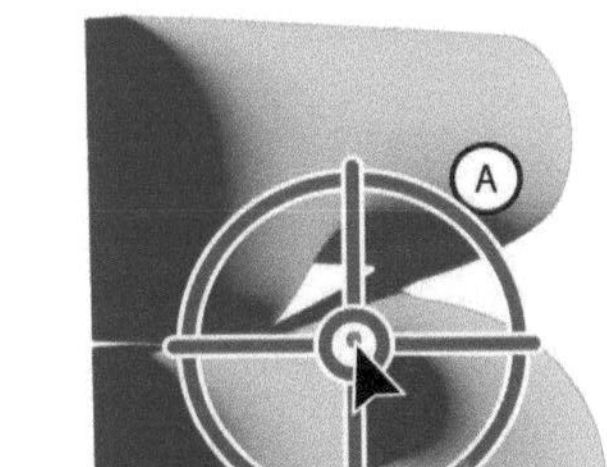

Scroll down to the "Rotation" section

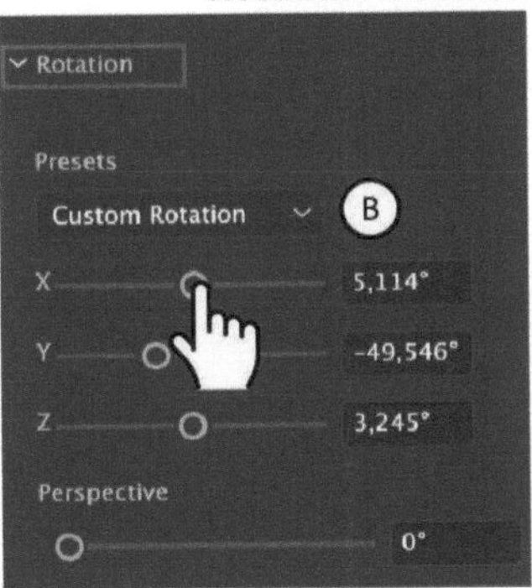

Step 4. In window **3D and Materials** that appears, you have the possibility of rotating the object manually (A) or using precise values (B). Also make use of the "Perspective" setting (C), you can achieve further interesting effects with this setting.

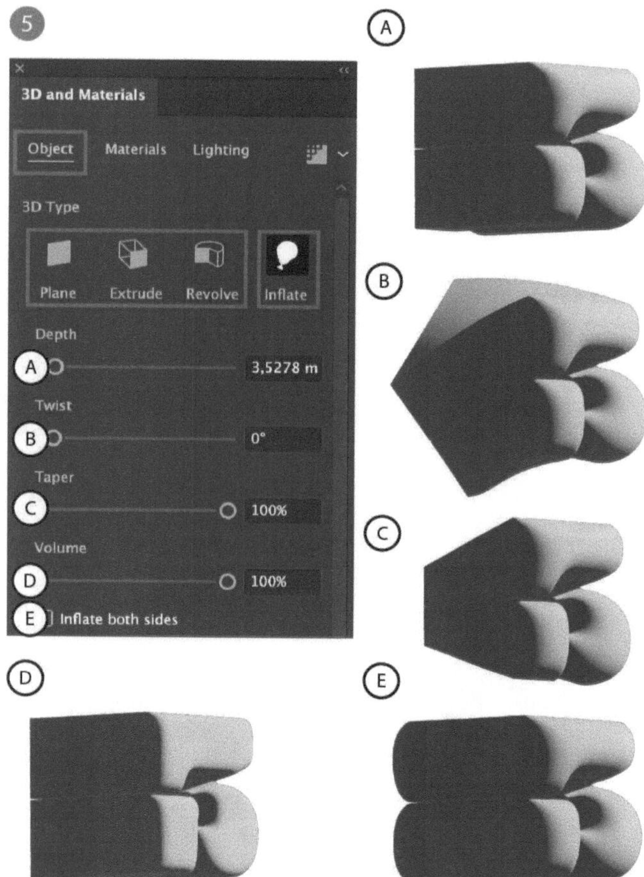

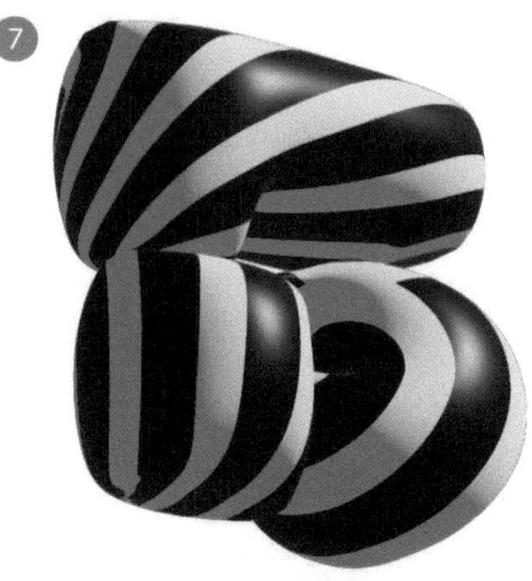

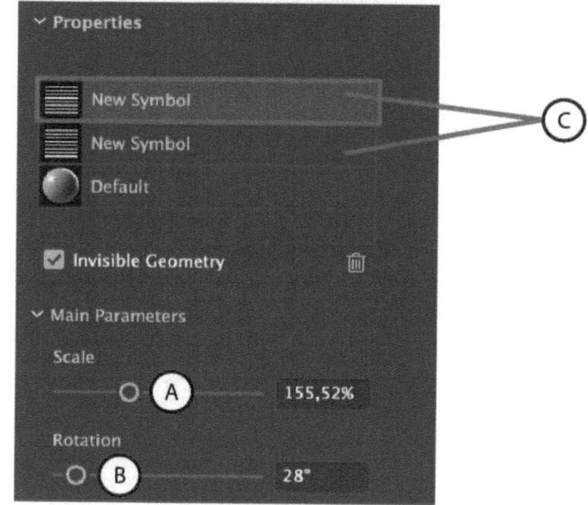

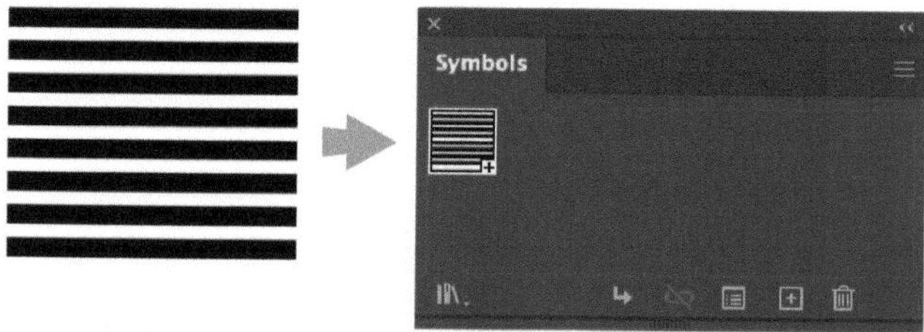

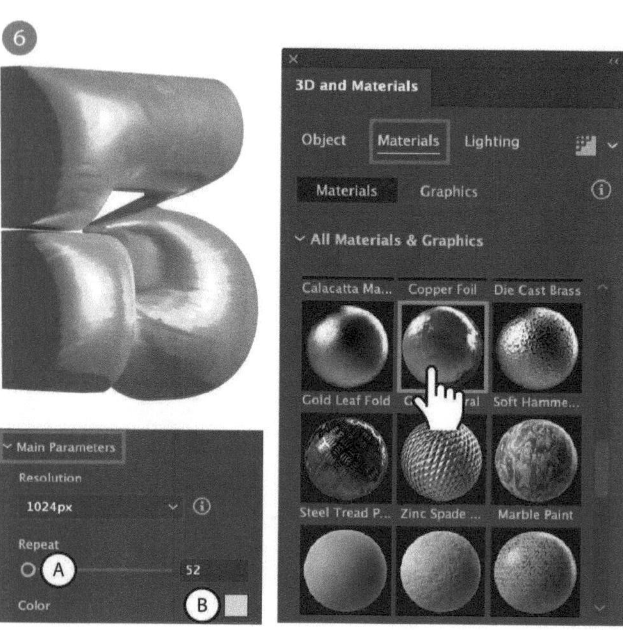

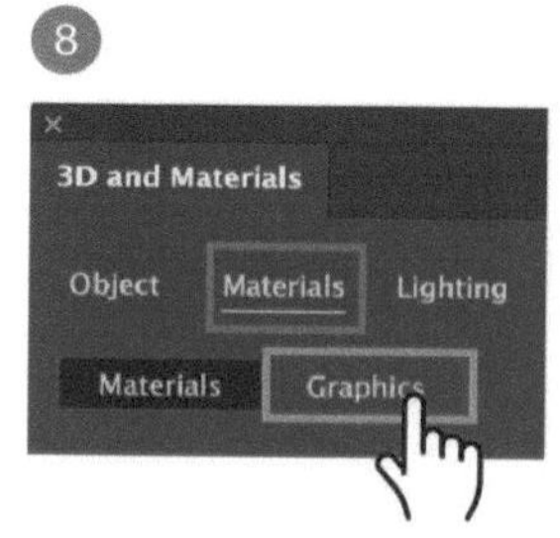

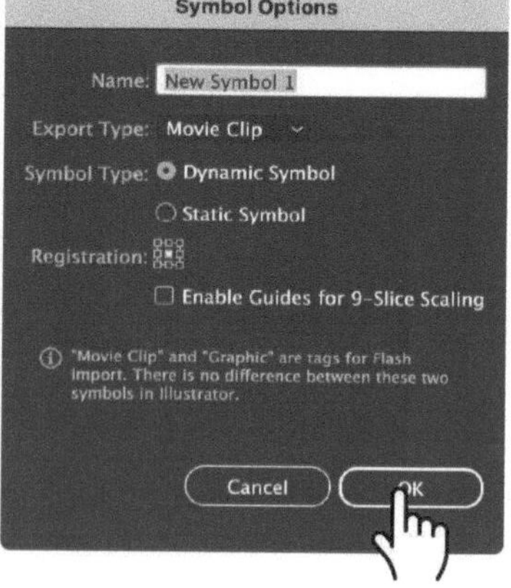

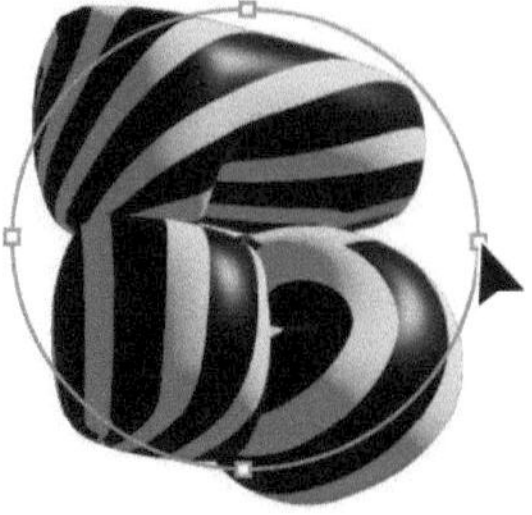

Step 5. The **3D and Materials** effect includes a lot of settings, only the most important settings are described here. You have to try out the most suitable settings for the respective project.

In section "Object" you will find the settings to adjust the shape of the object. You can manipulate settings **A** to **E** individually or in combination.

Step 6. In the "Materials" section you can apply different structures to the object, such as a golden surface. Please note, however, that with most settings the final result will only be visible after rendering.

For the "Materials" section you have many settings under "Main Parameters" such as **A** (repetition of the material pattern) and **B** (color of the material). Here you should also try out many settings.

Step 7. You also have the possibility to fill the 3D object with your own pattern. First create a pattern and drag it into **Window > Symbols**.

In the window that appears, confirm the settings with OK without changing anything.

Step 8. Switch now to the **3D and Materials** window , in the "Materials" section select "Graphics" and click on the new pattern that you just created.

Now you can move, rotate and scale the pattern to the desired location.

The pattern can be placed several times (C) on an object to fill all areas individually.

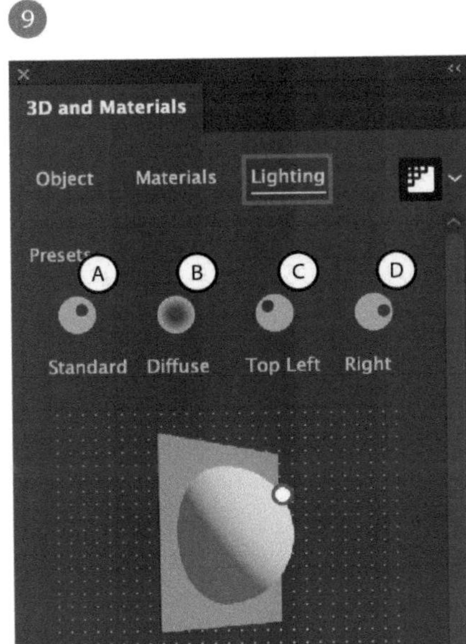

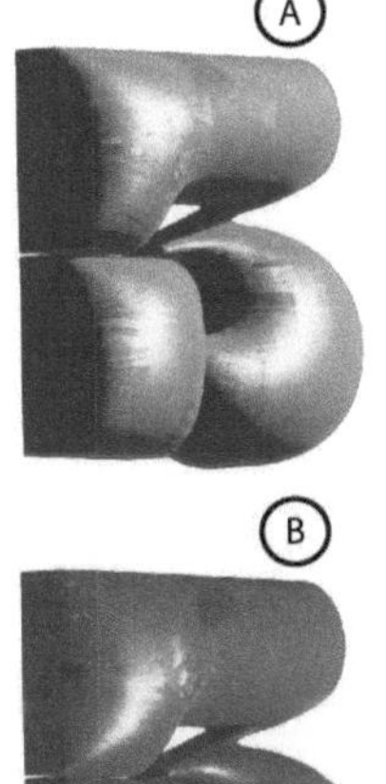

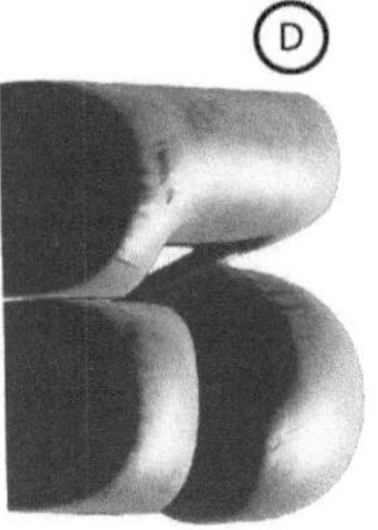

Step 9. In the "Lightning" section you can change the direction of the light.

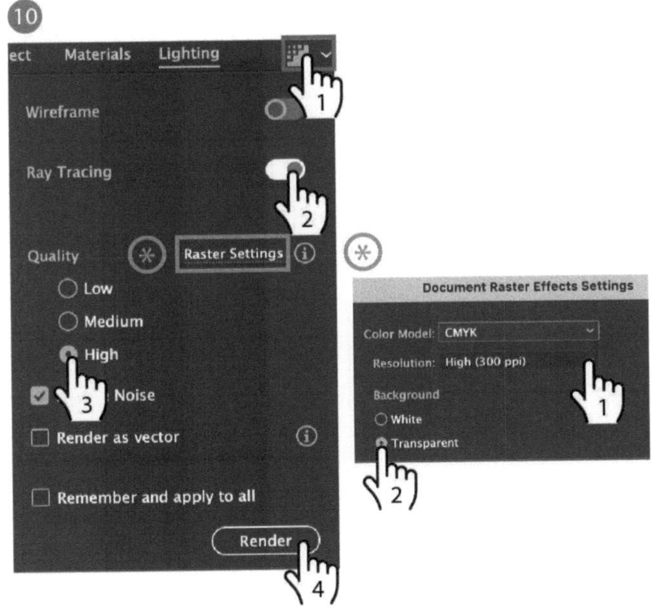

Step 10. In order to display the object in good quality with the right structures and right lighting conditions, it is necessary to render it.

Click on button "Render with Ray Tracing" and set the following settings. These settings may vary depending on the task.

In order to be able to edit the object later using additional filters and tools, it is recommended to create a copy of the object and expand this copy **Object > Expand Appearance**. This allows errors to be avoided during further processing but it's not a mandatory command.

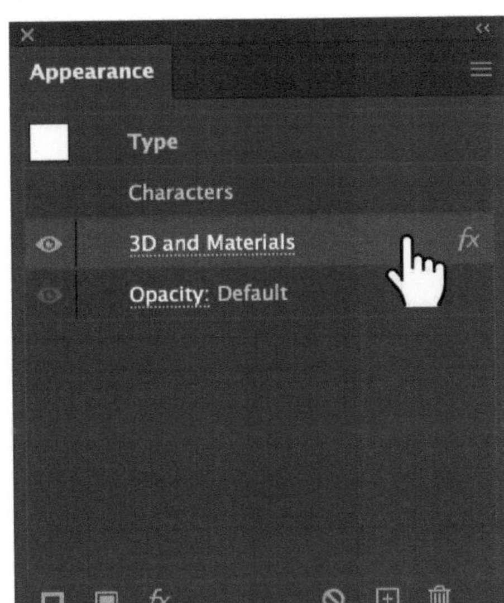

Step 11. In **Window > Appearance** you can always access the 3D settings again.

But make sure that this is only possible before you finally expand the object via **Object > Expand Appearance**. After that command you no longer have the possibility to edit the effects for the object. It also affects all other effects.